THE
LITTLE BOOK OF
SUFFOLK

THE
LITTLE BOOK
OF
SUFFOLK

CAROL TWINCH

breedon **books**
PUBLISHING

First published in Great Britain in 2007 by

The Breedon Books Publishing Company Limited

Breedon House, 3 The Parker Centre,

Derby, DE21 4SZ.

A catalogue record for this book is available from
the British Library.

ISBN 978-1-85983-587-6

Printed and bound by Cromwell, Trowbridge,
Wiltshire.

CONTENTS

Acknowledgements 6

ONE – This and That 7

TWO – The Coast 25

THREE – Churches and Chapels 45

FOUR – Epitaphs 64

FIVE – Suffolk Folk 74

SIX – Why is it called that? 100

SEVEN – Writers and Artists 112

EIGHT – The Dickens Connection 130

NINE – Particular to Suffolk 142

TEN – Miscellany 165

Bibliography 191

ACKNOWLEDGEMENTS

Grateful thanks to all those along the way who helped with local or specialised knowledge about the county of Suffolk, especially Suffolk County Council, Glemsford Mills, Trevor Kidd, Suffolk Moth Group, Albert Lain, Alan Mackley, Dr Priscilla Silver, Ipswich Transport Museum, Suffolk Library Service, Archant Suffolk and my husband Christopher, who accompanied me on investigative forays into deepest Suffolk.

ONE – THIS AND THAT

- ❖ SUFFOLK is bordered by Norfolk to the north, Cambridgeshire to the west, Essex to the south and the North Sea to the east. The southern boundary with Essex is only 50 miles from central London.
- ❖ In early Roman times, Suffolk was still part of the territory of the **Iceni** tribe. In AD61 the Iceni were led by their queen, Boudicca, into a disastrous rebellion against the Roman occupiers. The rebels managed to sack Camulodunum (Colchester in Essex) but were soon routed by the Roman forces. The Iceni returned home and submitted to Roman rule and entered the period of the **Romano-British**, which lasted until about AD450.
- ❖ In 1907 a **Rendham** schoolboy saw what he thought was a head in the River **Alde**. It was fished out of the water and for some years stood on a wall outside his house. It got forgotten until, some years later, a schoolmaster at nearby **Benhall** spied it and thought it looked interesting. He cleaned it up and, as he suspected, it was a Roman antiquity. Experts at the British Museum soon confirmed that the object was a bronze head of the Roman Emperor Claudius (died AD54) that had, in all probability, been looted from Camulodunum (Colchester) by the Iceni queen, Boudicca.

  In 1965 the head was sent to Sotheby's by the trustees of Miss Holland, on whose land it had been found, where it was sold for £15,500, the highest price fetched by an antiquity since the end of World War Two. It was bought on behalf of the British Museum, where it has been ever since, with replicas at **Ipswich** and **Rendham**.
- ❖ In about AD450 the Romans left Britain, leaving it defenceless, so that when the Saxons and Angles invaded they had little difficulty in conquering and occupying it. The Saxons and Angles divided Britain into several kingdoms and in AD575 the kingdom of East Anglia was founded, occupying almost the same country as the ancient Iceni. Gradually the people began to describe themselves as North-folk or South-folk. The name **Suffolk** derives from South-folk, which formed the southern half of the new kingdom. The earliest written reference to 'Suffolk' is found in AD1045, but it was probably used much earlier.
- ❖ The **East Angles** occupied Suffolk from the fifth to the seventh

centuries. They were a mixture of Saxons, Frisians and some Franks under the control of the Angles.

❖ In the ninth century the Danes began their invasions and it fell to the new king of the East Angles, **Edmund,** to defend the kingdom. He was just 15 years old when he was crowned on Christmas Day in AD855 and, only a few years later, he found himself at the head of an army defending East Anglia against the invaders.

In AD869 Edmund fought the Danes at **Thetford** and, although his army strove heroically, they could not contain the savage onslaught of the foreign barbarians. Retiring from battle, Edmund and his followers were captured. On 20 November AD869 Edmund was slain by being tied to a tree and shot with arrows and then beheaded.

King Edmund was both a historical figure and a legend and, although historians verify his death, the site of his martyrdom is more controversial. The strongest claim comes from **Hoxne**, where his body lay enshrined in a chapel in the woods. Some years later, when peace was restored, his body was moved to Beodricsworth (renamed **Bury St Edmunds**) and he was declared a saint. A great and powerful Benedictine Abbey grew up around his shrine, which rose to national, and then international, importance throughout the Middle Ages.

❖ **Saint Edmund** was considered the patron saint of England until the cult of St George, the dragon-slaying Turk, took on new dimensions during the Crusades and Richard I invoked his protection for himself and his army.

❖ According to legend, **Goldbrook Bridge** at **Hoxne** is so named because, in AD869, King Edmund hid under the bridge while retreating from the Danish invaders. He was betrayed when a bridal pair crossing the bridge saw the reflection of his gold spurs in the river. Since that time there has been a tradition of ill luck for any couples that cross Goldbrook Bridge on their wedding day.

❖ The Abbey at **Bury St Edmunds** was the wealthiest Benedictine house in Suffolk and the fifth richest in England, outstripped only by Westminster, Glastonbury, St Albans and Canterbury. At the Reformation in 1539 it owned lands and estates scattered throughout Suffolk, Norfolk, Lincolnshire and London.

❖ In 1536, **Butley Priory** was the second wealthiest monastery in Suffolk, having been founded in 1171 by the Augustinian Canons.

❖ Before the Dissolution of the Monasteries by Henry VIII, **Sibton Abbey** was the third wealthiest monastery in Suffolk and was the only Cistercian house in the county, founded in 1150.

❖ The Norman Conquest of 1066 brought sweeping and profound changes to British culture. Duke William of Normandy conquered England and was crowned king. Most of the lands belonging to the English nobility were seized, including those in Suffolk, and William I gave large tracts of the county to his followers. Two years later the king decided on a stocktaking exercise of his new country, the result of which was the **Domesday Book** of 1086, one of the most important documents in English history.

❖ The Domesday Book lists 71 'tenants-in-chief' in Suffolk (21 of whom also held lands in Norfolk and Essex). The town of **Ipswich** is listed under King William, as are most of the Hundreds of **Lothingland** and **Samford.**

❖ 'High Suffolk' refers to an elevated plain of clay land, roughly defined as extending from **Beccles** in the northeast to **Clare** and **Sudbury** in the southwest. It embraces that part of the county formerly known as the Woodlands (though most of the woodland has now disappeared). **Stowmarket** is generally said to be virtually in the centre of Suffolk. There are over 100 villages in High Suffolk.

❖ The fiscal administration of Suffolk and Norfolk remained under one Sheriff until 1575. The county boundary has altered little since then, except for coastal erosion. Parts of **Gorleston** and **Thetford** that were previously in Suffolk are now in Norfolk.

❖ The county of **Suffolk** was divided in 1888 by the Local Government Act into East and West Suffolk, with **Ipswich** and **Bury St Edmunds** the county towns respectively. However, the Local Government Act of 1972 saw East and West Suffolk, plus Ipswich, reunited to form the single county of Suffolk on 1 April 1974.

❖ The old motto of East Suffolk was *Opus Nostrum Dirige* (Direct Our Work), granted in 1935. It now appears as the motto for the Suffolk County Council as 'Guide Our Endeavour'.

❖ The county is divided into seven **Borough and District Councils,** which are (from west to east): Forest Heath, St Edmundsbury, Babergh, Mid Suffolk, Ipswich, Suffolk Coastal and Waveney. All districts except Ipswich also have parish and town councils, of which there are a total of 450.

❖ **Ipswich** is the 38th largest urban area in England.

❖ Part of **Newmarket,** with the adjoining parish of **Exning,** is the most westerly point of Suffolk and is peculiar in that it is surrounded almost entirely by Cambridgeshire, the old **Thetford** road serving as an isthmus that connects it with the rest of the county. It is 13 miles west of **Bury St Edmunds** and 13 miles east of Cambridge.

❖ The 34-acre parish of **Dallinghoo Wield** laid claim to being the smallest in England, but in 1980 boundary commissioners declared it an anachronism and got rid of it. In 1841 it was still called 'extra parochial' on the tithe map, which meant that it was outside the bounds of any civil or ecclesiastical parish and was exempt from some tithe payments. In 1894 most extra parochial places became civil parishes.

❖ **Mildenhall** is the largest parish in Suffolk and was once a port for the hinterland of West Suffolk on the River Lark. A fabulous cache of 34 pieces of fourth-century Roman silverware was discovered in Mildenhall in 1946 and is now on display in the British Museum.

❖ **Ness Point** in **Lowestoft** is the most easterly point of Suffolk and, therefore, the most easterly point of England. To mark the spot there is a compass and Euroscope. From that point it is 490 miles to Berlin, 814 to Warsaw, 133 to Amsterdam, 788 to Stockholm and 1,460 to Athens.

❖ **Ness Point** is the site of Suffolk's first and largest commercial wind turbine. Construction began on 7 December 2004 and was completed three days later. At 126m (413ft) it is the tallest wind turbine onshore in the United Kingdom and the ladders that go up to the nacelle unit (the hub or housing for the generator, gearbox and electrical control equipment) extend 80 metres upwards. The blade tips travel at up to 150mph.

The wind turbine produces 2.75 MW, enough electricity to meet the needs of 1,500 homes, saving around 6,215 tonnes of greenhouse gas emissions per year.

❖ The White Horse public house at **Edwardstone** was the first in the county to have its own nine-metre high wind turbine, sited in the pub grounds and used to power part of the business and landlord's accommodation.

❖ In February 2007 the 13th-century church of St Mary's at **Lidgate** became the first church in Suffolk, and the oldest in Britain, to install solar panels. The 10 panels are sited on the square tower roof. They are laid out in three sets of flat thermal collectors with an assembly of solar cells that are used to generate electricity. Initially the panels will save two thirds of the current power bills at St Mary's and any excess can be sold to the National Grid.

❖ **Rede** is on the highest land in Suffolk, over 400ft above sea level. For most of the county there is very little that is above 300ft above sea level.

❖ The ITV television transmitter at **Mendlesham** is 1,160ft high and 210ft above sea level. Building began early in 1959 and programme operation started on 27 October of that year. To prevent interference with European television services, while providing an adequate service to the coastal areas of Suffolk and Essex, the mast had to be sited in the south-east of the geographical centre of the required transmission area. The very low height of the Mendlesham site meant that the mast needed to be over 1,000ft. At the time of construction it was the highest television mast in Europe.

❖ The **BBC World Service Transmission Station** has been at **Orfordness** since the early 1980s. It uses a medium wave transmitter to provide coverage to Europe on the frequency 648kHz. The World Service began as the BBC Empire Service in 1932.

❖ BBC **Radio Suffolk** began broadcasting from St Matthew's Street, **Ipswich** in 1995. In 2004 it won Radio Station of the Year and received the accolade at the Sony Awards.

❖ Flint tools unearthed in **Pakefield** are 200,000 years older than the previous oldest finds. Until then it was thought that humans arrived in northern Europe 500,000 years ago. Soil samples from the Pakefield site reveal that the climate 700,000 years ago was similar to the present day Mediterranean region.

❖ In 1686 a government factory was established at **Brandon** to meet the demand for flints used in the English flintlock gun (invented in the 17th century). The flint factory was an offshoot of Grime's Graves, about three miles away, which is one of the earliest industrial sites in Britain. About 4,000 years ago, miners of the New Stone Age or Neolithic period dug through chalk to get at the jet-black band of flint. Flint has been used for tool-making and weapons for thousands of years and the flint-knapping industry at Brandon continued until the late 20th century.

❖ In the 19th century, flint knappers were paid on a piece-work basis, the standard rate being 1s 3d per thousand gunflints. They worked from 7am to 9pm and a master knapper could drop 3,000 gunflints a day into the biscuit tin receptacles. In 1813, the Brandon knappers were required to supply a monthly quota of over a million musket flints. After the army ceased using flintlocks, and the British contracts had consequently stopped, production of gunflints continued at Brandon for export to America and West Africa until the late 20th century.

❖ In the 1890s and early 1900s the Brandon knappers developed a cottage industry and made replicas of prehistoric flint tools and souvenirs, the last Brandon knapper retiring in the 1980s. The village is now on the western edge of **Thetford Forest**. The village sign depicts flint knappers and the Elizabethan inn is called the Flintmakers Arms.

❖ Until the 14th and 15th century, when clay tiles first came into general use, thatching was the normal form of roofing for most buildings in Suffolk, including public buildings and churches. Three main sources for material were cornfields, reed and sedge beds. The old Suffolk word for thatch is 'thak' (and the 'thakker' was the thatcher), a word still in common usage until the early 1900s.

❖ The village of **Dalham** reputedly contains the highest number of thatched cottages in Suffolk.

❖ Suffolk still has 22 **windmills** and 24 **watermills** with some or all of their machinery. Windmills have been part of the Suffolk landscape for over 800 years. One of the earliest references to a windmill is to one in **Bury St Edmunds** in 1191. In 1830 William Cobbett wrote that he had seen no fewer than 17 from a single vantage point near Ipswich.

❖ In their heyday of the early 19th century, around 500 windmills were at work in the county. Most were used for grinding corn, but wind power was also harnessed for drainage on the coastal marshes.

❖ The **Herringfleet Windpump** is the last survivor of the old-style Broadland windpumps, with cloth-spread sails and a boat-shaped cap turned manually by a tailpole and winch. The water is lifted by a 16ft diameter external scoopwheel. When the mill had to work all night to keep the marshes from flooding, the marshmen had to stay in a small area with only a fireplace and bench for comfort. The mill dates from 1820 and was in regular use until the early 1950s.

❖ A windmill built at **Aldringham** in 1803 was moved to **Thorpeness** in 1923 to pump water to the village water tower, which is the famous 'House in the Clouds'. Extra water was needed for Glencairn Ogilvie's holiday village and clapboard walls, windows and a pitched roof camouflaged the tower so that it looks as though a house is perched 'in the clouds'. When mains water came to the village the tower was converted into living quarters. The house folly was named after a children's poem entitled *The House in the Clouds* by Mrs Mason, the first tenant of the new accommodation. (See also Chapter Seven, Writers and Artists.)

❖ There have been tide mills at **Woodbridge** since the first of 1170 and the present building dates from 1793. It was saved from collapse in the 1970s and after major restoration was opened to the public in 1973 by the Tide Mill Trust. The mill had a 'pool bank' so that the incoming tide opened the sluice gates and filled the pool with water. When the tide turned, the pool gates closed, keeping the pool full so that the miller had enough water to drive the mill's machinery for about four hours.

❖ **Pakenham** is the only village in England to have both a windmill and a watermill both in working order. The watermill was built around 1814 on the site of a mill mentioned in Domesday Book. The windmill has a black-tarred tower and was in use until the 1950s.

❖ **Helmingham Hall** is the largest moated house in Suffolk. It was built around 1500 by Lionel Tollemache and although it has been remodelled several times since, it retained an early Tudor courtyard.

❖ In terms of county size Suffolk has 3,801sq km (approximately 1,500sq miles), and represents a 59th part of Great Britain. It has almost a million acres and is the eighth largest county in England.

❖ In 1836 the county was divided into 21 **hundreds** (or Registration Districts) with seven boroughs, consisting of over 500 **parishes**, 30 towns and around 1,000 **villages and hamlets**. A 'hundred' is an ancient subdivision of a county that has endured since the 10th century. Each hundred had its own judicial and administrative functions. It is thought that the name originated in the **Anglo-Saxon** era and probably consisted of 100 'hides' (a unit of taxation derived from a specified area of land, usually around 120 acres).

❖ In mediaeval times law and order was maintained by a system of 'frankpledge', whereby 10 or 12 householders formed groups which pledged responsibility to the manorial court leet for the good behaviour of each member. These groups were known as 'tithings' and if a member broke the peace or committed an offence against his neighbour he was reported to the township by the tithingman. Parishes often had an area of public land on which the tithing meetings were held, for example, that of Tye Green at **Glemsford**. When a murder took place the king fined the whole hundred. Early in the 12th century, for example, **Blything Hundred** had to pay Henry I a silver mark because a murder had been committed there.

❖ In the 18th and early 19th century unpaid Parish Constables took on the job of law enforcement. They often served their year's duty reluctantly and usually failed either to halt the rise of crime or to bring offenders to book. In all the hundreds, local associations sprang up in the towns and villages, dedicated to maintaining law and order, typical of which was **The Eye Anti-Felon Society**, which held its first meeting at the White Lion in July 1810. Detailed records were kept of all the officers' activities, especially the informers, who were encouraged to provide proof of guilt, and witnesses were paid 'beer money'. Although this and other such societies carried on their war against crime for many years, most thankfully handed over the task to the Rural Police Force, which was founded in East Suffolk in 1840.

❖ In 1836, **Ipswich, Bury St Edmunds** and **Sudbury** were the first to establish a professional police force, replacing the High Constable (responsible for the hundred) and the Parish Constable (for the villages and townships). Other smaller towns established similar forces over the next few years, followed by **East Suffolk** in 1840 and **West Suffolk** in 1845. In the late 1800s most of the East and West forces amalgamated, although it was not until 1967 that all the Suffolk forces finally combined to form the **Suffolk Constabulary**.

❖ In **2001** the population of Suffolk was **668,548**. This was an increase on the 1991 census figure, which showed a population of 633,098.

❖ There are 75 county councillors who are elected every four years. The county is divided into **electoral divisions** and there is a councillor for each division (in 12 of the divisions there are two councillors). On average each councillor represents over 7,000 people. The **County Council** meets at least six times a year.

❖ **Alton Water** is a man-made reservoir and is the largest area of inland water in Suffolk, with a circumference of over eight miles. A water shortage in the 1960s led to a study of 20 potential sites and Alton was finally chosen. The land was mostly agricultural, but Alton Hall was lost and Alton Mill dismantled and rebuilt at the Museum of East Anglian Life at **Stowmarket**. It took 13 years to construct and fill with water.

Although the reservoir is primarily used for the supply of water to Ipswich and surrounding areas, it is also used for water sports, bird-watching, scuba diving and fishing, with cross-country cycling on surrounding paths.

❖ **Havergate Island** is a coastal lagoon-type reserve in the River Ore below Orford. Purchased by the RSPB in 1948, it is two miles long and covers 267 acres plus a fair stretch of tidal saltings. Most of it is well below the level of high tides and if it were not for a drainage system and sea walls, it would be entirely flooded. In the 1930s cattle were still brought to the island for summer grazing. It is an important site for avocets, terns and other waders and is nationally important for its population of rare starlet sea anemone (*Nematostella vectensis*).

❖ A few miles to the north of Havergate Island is **Minsmere** RSPB Reserve, home to the **avocet**. This black and white wader, with a long curved-up beak, was thought extinct in the British Isles until 1947 when it reappeared at Minsmere. Originally there were six pairs and now numbers have grown to several hundred pairs. The avocet was chosen as the logo for the RSPB.

❖ In May 2000 about 2,000 twitchers from across Britain converged on **Corton** to witness a rare sighting of an alpine accentor, which is usually only found on European mountainsides. The bird spent much of the day in or around the churchyard before hopping off to the nearby sewage works. A spokesman for the *Suffolk Bird Report* told the local press that the species was usually found in mountainous areas between Spain and the Caspian Sea. 'There are two old Suffolk records' he said, 'one at **Oulton Broad** in 1823 and another at **Gorleston Pier** in 1894, although some authorities doubted them'.

❖ The 350-acre reserve of **Redgrave and Lopham Fen** is the only place in the British Isles where the Great Raft spider (*Dolomedes fimbriatus*) is found. This aquatic spider is capable of catching small fish such as sticklebacks just below the surface of the water. It is dark brown with a characteristic white or cream stripe along the sides of its body. The Great Raft spider was one of the first creatures to be put on English Nature's Species Recovery Programme.

❖ The parish of **Fritton** was moved from Suffolk to Norfolk during the county boundary reorganisation of 1974.

❖ The parish of **Gorleston** is five miles north of **Lowestoft** and plumb on the border between Suffolk and Norfolk. At one time it included the hamlet of **South Town**, sometimes known as Little Yarmouth, which was added to the Borough of Great Yarmouth (Norfolk) in 1681 and amalgamated with the same in 1891. St Mary's, South Town was built in 1831 as a chapel-of-ease to Gorleston and the registers were included in Gorleston.

The parish of Gorleston continued in Suffolk until 1815 when it, too, became part of Great Yarmouth although accounts of it are found under Suffolk until the early part of the 20th century. The bulk of its history belongs to Suffolk but, because of its geography and a certain lack of belonging, much of its story is lost.

❖ The parish of St Andrew's **Gorleston** is immortalised by a number of illustrated early 14th-century psalters including **The Gorleston Psalter** of 1320 and the **Douai Psalter** of 1330 (executed in Gorleston but unfortunately buried during World War One and consequently damaged).

In the 14th century there was a school of craftsmen producing illuminated psalters, associated with the church of St Andrew but also, possibly, connected to the local Augustinian Friary. The high quality of the psalter suggests a group of closely collaborating individuals, all with superior skills. Production of these psalters was a complex and expensive process, requiring parchment makers, scribes, artists and binders. It also needed a patron to pay the bills (who was usually the original owner) and the most likely candidate is **John, 8th Earl of Warenne** (1286–1347), as his arms are prominent, and rabbits in their warrens, jousting and riding the hounds that hunt them, populate the borders – a visual pun on the owner's name. Rabbits were also a common mediaeval symbol of lust. A commander in the king's army, the Earl had a colourful life and was excommunicated for multiple adultery.

❖ In 2003 one of the most important English illuminated manuscripts was discovered at Shirburn Castle in Oxfordshire, having lain on the shelves of the library of the Earls of Macclesfield for centuries. Executed in the 1320s, the 252-folio manuscript was named **The Macclesfield Psalter**, but it belonged originally to the parish church of St Andrew in **Gorleston** and was made by the local group of craftsmen based in or around the parish. Its name derives from its ownership at the time of discovery and although it was hoped to amend it to reflect its origins that has not, so far, happened.

The Psalter is a particularly fine example of Suffolk mediaeval art and the illuminations show devotional imagery, with exceedingly earthy glimpses of everyday life portrayed with ribald humour and uninhibited fantasy. Some of the compositions are almost identical to those on the **Gorleston Psalter**, suggesting that the artists reused themes and had stock motifs in their repertoire. A ploughing scene, David and Goliath, a cat and mouse sequence and a stag hunt all feature in both psalters with little or no alteration. Although there are rabbits on no more than five pages of the Macclesfield Psalter, it is possible that the Warenne family contributed to the production, although a single coat of arms has been identified as that of the Gorges family. The manuscript opens with two full-page miniatures, one of Saint Edmund and the other of Saint Andrew.

The Macclesfield Psalter is considered to be the most important English illuminated manuscripts to be discovered in living memory. A major fundraising campaign was launched to secure its future in England and it is currently kept at the Fitzwilliam Museum in Cambridge.

❖ The winter of **1946–47** was one of the severest winters of the previous 200 years. February was the worst month, the observer at RAF **Mildenhall** meteorological office recording temperatures of 7°F (minus 14°C). Snow was reported on 26 days of the month and, although the 1962–63 winter set new records for severe cold, the very low temperatures of February 1947 meant that the snow was light and powdery and easily whipped up into deep drifts by the frequent blizzards. At **Beccles** there were snowdrifts up to 15ft deep and at **Oulton Broad** cars were able to drive across the thick ice. The River **Waveney** was completely frozen over by ice a foot thick and the *Beccles and Bungay Journal* described it as an 'Arctic waste' and reported that the flooded areas were 'reminiscent of the Siberian tundra'. It was reported that an intrepid team of skaters was making the first attempt since the great freeze up of 1894–95 to skate from Beccles down to Oulton Broad. The skaters had to make a few detours but arrived at their destination without mishap and even had time for an impromptu game of ice hockey.

At **Southwold** a 'bulldozer turned turtle'. In an effort to clear a snowdrift near Quay Lane, about two miles from Southwold, a bulldozer skidded and turned over on its side. It took five hours to right the machine.

People living on boats had to thaw out their crafts at river level to prevent damage.

Wildlife suffered as blizzards buried feeding grounds and reed beds were under several feet of hard, frozen snow. Birds such as the bearded tit were all but obliterated and it took over 10 years for numbers to recover. Livestock farmers were unable to reach their animals and large numbers of sheep and cattle perished. Crops were damaged and potatoes were ruined when prolonged frost penetrated the clamps.

On 17 February a Keep-it-Moving campaign was launched in respect of coal supplies. The Central Electricity Board told members of the Coal Cabinet that they could not cope unless the factories implemented a staggering of work hours. Electricity was rationed by suspending supplies for three hours each morning and two hours in the afternoon and workers were laid off in workshops and factories. The County Surveyor said that it was costing £2,000 a day to clear the snow in East Suffolk.

On 22 February, the *East Anglian Daily Times* reported that the blizzards sweeping the county were further threatening coal trains and blocking roads. During one of the worst blizzards 13in of snow was strewn over a wide area and, in those coal-dependent days, schools were hard pressed to keep pupils warm as fuel shortages worsened. German and Italian prisoners of war were called in to assist with snow clearance but distribution of meat and sweets was badly affected and the Minister of Food announced a possible return to wartime rationing (though some commodities were still rationed).

At the beginning of March a deepening depression from the Atlantic moved rapidly across East Anglia and brought the worst gale for 100 years. Relief finally came towards the end of the month, though widespread flooding occurred as the snow began to melt and flooding caused further damage to thousands of acres of farmland. In the last week of that month temperatures rose to 55°F(13°C).

❖ At the other end of the scale, the summer of 1947 broke a different set of records. In June a heat wave saw temperatures peak at 90°F (32°C) and August had 280 hours of bright sunshine.

❖ **The Orwell Bridge** carries the A45 **Ipswich** bypass over the River Orwell between **Wherstead** and **Nacton**, taking traffic to and from London and the Midlands. Plans for a bridge were begun in 1965 but construction did not begin until December 1979 and was completed in December 1982. At the time it was one of the longest pre-stressed concrete bridges in Europe. Its main span is 190 metres and the total length is 1,287 metres. The total weight of each span is upwards of 2,600 tons and it contains 110,000 cubic metres of concrete. It cost £23.6 million. Sir William Halcrow & Partners designed it and the main contractor was Stebbings, a Dutch company (which caused an outcry in the town, as it was thought the contract should be awarded to a local firm).

It is, in fact, two parallel bridges with a space between the two carriageways. It is carried on 19 piers, which rest on piles going 131ft into the ground and 40m into the river bottom. The span over the navigation channel has a clearance of 126ft (38.3m) at high water, allowing large vessels to pass underneath.

More than 50,000 people walked across the bridge the day before the official opening. The Mayor of Ipswich, Mrs Beryl James, came up with the idea for people to walk the bridge for charity. The temperature was only five degrees above freezing, but there were babies in prams and people in wheelchairs.

❖ The gas-cooled reactors at **Sizewell A Power Station** occupy a 10-hectare site, which was chosen in 1959. Construction started in 1961, at a cost of £60 million, and it began generating electricity in 1966. Both of the A station reactors shut down for the last time on 31 December 2006. The two reactors were shut down within four hours of each other and the final moments were watched by more than 100 people via a live screen in Sizewell Sport and Social Club.

During the course of its operation it has been owned by Central Electricity Generating Board (1966–89), Nuclear Energy (1990–96), Magnox Electric Limited (1996–98) and between 1998 and 2005 it became a subsidiary of British Nuclear Fuels Limited. In 2005 the Nuclear Decommissioning Authority took over all the assets and liability of the operation.

❖ In 1980 the government announced its intention to build a PWR (Pressurised Water Reactor) at Sizewell, the only type of its kind in the country. The following year, the Central Electricity Generating Board submitted a planning application to build a nuclear reactor on land next to the older Magnox station at **Sizewell Beach**.

The resulting **Sizewell B** enquiry began in 1983 at **Snape Maltings**, chaired by Sir Frank Layfield QC, and at 340 days long it became Britain's longest public enquiry (only recently overtaken by Heathrow Terminal Five).

In 1987 consent was granted and construction began in 1988. Containment walls are 1.3m thick with another gas-tight steel casing within. Over 6,000 people worked on the construction and

Sizewell B became Europe's biggest civil engineering project to date. Since then only the Channel Tunnel construction has been bigger.

❖ In 1998, the Sizewell B site won the British Trust for Ornithology's Birds for Business Challenge with 160 species of bird, some very rare, spotted around the station's hinterland.

❖ The **Suffolk Wildlife Trust** used more than 60,000 recycled lemonade and cola bottles in a major refurbishment of the nature trail around the Sizewell station.

❖ Sizewell B is one of the largest employers in Suffolk, with 416 full-time staff, including 16 apprentices, all living within a 25-mile radius of the plant.

❖ **Felixstowe Port** is the largest container port in the United Kingdom and the second-largest in Europe. The container revolution of the 1960s brought new challenges to Suffolk's ports, not least the skills and equipment to deal with the 20ft container boxes.

In August 2005, the Port of Felixstowe welcomed what was then the world's largest container ship, the MSC *Pamela*, which measured 321m in length, with a gross tonnage of 107,200 and a breadth of 45.6m. The vessel is capable of a maximum speed of 25 knots.

❖ Suffolk is in the Province of Canterbury and until 1837 was wholly within the Diocese of Norwich. The Bishop of Norwich was assisted by the archdeaconries of **Sudbury** and Suffolk, each of which was subdivided into deaneries (eight for Sudbury and 14 for Suffolk). In 1837 the Sudbury Archdeaconry was transferred to the Ely Diocese, except for Stow and Hartismere, which were added to the Suffolk Archdeaconry.

❖ **Hadleigh** was a 'peculiar' of Canterbury and as such was outside the jurisdiction of the Bishop of Norwich – or, more importantly, the archdeacon – in whose diocese it was. For the Hadleigh parishioners, therefore, Canterbury held precedence over Norwich. Peculiars usually came about when the land in one parish was owned by a senior church dignitary who held high or privileged office in another, higher diocese. Hadleigh's peculiar was as a result of the will of Ealdorman Byrhtnoth of Essex, who bequeathed the town to the Priory of Canterbury Cathedral in the 10th century. The connection lives on in the name Canterbury Gardens, just below the almshouses. The peculiar was abolished in 1837 when great changes took place in the ecclesiastical boundaries.

❖ Other peculiars were **Monks Eleigh** and **Moulton** (peculiars to Canterbury) and **Freckenham** (peculiar to the Bishop of Rochester).

- ❖ The **Diocese of St Edmundsbury and Ipswich** came into being on 25 March 1914, when **Henry Hodgson** was enthroned as the first Bishop. So that the two counties of East and West Suffolk were represented, St James's in **Bury St Edmunds** was made the cathedral, while the residence of the new Bishop was **Ipswich**. The diocese has 479 parish churches, which includes parishes previously under the jurisdiction of the bishops of Ely and Norwich. 355 parishes from Norfolk merged with 177 from Ely to form the new diocese. The Bishop is assisted by the suffragan Bishop of Dunwich (whose ancient Episcopal See dates back to AD636 when Felix, the first bishop, was consecrated).

- ❖ Initially there was little or no structure to the church administration. The first Suffolk bishop was that of **Dunwich**, but when, in the late 11th century, Suffolk became part of the Diocese of Norwich, the title remained while the authority was lost. Initially there was a single archdeaconry but in 1125 an archdeacon was appointed for west and east Suffolk. The rural deans, who were a sub-division of the archdeacons, were responsible for areas that corresponded more or less with the secular hundreds.

- ❖ **Suffolk County Council** reported that between July 1996 and March 2005, 22,150 dwellings were built in Suffolk at an average annual rate of 2,530.

- ❖ In 2004–05, 63 percent of all housing completed in Suffolk was on previously developed 'brownfield' land, the highest level to date. This is the first time Suffolk has reached the national regional target of 60 percent.

- ❖ The Ipswich Associated Football Club (IAFC) was formed in 1878 at Portman Road, **Ipswich**, and became one of the first teams to use goal nets. It was not until 1936 that pressure mounted for the club to turn professional. **Ipswich Town Football Club** was launched at a luncheon at the Great White Horse and the toast was proposed by Stanley Rouse (later Sir Stanley), secretary of the Football Association and a Suffolk man. The football ground was on Portman Road, Ipswich.

- ❖ Captain John 'Ivan' Murray Cobbold (1897–1944) was the first chairman of the newly formed Ipswich Town FC.

- ❖ Two of the most famous managers of Ipswich Town FC were Sir Alf Ramsey (1920–1999) and Sir Bobby Robson. Sculptures of both men stand near the football ground at Portman Road, **Ipswich**.

- ❖ During Sir Alf Ramsey's reign, from 1955 to 1963, the team were nicknamed **Ramsey's Rural Rustics**, but they are now called the **Tractor Boys**.

❖ Soon after turning professional, Ipswich Town FC launched an open competition to find a club badge. The winning design was by John Gammage, a former postmaster and treasurer of the Supporters' Club. It included the **Suffolk Punch horse** because, said John, it was 'a noble animal, well suited to dominate our design and represent the club. And to complete the badge I thought of the town of Ipswich which contains many historical buildings, including the Wolsey Gate, and is close to the sea with a large dock area'.

❖ In 1995 the badge was given a facelift and the turrets of the Wolsey Gate (a relic of the 16th-century college founded by Cardinal Wolsey that stands on College Street, **Ipswich**) were moved to the top and the Suffolk Punch made bolder. The words Football Club replaced FC.

❖ Between 1942 and 1945 three million American military and auxiliary men and women passed through Great Britain. Because of the proximity of Suffolk to mainland Europe there were, in 1944, over 71,000 Americans in the county. For almost four years, one in seven people living in Suffolk was American.

❖ Nineteen new USAAF airbases were constructed in Suffolk during 1942 and 1943 for the use of the 8th Army Air Force. **Elveden Hall** was Divisional Headquarters and **Woodbridge** airfield was used as an Emergency Landing Group.

❖ The American airfield near **Alpheton** was used as the film setting for the classic *Twelve O'Clock High* (1949). Gregory Peck played Brigadier General Frank Savage, a World War Two flight commander taking over a struggling bomber group but eventually buckling under the strain of commanding countless bombing missions.

❖ Glenn Miller and his Army Air Force Band toured England during 1943 and 1944 giving over 800 performances, of which 500 were broadcast. In August 1944, only four months before he was killed, he gave an evening concert at **Parham** airfield attended by over 6,000.

❖ In 2006 the Adnams brewing company took delivery of the United Kingdom's largest commercial 'living roof' for its new brewery distribution centre just outside **Southwold**. The 2,382sq m roof is entirely covered in sedum, a living carpet of thick fleshy plants and grass that removes carbon dioxide and other pollutants from the air. Rainwater is trapped by the sedum and used in the depot.

The roof also has solar panels, which will heat 80 percent of the hot water on site, and waste water will be passed through a septic tank in reed beds for purification before being returned to nearby ponds.

The warehouse walls are 470mm thick and have a cavity wall constructed of two skins of blocks, which are filled with a hemp, chalk and lime mix. These bricks are claimed to be pioneer components in environmentally-friendly architecture.

❖ The East Anglian Ozone monitoring station is sited on the Lodge Wood Water Tower at **Sibton**.

❖ The Millennium Survey of British Butterflies was carried out between 1995 and 1999. The national database was updated annually and accumulated over 1.6 million butterfly records. Suffolk's contribution was 78,090 records from 1,088 tetrads (a tetrad is a 2 x 2km square).

❖ The piers at **Felixstowe, Lowestoft** and **Southwold** were built in the early 1900s by the Coastal Development Company, which ran the popular Belle steamers that brought day-trippers up to the Suffolk coast from London Bridge. Lowestoft has two piers; Claremont Pier is over 600ft in length and the South Pier forms part of the harbour wall. The original pier at **Southwold** was 810ft long and built in 1899.

❖ In 2002 the paddle steamer *Waverley*, Britain's only surviving sea-going steam passenger ship, resumed its tours of the Suffolk coast. The *Waverley* was rescued and restored by the Paddle Steamer Preservation Society.

❖ For many centuries the villages of **Culford, Ingham, Timworth, West Stow** and **Wordwell** were part of a single estate that covered some 10,000 acres. In 1935 around half of the land was sold to the Forestry Commission and was renamed the **King's Forest** in honour of George V's Jubilee.

❖ In 1996 an historic cast-iron bridge was discovered in the grounds of **Culford School** after years hidden behind reeds and undergrowth. The 28m bridge dates from 1803 and was considered so important that English Heritage immediately awarded it a Grade I listing. It turned out to be one of Britain's oldest iron bridges and one of the few left unmodified. Believed to be the work of Samuel Wyatt, the bridge has the earliest known example of hollow iron ribs.

Culford dates from the 18th century and was once the home of Lord Cornwallis, defeated commander of British forces in the American Revolution and later Governor-General in Bengal. Culford Hall has been a school since the estate was sold in 1935.

TWO – THE COAST

THE 50-mile coastline, from **Gorleston** in the north to **Felixstowe** in the south, is constantly at war with the superior might and force of the North Sea, and has been for centuries. There is no coastal road as such because the coastline is a series of estuaries, shingle, dunes and cliffs, which has helped, over the years, to maintain its timeless beauty. Almost everywhere now bears some evidence of modernity, yet sailing up stretches of the rivers **Deben** or **Ore,** it is likely that the tidal mudflats and marshlands are not dissimilar to those which the invading Vikings saw as they advanced up the Orwell to plunder and colonise the riverside communities. However, the coastline is changing all the time, constantly shaped and reshaped by the sea; the littoral drift, whereby sediments are moved along a beach shore, is always at work. High spring tides and waves do huge damage to the sandy shores, nowhere more obviously than at **Covehithe,** where the tarmacked road comes to an abrupt and jagged end, or in tales of the lost early mediaeval town of **Dunwich.** Extraordinarily high tides were recorded in the 16th century at **Butley** and in 1799 11 houses were demolished at one time by a high tide at **Aldeburgh.** In 1953 those living on the Suffolk coast were reminded of the might and power of the lethal combination of high tides and 90 mile an hour winds.

The Suffolk coast is a rare and beautiful thing except, of course, when storms and high winds cause the loss of ships and their crew. It is no accident that the lighthouses at **Orford, Southwold** and **Lowestoft** are within a few miles of one another, a clue to the treacherous nature of that part of the coast. In 1627, on one night alone, 32 ships were wrecked on **Orfordness** with barely a survivor among the crews. In one great storm in 1770, 30 vessels were lost off **Lowestoft** and in October 1789, 40 more ran aground off **Southwold.** In 1889, many ships sunk off the coast at Lowestoft and in December 1899 seven men perished when the **Aldeburgh** lifeboat capsized. Occasionally, if the gale was blowing in the right direction, ships were forced out across the North Sea and ended up in Holland. Here are a few stories about the nature of the coast, its mariners and some of its features:

❖ **The Armada Post**
   The Armada Post was erected on the High Street, **Lowestoft,** to commemorate the great battle that the English fought with the

Spanish Armada in 1588. Records show that the sailing vessel *Elizabeth* from Lowestoft was commandeered and used successfully as a fire ship in the battle against the Spanish fleet anchored off Calais. Although no ship was set alight, the fire ships scattered the Spanish galleons to such an extent that by the time they were able to regroup the battle was lost. The post was originally placed in 1688 and was renewed in 1788, 1888 and most recently by the Lowestoft and East Suffolk Maritime Society in 1998. The original purpose of the post, which bears the initials 'TM' (for Thomas Meldrum, owner of the *Elizabeth*), is unknown and there have been many theories as to its use.

❖ **Martello Towers**
Between 1805 and 1812, during the Napoleonic wars, 18 Martello Towers were built along the coast from **Aldeburgh** down to the Orwell Estuary. Looking like upturned flowerpots, or gasometers, 11 still stand and serve as a reminder of a time when the threat of a French invasion was taken very seriously. A recruiting leaflet of the time did not mince its words in the face of perceived danger: 'Bonaparte threatens to invade us. He promises to enrich his soldiers with our property, to glut their lust with our wives and daughters.'

Suffolkers in general, though, were unimpressed by the possibility of invasion, and a verse in an old song of the 18th century ran:

> The French are a comin',
> Oh dear, oh dear,
> They're all owd women,
> So we don't keer!

However, the politicians in London considered the east coast to be the likely point of invasion and it was left to Captain William Ford of the Royal Engineers to come up with an effective form of defence, should the French attempt beach landings. Not a man to do things by halves, and no doubt aware of the irony, Captain Ford recalled the troubles that had beset the British Navy in 1794 when they had been faced by a huge, French-built defence tower at Martella Point on the island of Corsica, Napoleon's birthplace. Sketches had been made of the Corsican tower and Captain Ford suggested a chain of similar towers along the British coast, starting at **Aldeburgh** and finishing at Newhaven in Sussex. The idea was not to maintain fully manned garrisons, but that each tower should have a long-range 24-pound cannon and enough manpower to engage the enemy sufficient for the navy to arrive. The towers were to be some 30ft tall, squat, ovoid-shaped and of immense strength (to withstand sustained bombardment) with only one or two narrow gun ports. They would be called Martello towers after that at Martella.

Captain Ford's proposal was approved, plans were drawn up for land purchase and building contractors commissioned. Each tower needed some 700,000 bricks, which came by barge from London, and the walls were thicker on the seaward side. By the summer of 1805 the beaches at **Shingle Street**, **Bawdsey**, **Alderton** and the cliffs at **Felixstowe** had become huge building sites. The **Aldeburgh** tower was the last to be constructed and its quatrefoil design is different to the rest.

While this frantic, and absurdly expensive building was getting underway, news came of Nelson's victory at Trafalgar, in October 1805, making an imminent French invasion of Britain less likely. Nevertheless, the French fleet had recovered before and, indeed, it looked as if Napoleon and his allies were yet more determined to invade and conquer Britain. Building of the towers continued until 1812 and Britain stood ready to repel the French invasion. By yet another coincidence this was the same year that Napoleon lost out on the Russian front thus making an invasion of Britain impossible. Not one Martello Tower ever fired a shot in anger and the string of newly built towers became one of the most costly coastal defences in English history.

❖ **The Tar Barrel on Woodbridge Church**

The Martello Towers were also designed to be the first link in a chain of signals that would have been triggered in the event of a French invasion. Should any of the Martellos send out a warning, church towers further inland would take up the semaphore action by lighting fires on high points and so alerting the entire county. In most parishes the highest point was the church tower and in **Woodbridge**, it was the tower of St Mary's. For many years a barrel of tar was kept ready on its roof to be fired as a signal. Mercifully it was never needed.

❖ **The Dunkirkers**

French invaders of an earlier age who did besiege the Suffolk coast successfully were the Dunkirkers, groups of pirates based at Dunkirk who attacked defenceless shipping and generally caused havoc on the high seas for the best part of the 17th century. As early as June 1604, Sir Julius Caesar, Judge of the Admiralty, wrote to King James' Council complaining of the outrages of the Dunkirkers in the seas off northern Europe and beyond.

On 23 September 1630, Captain Francis Sydenham was sent to **Orfordness** with instructions to repel the pirates by any means at his disposal, 'to take any of them or sink or fire them'.

During the Great Migrations of the 1630s, ships leaving for the New World crossed the seas together so as to afford some protection against these pirates. In 1630 **John Winthrop** of **Groton** (first Governor of Massachusetts) reported feared sightings of the Dunkirkers in his Shipboard Journal and, on 10 April, heard that the barque *Warwick* was taken by them.

John Rous, incumbent of **Santon Downham**, wrote in his diary of 1626 that the Dunkirkers 'troubled our seas' and that they had 'taken our shippes, and feared our merchants'.

❖   **Women Pirates**

Two of the most famous women pirates of the 16th century were Lady Mary Killigrew, the daughter of a Suffolk pirate from **Woolverstone**, and Mrs Peter Lambert, wife of a small time smuggler and pirate of **Aldeburgh**. While these ladies might not have captained pirate ships, though it is thought that Lady Killigrew might have gone to sea on her father's vessels, they were accessories to the act of piracy.

Lady Mary was the daughter of Philip Wolverston, squire of Woolverstone Hall and described as 'a distinguished gentleman pirate of Suffolk'. In about 1547, Mary married Sir John Killigrew (as her second husband), who belonged to a notorious and infamous Cornish family whose members perpetrated various piratical activities off the English coast and beyond. Elizabeth I tolerated them and other peacetime pirates, as such people were often useful in times of war. The Killigrews controlled several syndicates of pirates around the coast of Great Britain but they were careful never to steal from the Queen. However, Mary Killigrew fell foul of her sovereign when her mother-in-law, Elizabeth Killigrew, seized a stricken ship, murdered the crew and stole the cargo, which included jewels, silver and currency. Mary Killigrew was implicated as she was the family 'fence' and arranged for the disposal of pirated goods.

Although arrested and tried, the Queen almost immediately pardoned Mary Killigrew, knowing that she might one day be in need of the Killigrew family's services.

Mrs Peter Lambert was active in the late 1500s, working as her husband's on-shore fence and collaborator. Inevitably, Peter was duly caught and imprisoned in **Aldeburgh** gaol for his misdemeanours on the high seas. Mrs Lambert cooked a file in a meat pie, which got past the guard and was used to good effect. Peter Lambert escaped and returned to sea where, together with his wife, he continued his nefarious ways.

❖ **Lifeboats and Lighthouses**

In the 17th and 18th century, mariners off the **Suffolk** coast were helped by the placement of on-shore lights, to mark known hazards. This was done by means of a beacon fire, kept burning on the top of a stone or brick tower on a hill near the sea. At **Orford** the fire was kept burning on top of the castle keep and it was not until 1822 that the last of the beacons was replaced.

Lights (being tallow candles) were first displayed at **Lowestoft Ness** in 1609 (one on the beach, the Low Light, and another on the cliff top, the High Light) 'for the direction of ships which crept by night in the dangerous passage betwixt Lowestoft and Winterton'. A coal fire was used on top of High Light, but the Guild of Trinity House replaced it in 1676 with a 40ft high structure of stone and brick (not only the first to be built by Trinity House, but also the first in England to be built of brick). The Low Light was replaced several times but was finally dismantled in 1922.

Orford Ness was lit in 1634 when John Meldrum obtained a patent to build two temporary lights between **Sizewell Bank** and **Aldeburgh Napes**. The two timber towers were owned and managed by different owners over the years, some more diligent than others. In 1707, when Britain was at war with France, the Orford Ness lighthouse was attacked by a French Privateer who damaged a lantern and stole various goods, including the keeper's bed. Lord Braybrooke commissioned a new brick tower to be built in 1792 further back from the earlier lights, which remains to the present day.

Southwold lighthouse was completed in 1890 and had a range of

17 miles. Originally the light was generated from Argand burners but in 1938 electricity was installed.

Although ships were regularly wrecked off the coast, it was not until the early 19th century that the first lifeboats were organised. Up until then it was left to local fishermen to help in the event of a ship in distress, using their own vessels, which were usually fishing boats and barely adequate for the task.

In 1801, **Lowestoft** was the first to have a specially designated lifeboat (and it is the oldest lifeboat station in the British Isles), but its design proved unsuitable for the task. A few years later the first sailing lifeboat was built and named *Francis Ann*. Over the next few years a special 'Norfolk and Suffolk' lifeboat design was perfected, with an almost flat bottom, so that it could operate where the unseen and moving sandbanks often proved the undoing of deep draught vessels. A surviving example of the 'Norfolk and Suffolk' is the 44ft *Alfred Corry*, dedicated at Southwold in 1893 and remaining in service until 1918. She is now restored and on show at the Alfred Corry Museum at the seaward end of Southwold Harbour.

Organisations began to form to control the operation of the lifeboats, firstly the Suffolk Humane Society (formed at **Kessingland** in 1806), then in 1924 the Suffolk Association for Saving the Lives of Shipwrecked Seamen (a branch of the Royal National Institution for the Preservation of Life from Shipwreck, the original name of the Royal National Lifeboat Institution).

At the start of the 20th century plans were afoot to develop a marine internal combustion engine. In 1904 one was fitted to a lifeboat for the first time and in 1920 the first motor lifeboat was placed at Lowestoft and another at Southwold the following year.

In 1940, 19 Suffolk lifeboats went to Dunkirk to help with the evacuation of the British Expeditionary Force, including that from Southwold and the *Michael Stephens* from **Lowestoft**, which had only been in service a year. Twice rammed by motor torpedo boats, she completed her task and returned under her own power.

❖ *Watch The Wall, My Darling, While The Gentlemen Go By!*
There was never a time when smuggling did not take place off the Suffolk coast, mostly with Holland and northern France. Even in 1224 the people of **Orford** were urged to assist the Keeper of the Shore to prevent smuggling. During the 17th and 18th century,

though, it was at its height and exemplified by Rudyard Kipling's famous poem, *The Smuggler's Song*, which warned those awake at midnight not to draw back the blind or look into the street if they heard a horse's feet, as it was only the 'gentlemen' going by.

While smuggling went on all the time, the very high taxes of the 17th century both encouraged it and made it worth the risk. A pound of tea, for example, could be bought in Holland for 10 pence but the duty on it was twice that sum. Also, seamen discharged after the various wars ended, once home, found it difficult to find work but easy to throw their lot in with the smugglers. Local farm workers also welcomed the chance to earn a little extra as couriers or receive goods in return for their silence. Farmers allowed smugglers the use of their horses, an unspoken arrangement whereby the horses were returned along with a share of the booty. Due to stringent taxation there was a high degree of support for the smugglers, even from the clergy, who were not averse to accepting brandy from the 'gentlemen'. The Revd Francis Cunningham, vicar of **Pakefield**, was required to conduct a burial service over a 'dead seaman' at eight o'clock in the morning, only to discover later that he had read the service over a load of valuable lace. The Revd Meadows, rector of **Great Bealings**, was reputed to have left his stables unlocked, with the chaise and harness ready for the smugglers to convey goods to distribution points inland. The feet of a strategically driven flock of sheep invariably obliterated traces of human feet, wheels and horses' hooves.

The rivers, or runs as they were known locally, were an easy way of getting the contraband inland, although the major centre for smuggling was 40 miles inland, at **Hadleigh**, where the George Inn was the home of a notorious gang leader, John Harvey. **Ipswich** was easily reached by the Orwell and the Butt and Oyster at **Pin Mill** was a favourite resort of smugglers. **Martlesham Creek**, just a stone's throw from **Woodbridge**, was well used as a beach landing, as was **Aldeburgh**. The Queen's Head Inn at **Blyford** was a convenient stopping-off and storage place, where kegs of brandy were hidden above the fireplace and at the church across the road.

The inn at **Eastbridge** was peculiar in being a billet for dragoons, officers of the law, and also a meeting place for some of the leading villains of their time including Crocky Fellowes, Sam Newson and Quids Thornton, who operated a highly successful operation between there and the inn at **Aldringham**.

The Hadleigh and **Sizewell** gangs were notorious for violent encounters on the beaches with the preventative forces whose job it was to preserve the Revenue. The gangs numbered over a hundred men, each man with two horses, and made a formidable opponent for the stretched preventative services. On at least one occasion a huge consignment of contraband goods was landed on Sizewell beach and there were as many as 300 horses and 100 carts to be seen at one time loading tea, brandy and gin. Leonard P. Thompson, in *Smugglers of the Suffolk Coast*, records estimates of 4,551 horse-loads of contraband being run into Suffolk during 1745 alone. This is attributed to the fact that the Revenue boats were taken off smuggling duty in anticipation of a French invasion, with the intention of using them as tenders to the naval squadrons assembling on the East coast.

Early in the 19th century the authorities began to get the upper hand, chiefly by uniting various enforcement groups and ordering their cooperation with the Revenue officers. By the 1830s the law pertaining to excise was handed to the Admiralty and in 1856 foundations were laid for what became the Coastguard Service.

❖ **The Battle of Sole Bay**

During the 17th century, **Southwold** was England's chief fleet anchorage. Coastal erosion has since worn away **Easton Ness** to the north, and **Dunwich** to the south, but at the time it formed **Sole Bay**. It was here that the English fleet assembled for refits and victualling and here, too, that one of the most famous naval battles took place between the Allied Fleet of England and France against the Dutch.

On 28 May 1672 (the date sometimes appears as 7 June due to differences in the Gregorian and Julian calendars) hundreds of people lined up on the cliff edges of **Southwold** and **Dunwich** to watch the Battle of Sole Bay, played out over 14 hours. The morning fog, and later the smoke from the gunfire, made it difficult to see, but the noise was horrendous. Gunfire was heard as far away as London and smoke from the guns and burning ships drifted down the coast as far south as Essex. Some 50,000 men were engaged in the battle, approximately 25,000 on each side, although halfway through the French abandoned the fight, thus giving the advantage of numbers to the Dutch.

Admiral Michiel de Ruyter, a veteran of 32 sea battles, was in command of the Dutch fleet, and had at his disposal over 90 war ships and 36 fireships, which carried 4,202 guns. The Allied Fleet, in contrast, had over 120 vessels plus a number of fireships and pinnaces amounting to around 4,950 guns. The Dutch, though, had the advantage of surprise in that they caught the English and French napping. Having received intelligence that the Dutch fleet was safely anchored at Walcheren Island, approximately 90 nautical miles from Southwold, the fleet had assembled at Sole Bay to careen (run the ships ashore to remove barnacles from the hull) and to allow the crews shore leave. The Duke of York (later James II), together with the Earl of Sandwich and the French Admiral, Comte d'Estrées, made their headquarters at **Sutherland House** in the High Street. The plan was to defeat the Dutch Navy and deny the North Sea to Dutch shipping.

At 2.30am a French frigate reported that the Dutch Fleet had been sighted only two hours sailing away and was approaching from the North East with a good wind behind it. The Allied Fleet was put on immediate alert.

By 5.30am the English fleet had slowly put to sea, many of them having cut their anchor cables and, perforce, leaving hundreds of sailors not only stranded ashore but still asleep in the ale houses of Southwold, Dunwich and **Walberswick**.

As the Dutch onslaught began, things went badly for the Allies. As Admiral of the English fleet, the Duke of York had, in the course of the battle, to move his flag twice, finally to the *London,* as his flagships, the 100-gun *Prince Royal* and the *St Michael*, were taken out of action.

Losses were heavy on both sides. The Duke engaged de Ruyter head on, losing six ships through damage but disabling three of the Dutch. Then, the 100-gun *Royal James* (the newest and largest ship in the fleet), flagship of the Earl of Sandwich, was attacked by several fire ships and set ablaze, forcing the Earl to jump into the sea, where he drowned.

However, just when things began to look hopeless, the Dutch fleet fell into apparent disarray. The squadron of Admiral Willem Joseph van Ghent was in a state of confusion and the Duke realised he could take advantage of the situation. He sent his fire ships in among the Dutch fleet. It transpired that van Ghent himself had been killed and the chain of command was broken. The English ships began to sink or capture the Dutch vessels and by late afternoon the following day the battle was declared over.

The figurehead (a red lion) from one of the Dutch ships, the 48-gun *Stravoren*, was salvaged and can still be seen on the outside of the Red Lion Inn at **Martlesham Hill**.

The battle had been bitterly fought, although extraordinarily the English lost only the *Royal James* and a few fire ships, with eight vessels severely disabled. The Dutch had two ships sunk, one captured, and many more very badly damaged. Both sides claimed victory but the battle ended inconclusively. The English–French plan to blockade the Dutch was abandoned and it was the following year before the fleets met again at the Battle of Schooneveld.

All three combatants suffered considerable casualties: the English lost 2,500 men, the Dutch 1,800 and the French 450. For months afterwards, corpses and limbs were washed ashore and locals were paid a shilling for finding and burying a body. Over 800 wounded were landed at Southwold to be cared for in the town.

❖ **The Cannons on Gun Hill**
The six cannons mounted on Southwold's **Gun Hill** (previously known as St Edmund's Hill), pointing out across the North Sea, are not relics of the Battle of Sole Bay but are much older. They are thought to be 16th century, as they bear the Tudor Rose and Crown, and as such are among the earliest surviving in the country. The guns have a chequered history, and no one is quite sure where they stood originally, but in 1822 they came to the attention of George IV when they were fired in celebration of his sailing past Southwold on his way to Scotland. The king was not best pleased, as the guns were supposed to be out of service, but some 20 years later they were still capable of being fired to mark Queen Victoria's progress along the coast, also on her way to Scotland.

During World War One the guns were mistaken for fortifications, resulting in Southwold being bombarded by the Germans. The guns were removed and buried, being returned to Gun Hill in the 1920s. During World War Two they were again removed and buried. In his book *North-East Suffolk* Allan Jobson wrote, 'At present they are buried, but will come out again when the sun of Peace shines in full splendour', which indeed they did.

❖ During World War Two the borough of **Southwold** was designated a special Evacuation Area and the population was reduced to some 700. 2,040 warnings of the approach of enemy aircraft were recorded, placing the town under siege from the air. Many of the 700 people were firemen, air-raid wardens and bomb damage repair squads. The first aerial incident comprised a string of 100lb bombs that fell in Hotson Road. Altogether there were 28 incidents through the war and 77 buildings were destroyed. On 15 May 1943, 13 people lost their lives.

❖ **The Beach Companies**
On the pebbled foreshore north of Whapload Road in **Lowestoft** there are several old and very large anchors, marking the spot where the beach companies operated between 1762 and the 1940s. Their main business was recovering, or 'swiping', anchors which had been lost from vessels riding out gales in the offshore anchorages. Ships sometimes gathered in very large numbers waiting for a change in wind direction that would enable them to sail round Lowestoft Ness. The anchors would subsequently be sold to needy ships at a considerable profit.

The men of the beach companies used 'yoles' (often spelt 'yawls'), which were fast, seaworthy open beach boats about 50ft (15m) long. Their chief work was pilotage, salvage and, when the need arose, lifesaving from ships driven onto the treacherous offshore sandbanks.

❖ **Orfordness**
The spit at **Orford Ness** (now a National Trust Reserve) is the largest of its kind in Europe and the only one that bears any vegetation. It is formed by the rivers Ore and Alde on one side and the sea on the other. From 1913 to the mid-1980s it was a top secret military experimental station and important aircraft tests were carried out during World War One. A device for protecting aeroplanes against balloon barrage attack was developed here and much of the research carried out at Orfordness eventually led to the startling invention of radar by Robert Watson Watt and colleagues at **Bawdsey**, just prior to World War Two. The scientists called Orfordness 'the Island'. The Crown and Castle Hotel at **Orford** was a short boat trip away and a regular meeting place for the scientists. It was said that the sitting room at the hotel was an unofficial conference room.

❖ **The Home of Radar**
In 1935 **Bawdsey** was chosen as the new site for the development of

radio direction finding and the Manor House, close to **Bawdsey Quay**, became home to a small team of scientists led by Robert Watson Watt (1892–1973). In 1935, in a field near Daventry, Watson Watt and colleagues had demonstrated that an aircraft up to eight miles away could be detected using radio waves. After further research at their **Orfordness** base, Watson Watt and Arnold Wilkins had wanted to expand operations and looked round for a suitable site. Bawdsey Manor was up for sale, and as soon as the Air Ministry completed its purchase, the team of scientists moved down from Orfordness and began planning a series of experiments over the sea.

The estate was purchased from Sir Cuthbert Quilter, who had started building Bawdsey Manor in 1886 and carried on the process for another 20 years. It is a combination of Victorian Gothic, Tudor and Oriental styles but its proximity to the sea and relative isolation was just what the scientists needed. Stables and outbuildings were duly converted into laboratories and the new station was presided over by Squadron Leader (later Air Marshal Sir) Raymond Hart who became the first RAF officer at Bawdsey.

In February 1937 Bawdsey became the first radar training school in the world and the first of the proposed Chain Home radar stations round the English coast, which in Suffolk included a second station at **Darsham** (opened in the 1930s but demolished in 1957). In June 1939 prime minister Winston Churchill flew to **Martlesham** Heath and was taken to Bawdsey, where he was shown round by Robert Watson Watt, though the latter later recorded he might have been wasting his time trying to explain radar to the former!

By the outbreak of war in 1939 there were four 360ft transmitter towers in position and four lattice receiving masts so that aircraft could be detected from a distance of 140 miles. The use of radar to track incoming enemy planes was a vital factor in detecting day and night air attacks. There is no doubt that the development of radar contributed hugely to the progress of World War Two, with the Bawdsey station able to provide long-range early warning for the North Sea and Channel approaches, which bought the fighter squadrons valuable time in scrambling their aircraft to intercept the Luftwaffe.

❖ **The Bawdsey Boffins**
The word **boffin,** a slang term for a scientist or engineer engaged in technical or scientific research, was first used colloquially to

describe the group of brilliant scientists at **Bawdsey** and **Orfordness** in the 1930s and 1940s and has subsequently been applied to describe the stereotypical eccentric men in thick spectacles and white lab coats, obsessively working with complicated scientific apparatus with undoubted, if absent-minded, genius.

The name came from a restaurant called *Boffin's*, founded by the Boffin family at 107 High Street, Oxford (and later at the Central Tea, Coffee and Refreshment Rooms in Carfax), which was frequented by some of the scientists when they were at Oxford.

Besides being a real surname, the word turns up in the writings of Anthony Trollope, George Bernard Shaw, William Morris, J.R.R. Tolkien and Charles Dickens (in *Our Mutual Friend* there is a clerk named Nicodemus Boffin who is described as a 'very odd looking old fellow'.) It was also a naval term for an older naval officer and Sir Robert Watson-Watt himself thought it might be a combination of the word 'puffin' (a bird that is both serious and comical at the same time) and the Blackburn 'Baffin', an early British biplane described as having a Heath-Robinsonish appearance. Whatever its origins, it is certain that the word as applied to absent-minded professors came into general use during World War Two at Orfordness and has remained in common parlance ever since.

❖ Another of the boffins, Professor Robert Hanbury Brown (1916–2002), wrote a book about the development of miniaturised radar for installation in night fighters, which was entitled *Boffin* (1991). He joined the group at **Orfordness** and then at **Bawdsey** but in 1942 he was posted to Washington to assist the Americans in their radar developments. In 1947 he joined Robert Watson Watt in a firm of consultants on radar and related topics but developed an interest in astronomy and became the confidant of astronomer Bernard Lovell. Together they pioneered major new pieces of radio research that used the telescope.

❖ **Coastal Decoy Sites**
During the first year of World War Two the Air Ministry formed a secret department whose brief was to fool the German Luftwaffe pilots by constructing decoy airfields and other devices along the east coast. In charge of operations was Colonel Sir John Turner, a qualified pilot who had served in the Corps of Royal Engineers, who based himself at the Sound City Film Studios in Shepperton.

War conditions forced the film studios to be more inventive with their sets and, because of inconsistent daylight, they had developed expertise in clever lighting techniques. Colonel Turner wanted to utilise the knowledge of the film set creators and artists to build decoy sites along authentic military lines sufficient to draw the fire of the enemy bombers. The mock-ups had to be of an extremely high standard as enemy photography was known to be good and installations had to pass scrutiny from the air. There were no spare or obsolete aircraft so even they had to be constructed to be as realistic as possible. The film studios turned out lifelike replicas of Spitfires, Wellingtons, Hurricanes and Blenheims, mostly made from wood and, later, canvas which could be inflated. To mimic troop movement it was often necessary to move the decoy aircraft from one site to another.

The resulting decoys were so successful that even at ground level they could deceive. Many people thought that new airfields were being built but were confused by the lack of aerial activity. They also fooled the Allied pilots on occasions and a resident crew had to be stationed locally to warn off pilots attempting to land on the 'new' airfields. Ironically, the Decoy Men were probably the only servicemen who were actively inviting the Luftwaffe to bomb them, rather than their legitimate targets of real airfields, factories, towns and cities.

One of the first was at **Sutton Heath** where a dummy aerodrome was planned during 1939. Others were built at **Gislingham, Cavenham** and **Lidgate**. Night dummies were placed at **Kesgrave, Woolverstone, Waldringfield, Kirton** and **Trimley**, among others. Those used for night use were known as 'Q' sites and from the air would have looked like a runway flarepath. Naval 'Starfish' sites were added later to look like small towns or villages by day, while at night they would look as though bombs were exploding and buildings were on fire. Designed to lure the bombers away from **Lowestoft** and other ports, the Starfish were particularly crucial and the one at **Lound** did its work effectively throughout the war.

Evidence of the success of the decoys came in 1944 when a reconnaissance aircraft was brought down on **Wantisden Heath**. Camera equipment was discovered in the wreckage and the pilot's mission had been to obtain infra-red photographs of the **Hollesley** decoy site.

Other decoys included coastal gun sites and a particularly clever device known as 'Fortitude' that involved moving dummy convoys of landing craft, tanks and lorries. It was calculated that the decoys deflected over 2,000 tons of bombs that would otherwise have devastated large parts of East Anglia and beyond.

❖ **The East Coast Floods of 1953**
Shortly before midnight on 31 January 1953, the worst floods in living memory hit Suffolk. Without any warning, the rampaging North Sea smashed through existing coastal defences in what was to be one of the most violent and prolonged northerly gales in British meteorological history. By the time it subsided, over 100 lives had been lost (46 in Suffolk), 21,000 people were made homeless, 200,000 acres of farmland and pasture were under water, and countless cattle, horses, sheep and poultry had been drowned.

Many had gone to bed that night having heard news of the sinking of the *Princess Victoria*, a ferry running between Stranraer and Larne, five miles off the coast of Northern Ireland. Huge seas had burst open the doors on the car deck and 128 people lost their lives. During the day there had also been reports of serious flooding on the other side of the North Sea, in Holland, where vast areas of land were under water and there were initial reports of a high death toll. At no point was any warning given that the weather conditions surrounding these two incidents might be repeated on mainland East Anglia. Those who listened to their radios before turning in were concerned, but did not think that there was any immediate danger.

During the night of 31 January/1 February a combination of gale force north-westerly winds, with wind speeds of over 100 miles per hour, plus exceptionally high tides, caused havoc along the whole of the East Coast as billions of tons of sea water created a tidal surge. **Felixstowe** was one of the worst hit when flood waters from the River Orwell raced across **Fagbury Marshes** and swamped dozens of one-storey pre-fab houses. Over 50 beach huts and 100 boats from **Felixstowe Ferry** were swept on to the RAF base at **Bawdsey**. The river wall between Bawdsey and **Ramsholt** was breached in 53 places.

Huge trees were uprooted and in the countryside whole communities were cut off and without power, telephone lines were down, roads were blocked and railways severely disrupted. Hundreds of caravans were reduced to matchwood and not only homes but also shops, schools, businesses and the harbours were badly flooded or uninhabitable. Much of **Rendlesham Forest** was devastated in the space of 20 minutes as the mean wind speed of nearly 60 miles per hour continued unabated for nearly 10 minutes.

In the dark, and in horrendous weather conditions, families were evacuated from their houses as the rising tide forced many onto the roofs. At **Lowestoft,** where 400 homes disappeared under water almost immediately, a spectacular rescue of 40 youngsters and parents took place from St John's Church. The children had taken refuge in the church, but water poured in through the church door and forced those inside up into the chancel, where the verger 'sat waist deep in water playing nursery rhymes on the piano in order to take the children's minds off their ordeal'. Help eventually arrived in the form of two local fishermen, who rowed the children to safety.

Thousands of sandbags were filled and positioned in doorways but were useless as the tide rose. Most at risk were those living in seaside bungalows, prefabs and ground floor or basement rooms.

Four men later received flood awards, including Leading Fireman John Barley of Lowestoft, who received the BEM for exceptional bravery when, 'without thought for his personal safety he waded neck-deep into the swirling water to save an unconscious man with great difficulties and attendant dangers'.

Councillor Jenson was also awarded the BEM for 'gallantry shown during the flood when he waded from house to house giving assurance to people, saving pigs and other livestock and working tirelessly for 15 days in the Whapload Road area'.

Southwold was completely cut off for 48 hours and some 300ft of the South Pier structure was washed away. The dining room of the White Lion Hotel was under four feet of water and many records kept at the **Moot Hall** had later to be dried out. Some were damaged beyond repair. Four people drowned and a fifth body was never recovered.

Arriving at Ipswich Station, the **Ipswich Town Football Club** team was marooned there for almost five hours. The football ground at Portman Road was under several feet of water and a pump was used to reduce the volume of water from the main stand enclosure. Three weeks later, a strong Ipswich Town team beat a Royal Navy XI 3–1 in aid of the East Coast Flood Relief Fund, in a match that raised £158 2s 6d.

Help came from many quarters, including the British Red Cross Detachment at **Claydon** and 2,000 cadets from **HMS *Ganges*.**

Assistance came, too, from the Salvation Army (who provided tea wagons), the East Suffolk Police force, **RAF Wattisham** and the American airbase at **Bentwaters**. Tales of bravery and tragedy were numerous and it was many months, even years, before the memory of that night was wiped from people's minds. The rescue services were stretched almost beyond endurance and many of those who returned to their homes days later found they had lost everything. Others found mud, rotting debris, sewage and water damage that made thousands of homes uninhabitable.

❖ **European Gateway Disaster**

At 22.30 hours on 19 December 1982 the MV *European Gateway* left her **Felixstowe** berth, bound for Rotterdam Europoort. On board were 34 crew and 36 passengers, mainly long-distance lorry drivers. Twenty minutes later the ferry was in collision with Harwich-bound *Speedlink Vanguard*, which tore a 200ft gash in the side of the *European Gateway*'s shell plating. More than 10,000 tonnes of water poured into the ship. The two vessels locked together, the *European Gateway* impaled on her starboard side. The *Speedlink Vanguard* pivoted and the ships broke free, sending a huge shower of sparks up into the night skies. The *European Gateway* keeled over on to one side and, amid high seas and a vicious south-westerly force six gale, a wall of water 3ft high swept through the ship from starboard to port. Within minutes the *European Gateway* ran aground, the main freight deck submerged, and she capsized on her starboard side, coming to rest close to the Felixstowe Ledge Buoy and just clear of the shipping channel.

Officers sounded the Mayday signal and a full-scale rescue operation got underway. Lifeboats and tugs in the immediate area joined pilot launches and four helicopters were scrambled. The men from the Trinity House pilotage were among the first on the scene and managed to save 48 lives. The 40ft Trinity House launch *Valour* made several runs under the dangerously listing superstructure of the ferry as lorries and containers began to shift in the holds or slide off the decks into the sea. Drums of poisonous and inflammable chemicals also rolled into the sea and many were later washed up on the shore. The men of the *Valour* lived up to the name of their launch that night as they first had to rescue the lifeboat which, due to the list, was dangling too far away from the ship for boarding. Once it hit the water the launch pushed the lifeboat back towards the side of the ferry and held it alongside. With debris crashing down around them and the constant threat that the ship would roll over on top of them, they allowed 28 men to use it as a bridge to the *Valour* and to safety.

Inside was chaos. Within minutes of the impact the engineers down below looked up to see a wall of water crashing through the open watertight door, which then poured through to the stabiliser and main engine rooms. Almost immediately the starboard generator packed up and, starved of fuel, the main engines stopped working. On the night of the collision, all three watertight doors were still open and once flooding occurred the two doors to the generator room needed to be closed within 50 seconds in order to save the ship. It was impossible and as the vessel began to list the engineers abandoned the task.

Six lives were lost and 64 people were rescued. The body of one of the crew, Joseph Topp, was not found until April the following year.

The 35-day Government inquiry found that the collision was caused jointly by both captains, the captain of the *European Gateway* being found guilty of serious negligence in navigation by attempting to cross ahead of the *Speedlink Vanguard*. Both captains were allowed to keep their master's ticket and neither was suspended.

The *European Gateway* wreck lay on a sandbank just off Felixstowe for three months until an ambitious, and eventually successful, £1 million salvage operation got under way. After being righted by Dutch salvage engineers in February 1983, she underwent repairs and was sold on for service in Greek waters.

❖ **The Scallop on the Beach**
Scallops mean different things to different people. Its meat is a favourite with both Eastern and Western seafood lovers and its shell is generally associated with mediaeval pilgrims, St James of Compostella in particular. In the days when a pilgrim need only present him or herself at a church, castle, abbey or manor house in order to be given sustenance, the provisions were not unlimited but as much as could be taken with one scoop of the scallop. The scallop is also a fertility symbol, perhaps because it is hermaphroditic, and its wavy patterned shape appears in heraldry, art and on countless logos, including that of a multinational oil company. To this list may now be added the scallop sculpture on

Aldeburgh beach which, in the three short years since it was put there, has attracted enough controversy to make it one of the best-known sculptures in England. It has earned untold kudos for its creator, the internationally renowned artist Maggie Hambling. Thus, a work by a Suffolk artist to commemorate a Suffolk composer (Benjamin Britten), who in turn was inspired by a Suffolk poet (George Crabbe), has had nine alternative sites investigated and rejected, is regularly vandalised (11 incidents to date) and there have been numerous local protests and petitions to have it removed or at least moved to another part of the beach.

Endless columns and Letters to the Editor in the local and national press have been devoted to it and its nicknames include 'the tin can' and 'the tin man'. It is, say detractors, quite simply in the wrong place and spoils an otherwise uncluttered and beautiful shingle beach which Britten himself loved for that very reason. Conversely, its supporters say it is a work of art that enhances the landscape and 'forms a conversation with the sea' as intended by the artist.

The 11ft (4m) high steel sculpture, named *Scallop* but dubbed 'The Scallop of the East', was unveiled on Aldeburgh beach in November 2003. It cost in the region of £70,000 and was built by steel fabricators J.T. Pegg's of Aldeburgh under the supervision of Maggie Hambling, who lives near **Saxmundham**. *Scallop* is anchored in beach shingle and made in two separate pieces. Along the top edge of the upright shell is pierced the phrase 'I heard those voices that will not be drowned' from *Peter Grimes* (an opera composed by Britten from Crabbe's poem of the same name). Part of the structure is treated to allow it to 'rust'.

In 2005 *Scallop* won the Marsh Award for Excellence in Public Sculpture, awarded by the Public Monuments and Sculpture Association. In spite of vociferous and on-going protests, including those from a specially-formed group called The Voice of the People, *Scallop* remains on Aldeburgh beach and has spawned a small industry in scallop-related memorabilia, postcards and mugs. By virtue of divided local opinion *Scallop* has created a central and insoluble problem that looks unlikely to be solved in the near future. Maggie Hambling continues to be unfazed by criticism, saying 'It's always like that with works of art. You can't expect everyone to say "how wonderful,"' although her original hope that 'perhaps people will change their minds when the sculpture is there' proved to be misjudged.

❖ **Benjamin Britten** (1913–1976) founded **The Aldeburgh Festival** in 1947 and the first performances took place the following year. Concerts were given in Jubilee Hall for the first 17 years but in 1965 it was decided that the festival had become so successful that it had seriously outgrown its first home. Part of the old **Snape Maltings** complex was purchased and in June 1967 the new Concert Hall was opened by HM the Queen. Although arts performances of all kinds are held at Snape, the original Festival still takes place in June each year.

THREE – CHURCHES AND CHAPELS

THE churches and chapels of Suffolk are indisputably the most prized of the county's assets and are scattered like precious jewels across the landscape, each one unique in its evolution and many encapsulating history as far back as we can visibly go. In the mediaeval period there were at least 500 ecclesiastical parishes and there is barely one that cannot lay claim to having had a church at some time in its history. Inevitably they are not all still there. Some of the smaller parishes have been swallowed up by larger ones, much church fabric has been destroyed by the ravages of time, and several churches deconsecrated to serve as private homes. But those that remain are testaments to living, breathing communities, which have inhabited the towns, villages and hamlets of Suffolk for two millennia and each one has evolved in a unique way.

Happily, the study of Suffolk's ecclesiastical heritage has no end and, in spite of being pored over for centuries by historians, architects, antiquarians, and generations of chapel and church-crawlers, there is always something new to learn or discover, always a new angle to be seen or weighed. Here are a few snippets from the inexhaustible supply.

❖ **The Magna Carta**
One of the most important events in the history of England took place at the now ruined altar of the majestic Benedictine abbey at **Bury St Edmunds.** Here, on 20 November 1214, Cardinal Langton and 25 barons swore at St Edmund's Altar that they would obtain from King John the ratification of **Magna Carta** (or Great Charter). Fearful that their meeting might be discovered, they met under pretext of pilgrimage to the shrine of Saint Edmund (20 November being Saint Edmund's Day), but instead vowed that they would unite to compel the king to restore to the people their right to freedom from oppression and, if need be, by force of arms. These influential barons formed the alliance that eventually led to King John signing the Magna Carta at Runnymede on 15 June 1215.

The shrine of Edmund, King and Martyr, in the great Benedictine Abbey, and the gathering of the barons at the high altar gave **Bury St Edmunds** its motto – 'Shrine of a King, Cradle of the Law'.

As one of the Charter Towns, **Bury St Edmunds** takes part in the three-yearly celebrations that rotate among the five towns accorded the title. The celebrations are organised by the Magna Carta Trust, formed in 1957 to perpetuate the principles of the Magna Carta and preserve for 'reverent public use' sites associated with its origins. In 2004 it was Bury's turn to welcome visitors from Runnymede, St Albans, Canterbury and the City of London.

❖ **Acton's Famous Brass**
In the church of All Saints **Acton** is found the earliest church brass in Suffolk and one of the oldest to be found in England. **Sir Robert de Bures** (died 1331) is shown clad in chain mail beneath a surcoat, (a sleeveless cloth garment which protected the armoured wearer from being 'baked' in direct sunshine). The style of armour is that of the 1300s and Sir Robert is wearing elaborate knee guards and the surcoat is slit up the middle so that the wearer can mount and dismount easily. He wears a broad belt and has a sword and a shield with two lions. His hands are clasped in prayer and his feet rest on a smiling lion. Several authorities have singled this out as 'the finest military brass in existence' and, at 79 inches, it is one of the largest.

❖ **The Pickled Head of an Archbishop of Canterbury**
At St Gregory's **Sudbury** is one of the most extraordinary exhibits in any Suffolk church. It is the pickled head of **Archbishop Simon Theobald** of Sudbury who was beheaded by a mob of rioters in 1381 when, as Chancellor of England, he became embroiled in the politics of the hated Poll Tax, the imposition of which sparked off the Peasants' Revolt.

It all started well for Simon, who was born in Sudbury in 1317, the son of a wealthy local merchant. He received a good education and worked his way steadily upward in his career as a churchman, eventually being appointed chaplain to Pope Innocent VI. In 1375 Pope Gregory XIII appointed him Archbishop of Canterbury. In those days the grandees of the church wielded considerable power and the position of Lord High Chancellor of England, to which Simon was appointed in 1380, was the most powerful of all. Thus it was that Simon of Sudbury was passed the poisonous chalice of imposing the Poll Tax, which demanded one shilling per head for everyone over 16 and only the very poor were exempt. Feelings were running high in protest against Richard II's insatiable need for money (see also Chapter Five, Suffolk Folk). As Archbishop, Simon had crowned King Richard, and as his Lord Chancellor he was required to impose whatever taxes he could to finance the French wars. Soldiers were deserting in default of wages, the Crown Jewels were in pawn and the king himself was steeped in debt.

In 1381, Simon imprisoned one of the leaders of the Peasants' Revolt, the Revd John Ball, for 'beguiling the ears of the laity by invective, putting about scandals...and using dreadful language, such as shocks the ears of Christians'.

Ball's followers stormed and sacked the Archbishop's palace at Lambeth and demanded that he be given to them as a 'traitorous minister'. He took refuge with the king in the Tower of London, where he celebrated Mass for the last time. Richard then left the Tower to meet the rebels at Mile End, leaving Simon in the chapel.

On 14 June 1381, the mob broke into the chapel, seized Simon and beheaded him 'with great brutality' on Tower Hill. After order was restored his body was buried in Canterbury Cathedral, but his head was returned to Sudbury, where it was placed in a recess in the vestry wall of St Gregory's Church, hidden from general view by a green door.

The Peasants' Revolt lasted for only two weeks and King Richard later revoked most of the freedoms he had granted under duress. He sent his troops out to round up the rebels and summary justice was severe, especially in **Bury St Edmunds** where the townspeople had taken advantage of the situation to storm the Abbey and demand their own freedoms from the Abbot. Abbot Richard de Cambridge was among those murdered by the mob. When a national amnesty was declared, Bury St Edmunds was the only town in England to be excluded, because of the ferocity of the rebellion there.

❖ **The Oldest Chapel in Suffolk**
Suffolk has a strong tradition of Non-Conformity stretching back to the early 17th century and the old meeting house at **Walpole** near Halesworth is the oldest in East Anglia and the second oldest in the country. It is over 300 years old and is the same inside now as when first opened for worship in 1647, having been built on the site of an even older house. There is a double-decker pulpit, old box pews and in the centre a ship's mast said to have been brought from Great Yarmouth (Norfolk).

❖ **St Petronilla**

Whepstead church is the only one in England to carry the unique dedication to the obscure Saint Petronilla, said to be the daughter of Saint Peter.

Petronilla was a Roman virgin and martyr venerated from the first century but, while she appears on the occasional mediaeval rood screen in England, very little is known about her life. Her attribute in religious art is a bunch of keys, apparently for no other reason than that her supposed father held the key to the kingdom of heaven.

History leaves no certainties as to why this church should be dedicated to her although, in 1535, part of the income of the leper hospital of Saint Petronilla, which stood near the south gate of the Abbey in **Bury St Edmunds,** was derived from 'temporalities' in Whepstead.

Saint Petronilla also appears in mediaeval stained glass at **Wilby** and on a screen panel at **Somerleyton**. There was also a chapel of St Petronilla in **Little Wenham Hall** (see also Chapter Ten, Miscellany).

❖ The parish church at **Euston** is the only one in the county dedicated to Saint Genevieve. The mediaeval church was rebuilt in 1676 by Henry Bennet, Earl of Arlington, and in *Suffolk Churches*, D.P. Mortlock declares that it is 'one of only two classical designs in the county'.

❖ **Ralph's Squint**

On the north side of the nave of St Gregory's **Hemingstone** is an annexe, now used as a vestry and accessed by a connecting passage from the chancel. It was built some time in the 1550s by Ralph Cantrell, whose family had lived at Wealden Farm (now Stonewall Farm) in Hemingstone since at least the early 15th century. At the Reformation, when Catholics were no longer allowed to practice their religion, the Cantrells doggedly retained their loyalty to the Old Religion. However, Henry VIII required his subjects to attend the new Protestant services on pain of severe penalties, which put the Cantrells in an awkward position. To solve the dilemma, Ralph built the annexe with a slit, or squint, built into the church wall through which he could observe the service. This salved his conscience as he was not really in attendance.

❖ **The Holy Well of Exning**

Although the church at **Exning** is not dedicated to Saint Etheldreda (died 679), but to Saint Martin, the village is nevertheless renowned for **Saint Etheldreda's Well,** said to contain water good for ailments of the eye and sought by mediaeval pilgrims. Princess Etheldreda was the daughter of Anna, king of the East Angles, and Saint Felix is said to have visited Exning and baptised Etheldreda and two of her sisters. The well where the baptisms took place became known as Saint Etheldreda's Well, although it is occasionally known as Saint Mindred's Well, Mindred being another name for Wendreda.

Etheldreda was at one time the most popular of the Anglo-Saxon women saints. Her three sisters, Sexburga (died 699), Ethelburga (died 678) and Withburga (died 743) were also honoured as saints in East Anglia and beyond. Among the many churches where Etheldreda is found are **Mildenhall, Rattlesden, Ampton, Dalham, Bramford, Campsea Ash** and **Ufford.**

At **Melton** the church dedication used to be for St Andrew and St Etheldreda, but when the new church was built in the 1860s only the former was retained because, it is believed, of the association with the nearby mental hospital, Saint Audrey's. Audrey is a corruption of Etheldreda and the word 'tawdry' comes from the cheap lace, toys and knick-knacks that were sold at Saint Audrey's Fairs across East Anglia. Necklaces were sold at the fairs and were particularly associated with Etheldreda as, in her final years, she suffered a throat tumour. When the tumour was lanced she said it reminded her of a necklace and that it was punishment for her pride in wearing fine necklaces in her youth.

❖ **The Three Trimleys**

There were once three churches in the three parishes of **Trimley.** Trimley St John disappeared as a parish in around 1362 when it became part of Trimley St Martin. The site of the old church of St John is approximately where **Alston** is now (previously called Alleston). The remaining two, **Trimley St Martin** and **Trimley St Mary,** retain their churches in the same churchyard. In the 1980s St Mary's ceased to be used and in 1990 took on a multi-purpose role as an alternative to total redundancy. A small strip of land that runs between the two churches was the parish boundary and for many years was known as No Man's Land. Both the Trimleys are more or less suburbs of **Felixstowe.**

❖ **Doomed!**

The late 15th and early 16th century congregations at St Peter's **Wenhaston** no doubt paid rapt attention to the Creed, especially when the priest spoke the words 'and He descended into hell', no doubt followed by an uncomfortable shuffling in the pews. They had little need to imagine an abstract vision of the ghastliness of hell, they only had to look up at an explicit painting of what might happen to them if, after death, they were found wanting. The **Doom** painting, which would then have been mounted on the rood beam (called the 'candlebeam' in Suffolk) and spanning the chancel arch, was intended as an example of what would befall those who chose not to repent of their sins. Among the paintings on its 11 horizontal timber planks, the devil is seen scooping up the dammed, chains forcing them into the jaws of hell (depicted as the gaping mouth of a fish) and imps are seen tipping the scales in their favour against those who are yet to be judged. To the left an angel with a beatific smile is seen welcoming the just and righteous into heaven.

The church had a vested interest in nurturing the prospect of hell, the notion of perpetual suffering, and of the converse glories of a beautiful, peaceful heaven. In order to attain the latter, and as one of the ways to ensure a constant source of revenue for the church, indulgences were offered, whereby the sinner could be pardoned (or at least have his expected time in Purgatory reduced) by donations to the parish church or pilgrimage to holy shrines.

The Doom was painted around 1520, the Wenhaston parishioners having had to save up for some 30 years before work could begin. A bequest from John Townysend from **Thorington** (the neighbouring parish) bequeathed twelvepence 'to the new candlebeam in Wenhaston church' in his will of June 1489. Bequests on such a small scale would need to have accrued over many years.

That this extraordinary relic of mediaeval Suffolk should have survived at all is little short of a miracle, as is the story of its accidental discovery (and near destruction) in 1889.

The Doom must have been whitewashed sometime in the 16th century to protect it, either from the destruction of the reformers at the Dissolution of the Monasteries, or in response to Edward VI's edict that roods were to be abolished and church walls should be whitewashed. The sculptured figures were removed (the holes through which the bolts passed fixing the figures to the Doom are visible) and probably destroyed. The (now flat) rood screen was boarded up and whitewashed, then painted over with passages from the scriptures. There it remained until 1892 when plans to renovate the east end of the church were mooted. A few years later the renovations reached the chancel arch and the whitewashed Doom was taken down, plank by plank, and the boards discarded in the churchyard. That night it rained heavily and in the morning the whitewash had dissolved and the figures could be seen for the first time in almost 400 years. The Doom could not be returned to its former position, since the new chancel arch was too narrow, and after being moved to various sites in the church it came to rest in its present position on the north wall.

The Wenhaston Doom is considered to be the finest of its period in England and highly unusual in that sculptured figures of Christ on the Cross, the Virgin Mary and St John were once attached to the wooden planks instead of being merely painted on. There are other Dooms, or partial remains, at **Chelsworth**, **North Cove**, **Earl Stonham**, **Cowlinge**, **Bacton** (near **Stowmarket**), **Stanningfield** and **Yaxley**. St Michael Weighing Souls is seen at **Wissington**.

❖ **The Saints**

There were once 12 villages and hamlets between **Halesworth** and **Bungay**, which cause that part of Suffolk to be known as 'The Saints'. They are situated roughly along the route of the Roman 'Stone Street'. The parishes' churches are similarly named.

The five **Ilketshall** saints are Andrew, John the Baptist, Lawrence, Margaret and Michael. Ilketshall Saint John is on the fringes of Bungay. The foundations of Ilketshall Saint Lawrence church are late 12th and early 13th century and in its walls are found sections of recycled Roman tiles.

The seven **South Elmham** Saints are James, Peter, Margaret, Michael, Nicholas, Cross and All Saints. The oldest church is that of Saint James. The parish of All Saints-cum-Saint Nicholas once had two churches.

At South Elmham Saint Cross are the ruins of a church known as the Old Minster that was, according to tradition, founded by Bishop Felix in the seventh century. The parish church of Saint Cross is the only one in Suffolk dedicated to the Holy Cross and is one of the few to have an alternative dedication, that of St George.

❖　In 2004 lightning struck the church at **Ilketshall St Andrew** not once but twice, and in doing so revealed spectacular wall paintings dating from the 14th century. The first strike was in December 2001 when the Norman building's tower took the full force of thousands of volts during a storm. Shortly afterwards a workman discovered the mediaeval church art. Nothing much was done to conserve the paintings as the work was going to be too expensive. However, in August 2004 another strike hit the tower and left a mark where the lightning struck an iron fixing which burst out and took some flints with it. The parishioners decided that 'the guy upstairs' was trying to tell them to get going on uncovering the wall paintings.

The paintings were found to contain depictions of angels believed to date to 1320 and conservators were excited to discover a Wheel of Fortune on the south wall. This picture, with fate standing at its centre, shows a king climbing up the left side with the words 'I rule' written above his head in Latin. He then falls down the right side, having lost his crown.

There are also people, including naked women, climbing out of coffins immediately to the left of the wheel, in scenes depicting the Day of Judgement. The earliest image included a fresco sketched out in the early 1100s.

❖　**Lost Church**
The church of King Charles the Martyr **Shelland** (near **Onehouse**) is one of only four such dedications in England to King Charles I. For some reason, the location of both the church and the village is invariably missed off maps.

❖　**A Victim of the Witch Finder**
On the north wall of **Brandeston** church is a list of vicars, which includes the name of 80-year-old John Lowes, who was vicar there for nearly 50 years from 1596. He became one of the victims of Matthew Hopkins, who assumed the title Witchfinder General and terrorised Suffolk in the 1640s during the English Civil War, searching out witches and extorting 'confessions' through torture. After 'brainwashing', which involved being kept awake for several nights and forced to run until he was breathless, the Revd Lowes 'confessed' to employing imps to sink ships at sea and of trafficking with Satan. After being found guilty of these, and other such

unlikely 'crimes', he was hanged at **Bury St Edmunds** in 1646 having first read the Burial Service over himself.

❖ **The Rare and Mysterious Sciapod**

There are many unique and unusual aspects of St Mary's **Dennington**, but none more so than the famous **Sciapod**, carved onto the sixth bench-end in the centre aisle. It is the only example in an English church and is one of 76 intricately carved mediaeval bench-ends depicting animals, birds and exotic creatures.

The Sciapod is a mysterious and strange mythological creature surrounded by folkloric tales. The first-century Roman historian, Pliny the Elder, had read of them as creatures of 'another race of men, who are known as *monocoli*, who have only one leg, but are able to leap with surprising agility'. The same people were also called *Sciapodae*, because they were in the habit of lying on their backs, during times of extreme heat, to protect themselves from the sun by the shade of their outlandishly large feet.

The artist who executed the Dennington Sciapod in the 15th century perhaps decided that Suffolk people might not go much on a one-legged race so he gave him two feet, the better to shade himself with. He also added three small figures, which enjoy the shade from their host's feet, thought to be Brachmani, miniature cave dwellers. They are given shelter under the Sciapod's feet (some say from the rain as well as the sun), which are at least as long as the figure's body.

Dennington's other bench-end carvings include a pelican, a bear (or dog) wearing a saddle, a mermaid and a tortoise that is, like the Sciapod, a unique example. There is also a stooping eagle and a double-headed eagle.

Modern copies of many of Dennington's mediaeval menagerie can be found at All Saints Church, **Hollesley**, including the Sciapod.

❖ Another rarity also to be seen at **Dennington** is a sand tray that was used to bring rudimentary education to village children early in the 19th century. It pre-dates the blackboard by many years and is a long, shallow tray filled with sand into which the teacher would trace figures and numbers for the children to copy or learn. Like chalk, the sand could easily be erased and new images marked into the sand. Before the purpose-built schools of the 1840s, usually paid for by subscription by local worthies, the only education available for those who could not afford to pay was from the National Society for the Education of the Poor in the Principles of the Established Church (founded in 1811), or in other words, Church Schools. The churchwardens of Dennington church were obviously proud of their efforts with the sand tray as the sexton was photographed with the sand tray outside the church and the picture made into a postcard.

❖ **Upside Down Bells**
In 1525 the parishioners of St Mary's Church, **East Bergholt,** started work on a bell tower that was sponsored by the influential local boy made good, Cardinal Thomas Wolsey (1472–1530). Wolsey, who was born in **Ipswich,** was at the height of his influence with Henry VIII and no one saw any reason to doubt that his promise of support should not bring the tower project to fruition. It was to be on the west of the church and the whole thing got off to an optimistic and rousing start.

Alas, Cardinal Wolsey fell from grace and died in 1530. With him went all hope of a new bell tower. No alternative source of finance was available and it was impossible for the parish to raise even a fraction of the money required to complete the building work. But what was to happen to the bells that were left standing in the east part of the churchyard? In 1531 it was decided that a temporary bell cage should be erected, causing them to become known as the 'imprisoned bells'. A verse dating from the 16th century was once inscribed on the bell cage:

Bells ring for joy and eke for sadness
For solemn requiem
Or in the marriage peal of gladness
Do though like them
Fitly employ thy voice.

Unfortunately, the Chaplin family at the nearby Old Hall did not like the sound of the bells being employed and in the 17th century they were moved to another part of the churchyard, at the expense of Joseph Chaplin, where they have remained to this day. It is possible that one or more of the bells from the 17th century were added at this time and the bell cage enlarged to accommodate them.

Even though they are not counterbalanced, the bells continued to be rung by pure force of hand applied directly to a wooden headstock and not by rope and wheel, which accounts for them being 'hung' upside down. If hung downwards they would be almost impossible to ring. This is an extraordinary feat since they are the heaviest set of five bells currently being run in England, with a total weight of 4.25 tons (or 4,400 kilos).

The oldest bell (and the only one that has not been re-cast or modified) carries an inscription, 'Here sounds the bell of faithful Gabrielle'. The next is from 1601 and others are from the 17th, 18th and 19th century.

The bells were removed from the cage in 1972 for restoration work and were rehung, this time on ball bearings, but it still takes two years for someone to learn to ring the bells.

❖ **Millennium Belfry**
At All Saints Church **Sutton** is a new wooden free-standing belfry, just south of the chancel, a Millennium project.

❖ **The Wooden Chancel**
The wooden 15th-century chancel of All Saints **Crowfield** is unique in East Anglia. It has the appearance of a half-timbered Tudor cottage, with wooden mullioned windows and a priest's door on the south side. Inside, on either side of the chancel step, is a group of kneeling angels carved in the 19th century by James Wormald and Willy Polly.

The Wormald and Polly poppyheads of the pews have an extraordinary collection of fruit, corn and foliage carvings including apples, gooseberries, hops, ivy, beech and maple.

❖ **Barsham's Treasures**
The Church of the Most Holy Trinity **Barsham with Shipmeadow**, near **Beccles**, is a church with unique architectural features and very famous connections, both old and new. Catherine Suckling, mother of England's great naval hero, Horatio Nelson (1758–1805), was born at Barsham Rectory in May 1725. She met her husband, the Revd Edmund Nelson, when he was appointed curate at nearby **Beccles**, and the two married in Beccles Parish Church on 11 May 1749. Horatio was their second son and it was Catherine's brother who took the young Horatio on his first sea voyage.

The Sucklings had a long and distinguished association with Barsham and several lie buried in the churchyard. The central window in the nave is the Trafalgar Window, installed in 1905 to mark the centenary of the great English sea battle of 1805, a victory for the English against the French but which claimed the life of Viscount Nelson of the Nile. The window is dedicated to members of the Suckling family, though it fails to mention Rear Admiral Benjamin Suckling who was a midshipman aboard HMS *Victory* at Trafalgar.

Over the years Nelson made frequent visits to Suffolk and in 1798 he purchased a property just outside **Ipswich** and installed his wife and father-in-law there as a means of removing them from London. He visited only twice, the second time accompanied by Sir William and Lady Hamilton (Emma Hamilton at the time pregnant with Horatia, Nelson's daughter). Finding his wife out (she had gone to London to visit him) Horatio and the Hamiltons put up at the Great White Horse in Ipswich and returned to London the following day.

Barsham's more recent hero is the writer Adrian Bell (1901–1980) who lies here with his wife, Marjorie. Adrian Bell was one of the foremost writers about Suffolk, and books such as the trilogy *Corduroy* (1930), *Silver Ley* (1931) and *The Cherry Tree* (1932) have become classics of their kind. Adrian is the father of the white-suited former independent MP, Martin Bell OBE, and in addition to his books and journalism he was the first compiler of *The Times* crossword, which first appeared in January 1930. He set around 5,000 puzzles between 1930 and 1978. He lived at a number of different places across the county but his final home was a very run-down Crake's Hall, Barsham but which, said Adrian, 'gazed at me with the appealing patience of an old horse's dusked eyes'.

The external criss-cross latticework on the chancel east wall brings visitors from all over the world to marvel at its construction and design. Its precise date is uncertain, as the stonework had to be restored in 1906 after a lightning strike did extensive damage to the building, but it is thought the design dates from the 15th century.

❖ **Sotterley Chapel**
A most unusual octagonal-shaped chapel stands in the parish of **Sotterley**, at the crossroads where the roads to **Hulver, Shadingfield, Stoven** and **Wrentham** all meet. The chapel and cemetery were consecrated by the Bishop of Norwich in 1883 and constructed at the behest of the Barne family in 1882. Built in the Gothic style, in local

red brickwork, it has stone buttresses and large porches to the north and south. The cemetery is the only active local graveyard in Sotterley.

Close to the chapel are the War Memorial and a bench, where passing cyclists are often seen to assemble.

❖ **Haughley's Fire Buckets**

There can be few churches as well equipped in the fire dowsing department as that of The Assumption **Haughley**, where four of the wonderful collection of 18th-century leather fire buckets are found hanging from the vestry ceiling.

There were 35 fire buckets in the original collection and they were clearly intended to be hung from the porch ceiling, where there are several rows of pegs. They are painted with their dates (between 1725 and 1728) and 'Haughley' and some bear crosses and stroke marks.

Until the late 19th and early 20th century, the threat of fire was a constant and serious worry as most houses were constructed of flammable materials (particularly thatched roofs) and outbreaks were extinguished by means of a line of buckets manned by local villagers. In Haughley it was obviously decided that the most central and convenient place to keep the fire buckets was the church porch, thus ready for immediate use – a reminder of the central role the church played in all aspects of life and not just as a venue for church services.

❖ **Part of the Holiday Village**

The building of St Mary's **Thorpeness** by Glencairn Stuart Ogilvie was completed in 1938, in which year it was dedicated but not consecrated. The initial cost of construction was estimated at £3,000 with £300 for the furnishings. However, when Glencairn died work stopped and it was never finished. It was designed by William Gilmore Wilson and was part of the on-going development of Glencairn Ogilvie's original holiday village (see also Chapter Seven, Writers and Artists). The expense was borne by Glencairn's mother, Margaret (a Quaker), who wished that it should be left unconsecrated so that 'people of all denominations would feel welcome'. Before World War Two the church was 'packed to the rafters' at every service, with people attending in their tennis clothes or holiday outfits, on the way to the beach or to take part in a sports tournament.

St Mary's was built originally in a neo-Norman style to resemble a French fortress and constructed of rendered concrete and brick with stone dressing. It was designated a listed building in 1995 and in 2005 it was converted to five private residences.

❖ **Your Country Needs You!**
The Chevallier family have been associated with **Aspall** for generations and in 1845, Anne Frances Chevallier married Henry Kitchener in the church of St Mary of Grace. She travelled with him to Ireland, where she became the mother of **Horatio Herbert Kitchener,** the future Earl Kitchener of Khartoum (1850–1916). As British Secretary of State for War from 1914, he modernised the British forces and his portrait appeared on posters encouraging men to sign up in World War One with the famous caption, 'Your Country Needs You!' Among his many titles was 'Baron Kitchener of Aspall in the county of Suffolk'.

Lord Kitchener drowned in a torpedoed ship and a plaque to him in the church is a tribute 'of love and grief from countrymen overseas' from the Overseas Club, Kitchener Branch, Santa Barbara, California.

There is another memorial to Lord Kitchener at **Lakenheath** where a forebear was once bailiff to the Lord of the Manor. It was placed there by the London Society of East Anglians (of which he was president).

❖ There are over 150 churches in Suffolk which bear a dedication to St Mary, or the Blessed Virgin, but St Mary of Grace at **Aspall** is the only one that takes this particular title.

❖ **Star of David**
In the churchyard of Our Lady of Grace **Aspall** is found a unique example of a Star of David engraved on a gravestone in an Anglican churchyard. Here lies the famous Hollywood screenwriter and novelist, **Emeric Pressburger** (1902–1988), who lived at Shoemakers in nearby **Debenham**.

Pressburger was a Hungarian Jew who went to work in Germany but came to England in 1935. He began a long and successful career in films among which was *49th Parallel* (1941), *Ill Met by Moonlight* (1957) and *The Red Shoes* (1948), a hit film starring Moira Shearer.

Having expressed a wish to be buried at Aspall, the family received a message from a long-forgotten cousin who rang from Belgrade to ensure that Pressburger was given a Jewish burial. As far as anyone knew he had not been a practising Jew, but as a gesture of goodwill the Anglican vicar allowed the Star of David to be engraved on the gravestone.

❖ **Barrow's Guardian Angel**
All Saints **Barrow** would seem to have a 21st-century guardian angel that is keeping an eye out for anything untoward. In 2003 a haul of valuable silver, including goblets and chalices, was stolen from the church. However, thanks to security marks it was thought that the burglars decided that they would not be able to sell their loot and within days of the theft dumped their loot outside a monastery in Holloway, London. That it was deliberately placed at a site where its return was ensured, rather than sold for melting down or simply thrown in the Thames, was thought to be a miracle. The parish priest organised a thanksgiving service.

Two years later a potentially devastating fire tore through floorboards, but mysteriously stopped just in front of the altar. Father Peter Macleod Miller was quoted as saying that the abrupt quelling of the flames was 'apparently inexplicable using mere mortal logic'. Although an altar rail and a prayer kneeler were destroyed – and a large hole burned into the floor of the 1,000-year-old church – the incident caused the local press to suggest that the church had its own guardian angel.

❖ Perhaps encouraged by Barrow's guardian angel, The Assumption of the Blessed Virgin Mary **Haughley** cleaned up the faces of their 18 oak angels in 2004. The angels are thought to have been part of the Victorian restoration of the church and date back to the mid-1800s. The angels had their wings fixed and one had its feathers restored – just in case there was some future guarding to be done!

❖ In 2000, St Mary's **Great Bealings** commissioned new angels for its Tudor porch to prevent the crumbling originals from becoming fallen angels. The two new replicas are made from Ketton stone and, it is hoped, they will grace the church porch for as long as their predecessors.

❖ **In The Stocks**

At All Saints **Saxtead** stand the village stocks bearing the inscription 'Fear God and Honour the King'. Their original location is unknown but they now live in the church porch. The Saxtead stocks have three sets of leg holes, graded in size, presumably so that miscreants of all ages were accommodated. The people of Saxtead would seem to have been law breakers on an appreciable scale, as there is attached a sturdy whipping post, complete with metal wrist clasps.

There is a similar version of the stocks in **Athelington** porch, but not built on quite so grand a scale as those at Saxtead.

❖ **The Virgin's Crant**

In St Mary's **Walsham le Willows** is a curious pendant memorial known as the Virgin's Crant (the garland carried before the bier of a maiden and hung over her grave) or Maiden's Garland. A white stone medallion, about 9in long, hangs by a wire from a rod projecting from the nave wall. One side bears an arrow pointing to a heart with the name Mary Boyce cut in rough lettering, on the other is her date of death, 1685. The crant for Mary Boyce, who died a virgin at the age of 20 of a broken heart, is a remnant of a mediaeval custom of marking the pews of unmarried girls who had died young. At Walsham le Willows it was for many years a tradition that the young men of the village hung a bridal garland over the stone on the anniversary of Mary Boyce's death.

❖ **Home of the Iceni**

Icklingham was once two distinct parishes and although they are now united the village retains not one but two mediaeval churches within half a mile of each other, All Saints and St James's. Named for the Iceni tribe, of which Boudicca was the last sovereign, Icklingham was traversed by the old Roman road **Icknield Street**. There was a Roman camp here called Kentfield, which occupied about 25 acres. The immense importance of Icklingham in Saxon times is illustrated at nearby **West Stow Anglo-Saxon Village** where, following rich archaeological discoveries on Stow's heath, there is now a reconstructed Saxon village and visitor centre. West Stow was excavated between 1965 and 1972 and revealed a pagan village of national and international importance, which was occupied from AD420 to 650.

All Saints, which is thatched and of Norman origin, was declared redundant over 100 years ago and is under the care of the Churches Conservation Trust.

❖ **Time Capsule**

In 2005 a time capsule was buried in the vault of **Boxted** church next to two ancient coffins. The coffins contain the remains of John Grimwood (died 1832), a former recorder (or judge) at Colchester, and his wife. The vault had not been opened since 1968 and was re-sealed after repairs were completed and the capsules put into a locked metal box alongside the coffins.

❖ **The Father of Scientific Archaeology**

In January 2000 a monument was unveiled in St Bartholomew's **Finningham** to the first man in Britain to recognise palaeoliths for what they were. John Frere, FRS, FSA (1740–1807) made this discovery in 1797 on a chance journey through **Hoxne** on his way to **Eye** when he stopped to watch some workmen digging clay for bricks in the pit now well known as the site of the Hoxnian Stage of the British Quaternary. This led to groundbreaking discoveries in relation to the valleys of the Dove, Waveney and Gold Brook rivers, which he reported in a letter to the Society of Antiquaries of London in 1797. He recognised the flints as of human workmanship, noting that they were 'fabricated and used by a people who had not the use of metals'. This was, he realised, a practical application of the idea of the Roman author Lucretius who had written that an 'age of stone' had preceded those of bronze and iron.

John Frere was born at Finningham, which was the ancestral home of the illustrious Frere family. He married and had seven sons and two daughters.

A party of people interested in the Palaeolithic period visited the area in 1997 and noted that, although there were many monuments to the Frere family in Finningham church, there was nothing to celebrate the man hailed by The Prehistoric Society as 'the father of scientific archaeology'. An appeal was made for funds and a memorial commissioned. The tablet is cut in Welsh slate, and includes a replica of one of the 300,000-year-old flint hand axes that sparked Frere's conclusions. Made by Phil Harding (of *Time Team* fame) the legend reads, 'from his discoveries at Hoxne was the first to realise the immense antiquity of mankind'.

Frere's discovery of the hand axes was made not far from where the **Hoxne Hoard** was discovered, a Roman treasure found in 1992 by a retired gardener using a metal detector to try and locate some lost tools in an arable field. The hoard consisted of over 14,700 coins and some 200 other gold and silver objects. It is one of the biggest hoards of Roman treasure ever discovered in Britain and its importance is enhanced by the fact that it was professionally excavated, enabling details to be recorded which revealed new insights into the early fifth century AD when it was buried.

One of the finest of the silver objects is the solid-cast statuette of a prancing tigress, whose stripes are inlaid in niello (black silver sulphide) and which was once part of a large silver vase. Most of the objects were carefully wrapped in cloth and packed in wooden boxes, some with tiny silver padlocks.

During excavations of the Hoxne treasure site it was confirmed that people had been living there for between 1,000 and 1,500 years before the hoard was buried. Prehistoric evidence was found, including fragments of handmade pots and pits containing domestic debris. The archaeology enlarged and confirmed what John Frere had discovered almost 200 years previously.

❖ **Men Only**

All Saints **Laxfield** is famous for the unusual and varied types of pews that illustrate five centuries of changing fashion and style of church seating. First are the box – or family - pews, many of them constructed from an assortment of panelling in the 18th century. There are also bench pews, the oldest made before the 1550s, and one of which has a pew end with a carving of a chalice and wafer.

The surviving gallery pews were strictly for the use of the 'Young Men and Boys' who were given free education on condition that they attended Sunday service. The top row was for Men Only and the lower ones for Men and Boys, the painted notices still visible written in black along the ledges. Lest any woman or girl was tempted to use them, the pews were enclosed and a notice inscribed on the door that these were 'Seats for Young Men and Boys' only.

The interior of the church is unusually spacious, the nave being approximately 36ft wide, one of the widest single-aisled churches in East Anglia. The massive oak beams in the trussed-rafter roof stretch across like a pair of open scissors.

Among the many treasures of Laxfield church is an enormous parish chest, iron banded, with an array of locks, one of which requires two keys to be turned in contrary directions.

❖ **Four Generations**

The present Rector of All Saints **Waldringfield** is the fourth generation of his family to hold the position, an unbroken line since 1862. The Waller family, who also farmed at **Ramsholt**, began with Thomas Henry Waller (1862), followed by Arthur Pretyman Waller (1906) and Trevor Waller (1948). The present incumbent, John Pretyman Waller, took up the rectorship in 1974.

In the church is a notice of a 'Benefaction' left by Captain Francis Waller, BA who in 1855 left £20 to the poor of the parish to be spent on bread and distributed 'on the Sunday nearest to January the 19th and April the 3rd'.

FOUR – EPITAPHS

MANY parishioners, or their relatives, who worshipped in the county's churches left messages in the form of written epitaphs, sometimes on plaques and at other times in the registers or on gravestones. These links with those who have gone before are among the most intriguing facets of church buildings.

❖ One of Suffolk's most famous epitaphs is found in **Little Glemham** church and records the word **'sylly'**, which gives rise to a wilfully misinterpreted 'Silly Suffolk' as opposed to its true meaning of 'Holy Suffolk'. It appears on a shield belonging to **Thomas Glemham** (1571) and begins: 'This sylly grave the happy cynders hyde'.

   The word (although spelt differently) is found again at **Huntingfield** where there is a very long epitaph on the tomb of a member of the Paston family including: 'Againste the seelie needy soule his purse was never shutt'.

❖ Inscribed on a stone at St Peter's **Redisham**, is a verse by a mother for her illegitimate baby, Eliza Westrup, who was only 11 months old when she died in 1810. The baby's father never acknowledged her as his own and to remind him of their dead child and his own shame, the mother placed the stone, which the man would pass each day on his way to work:

> Remember me as you pass by,
> Though you my Father did me deny.
> Glad were you to hear the Sound
> Of the Bell that tolled me to the ground.
> If you were free of sin as I
> You would not be afraid to die
> As I am now so you will be
> So be prepared to follow me.

❖ An epitaph to Mrs Anne Butts (1609), mother-in-law of Sir Nicholas Bacon, is found in St Mary's **Redgrave**:

> The weaker sexes strongest precedent
> Lies here belowe: seaven fayer years she spent
> In Wedlock sage: and since that merry age
> Sixty one years she lived a widowe sage

❖ At St Michael's **Hunston** is a short tale of the sudden death of Junior (or John) Jiggins, who died in 1846.

Verses on his stone begin:

> It was so suddenly I fell,
> My neighbours started at my knell:
> Amazed that I should be no more,
> The man they'd seen the day before.

❖ In Holy Trinity **Blythburgh** is a tablet to **Elizabeth Crofts**, only child of Ernest Crofts RA and Elizabeth his wife:

> What we bury in the grave is but an earthly clothing
> What we love lives on.

Royal Academician, painter and illustrator, **Ernest Crofts** (1847–1911), lived in Blythburgh and has the dubious distinction of being the first person to die in a motor accident resulting from a collision between 'two horseless carriages'. The accident occurred just outside Blythburgh.

Another tablet in the church is in memory of **Sir John Seymour Lucas** (1849–1923), a friend of Ernest Crofts, who lived at The Priory, Blythburgh. Although trained as a sculptor, Sir John was also a painter of portraits and historical subjects.

❖ At St Andrew's **Great Saxham** is buried the adventurer, merchant, citizen and clothworker of London, **John Eldred** (died 1632), who received a Grant of Arms in 1592 and bought the manor of Great Saxham in 1597. His imposing tomb and brass portrait were erected by his son, Revett, who included in the epitaph:

> Might all my travels me excuse
> For being dead and lying here.

John built a large house at Great Saxham, which he called Nutmeg Hall to commemorate the fact that he was the first to bring nutmegs to England from the Middle East in 'the richest ship that ever was known to this realm'. However, Revett might have had his fill of his father's endless travel tales as he ends the verse:

> But Riches can noe ransome buy
> Nor Travells passe ye destiny.

❖ Edmund Gillingwater, in *St Edmund's Bury*, points to an epitaph in the Great Churchyard of **Bury St Edmunds** to Joan Kitchen:

> Here lies Joan Kitchen, when her glass was spent,
> She kick'd up her heels, and away she went.

He also points to nearby memorials for two remarkable women

who had both been midwives. One had brought 2,237 babies into the world and another 4,323 living children!

❖ **Woodbridge** seems to have attracted a high number of benefactors and philanthropists, not least **Thomas Seckford** (1515–1587) the greatest of them all. He was born at **Great Bealings** and rose to great heights during the reign of Elizabeth I, in spite of the Queen once having complained about the odour of Seckford's boots. She was silenced by 'the gentleman's reference to the equally offensive odour of the unpaid royal debts'!

A plaque to **Henry Silver** (died 1910, aged 83 years) in St Mary's declares:

> Duties and friendships and charities
> Were more to him than fame and honour.

A tablet to another of the town's benefactors, **John Sayer**, bears the lines:

> Reader, thou shalt find
> Heaven takes the best, still leaves the worst behind.

In 1635 'John Sayer of this parish, yeoman' provided a Dole Cupboard (seen in the North Porch) in which to store loaves that formed part of his bequest. He provided bread, which was to be distributed 'amongst the poor of this parish every Sabbath Day for ever'. Not surprisingly the practice did not last 'for ever' but it did survive until World War One. (There was a similar bread charity at **Laxfield** where an 18th-century shelf can be seen behind the back pew that housed the loaves that the poor took home with them after the service. It, too, ceased in around 1914.)

In the churchyard there is a surprisingly lighthearted epitaph on the gravestone of the unfortunate **Benjamin Brinkley**, which reads:

> Here lieth the body of Benjamin Brinkley
> Who though Lustie and Strong was one
> That by misfortune shot Himself with's Gun
> In the 23rd year of his age
> He departed this life to the grief of his parents
> Spectators and Wife.
> March the 27, 1723

❖ In St Gregory's **Sudbury** is a Latin epitaph on the side of the tomb of a town benefactor who died in 1706:

> Traveller, I will tell a wondrous thing
> On the day on which Thomas Carter breathed his last
> A Sudbury camel passed through the eye of a needle.
> If thou art wealthy go and do likewise.

❖ In St Mary's **Huntingfield** is found a memorial to the Revd Edmund Stubbe who was Rector there for 38 years, through the Civil War and Commonwealth, dying in 1639. Both he and one of his sons were men of learning and a Latin inscription is under an arch of books supported by stacks of others. It ends:

> Oh Reader, these books stand before thine eyes,
> Know though thyself art like a little book of which
> The title is thy birthday and the last line, thy death.

In the same church is a memorial erected by Edward Coke to his mother-in-law, Anne, who died in 1595:

> She was a godly, wise and virtuous woman, and kept a
> beautiful house at Huntingfield, especially for the poore,
> nere fifty years. She departed this life in her good old age,
> 20th June 1595.

❖ On a small plaque in St Andrew's **Hasketon**, with a cherub at the top and skull and crossbones below, is an epitaph to the Revd William Farrer's 15-year-old son:

> Here lies his kindred's hopes, his parents' joy
> A man in manners, though in years a boy.
> If on his yeares you looke, he dy'd but young
> If on his virtues then hee lived long.

The Revd Farrer was Rector from 1620–30 and died in 1637.

❖ All Saints **Hawstead** has more monuments than any other church in Suffolk, many of them to the Drury family. In the 16th century Sir Robert Drury's daughter died aged four years old:

> She, little promised much, too soon untied,
> She only dreamt she lived, and then she died.

Nearby is an alabaster figure of Sir Robert's elder daughter Elizabeth, with whom Prince Henry, brother to the ill-fated Charles I, is said to have been in love. Two watchdogs stand guard and she lies resting her head on one arm while a woman scatters flowers around her.

❖ At the church of the Most Holy Trinity **Barsham** are inscriptions in Latin and Greek to Thomas Missenden, rector here from 1740–74. There are variations on the translation but the Greek at the head reads roughly:

> I've entered port, Fortune and Hope adieu!
> Make game of others, for I've done with you!

The Latin at the foot reads:

> The present hour is thine: The next no man can claim.

❖ **Bramfield** Church has an unequalled number of intriguingly narrative epitaphs concerning the Nelson, Applewhaite and Rabett families contained on chancel floor slabs. The most famous is that to **Bridgett Applewhaite (née Nelson)**, which is 32 lines long and includes the vital statistics of her 44 years, including what appears to be an arduous marriage to husband Arthur (who lies nearby):

After the Fatigues of a Married Life,
Born by her with Incredible Patience
For four Years and three Quarters, baring three Weeks;
And after the Enjoiment of the Glorious Freedom
Of an Early and Unblemisht Widowhood,
For four Years and Upwards,
She resolved to run the Risk of a Second Marriage Bed.

However, Bridgett would never know if the risk paid off as death intervened by the means of an 'Apoplectick Dart' that 'touch't the most Vital part of her Brain', which affliction had also dispatched her mother. Her death throes are recorded for posterity in extraordinary detail:

She must have fallen Directly to the Ground
(as one Thunder-strook)
If she had not been Catcht and Supported
By her Intended Husband
Of which Invisible Bruise
After a Struggle for above Sixty Hours,
With that Grand Enemy to Life
(But the certain and Merciful Friend to Helpless Old Age,)
In Terrible Convulsions Plaintive Groans or Stupefying Sleep
Without recovery of Speech or Senses,
She dyed on the 12th day of Sept. in ye Year of our Lord 1737.

Mary Nelson (died 1710) was Bridgett's mother and her demise is noted as having been 'carried off by an apoplectic fit'.

The epitaph of **Mrs Bridget Nelson** contains the family saga (the 'Mrs' is surely a courtesy title):

The body of Mrs Bridget Nelson, born in this parish, June 26th, 1672, was buried here, September 19th, 1731. Though never married, she freely underwent the care of a wife and mother, and often the fatigues of a true friend, for any of her acquaintances in sickness or distress.
She was a devout member of the established church; charitable, prudent, chaste, active, and remarkably temperate,

yet often afflicted with great sickness, and for above three
years before her death with a dropsy of which she died after
having been tapped five times.

The Rabett family lived at Bramfield Hall for over 400 years and
spelling variations of the name include Rabbit and Rabit, which
accounts for the three rabbit heads in their arms. The name is first
found in Suffolk where they were 'seated' and given land by
William the Conqueror for distinguished service at the Battle of
Hastings in 1066. **Bridgett Rabett**, wife of Lambert Rabett, died in
1680:

Stay traveller, let your eyes, dry from much weeping, flow.

A true woman has died, a rare woman lies beneath.

She, happy for long, but ailing at length, rejoices.

She left a daughter and soon the dutiful child, sadly
surviving, had closed the tomb as the colic closed the life of
her dear one and here you have the sad stone to bear witness.

Edward Nelson (died 1726) was a man who 'readily but unwisely
took upon himself the under shrievalty of this county' and,
'weakened by illness and by the wasting of his body', he caught a
severe and feverish chill. The story goes on:

Afflicted by the daily pressure of corrosive care and
daily depression,

He succumbed to a debilitating cough and raging fever
and a progressive wasting away.

Scarcely at length had he discharged his office with the
greatest praise than eaten away by consumption of the lung
(oh sorrow) he died'.

❖   At the redundant St Nicholas **Wattisham** (now looked after by a
Church Trust) is an 18th-century epitaph for John and Mary
Downing and their six children:

This inscription Serves to Authenticate the Truth of a
Singular Calamity

Which Suddenly happened to a poor Family in this Parish
Of which Six Persons lost their Feet by a mortification not to
be accounted for.

A Full Narrative of their Case is recorded in the Parish
Register for 1762.

On Sunday 10 January the eldest daughter Mary, aged 15,
complained of pain in the left leg. By nightfall it had become
excruciating and she likened it to being gnawed at by dogs. A

second daughter became afflicted and the next day the mother and another child followed. By Tuesday the entire family except John Downing and the baby began to develop blue spots on their feet and the diseased limbs turned black and gangrenous. The surgeon was summoned and he did the best he could by amputating the affected legs below the knee. Mary died some weeks later but Mrs Downing survived, though she lost both legs. Robert, aged eight, lost both legs while Edward, aged four, lost his feet. The baby died but John Downing survived almost unscathed.

Initially the 'calamity' was put down to witchcraft, but it was eventually decided that the family had somehow poisoned themselves, perhaps by contaminated food or by drinking water from a stagnant pond.

❖ In the churchyard of St Mary's **Newbourne** (the 'e' seems to be optional and interchangeable) is the tombstone of the Suffolk Giant, George Page. George was 7ft 7in tall and, together with his brother Meadows (who was only a few inches shorter), they toured the country in fairs and circuses as exhibits in sideshows. To emphasise his height the grave footstone is extended well beyond others alongside him. George died when he was still very young but Meadows continued working until 1875 and had a daughter. The (now badly eroded) inscription begins:

George Page, The Suffolk Giant
Died 20th April 1870 age 26 years
He was exhibited in most towns in England but his
best exhibition was with his Blessed Redeemer.

George Page became the inspiration for a novel by Frank Elias (1888–1949), who lived at **Felixstowe** and wrote under the pen name of John Owen. Elias, who first came to Suffolk in 1915 with the Suffolk Regiment, visited the grave at Newbourne in 1926 and wrote *The Giant of Oldbourne* plus 40 other novels, mostly about Suffolk.

❖ In the churchyard of St John the Baptist **Badingham** is an 18th-century tombstone of a blacksmith's family, ending:

My coal is spent, my iron gone,
My last nail's driven, my work is done.

❖ A roundel is found in St Peter and St Paul **Pettistree** which records the sad death of Ann Carter, who died in childbirth in 1790:

How dear the Purchase! How severe the Cost!
The Fruit was sav'd, the parent Tree was lost!

❖ The epitaph on a wall tablet to Elizabeth Hyam in **Boxford** church shows her to have been busy in the marriage stakes but might contain an exaggeration of her age:

In memory of
ELIZABETH HYAM
Of this Parish, for the
Fourth time Widow,
Who by a Fall, that brought on a Mortification,
Was at last hastened to her End on the
4th May 1748 in her 113th year.

❖ A desperately sad epitaph is found at **Westhorpe** where Maurice, the dearly loved child of W.H. and M.J. Symes, was killed in October 1901, aged 3½ years:

The event has left a wound, no time can heal
Which poets cannot paint, but mothers feel.

❖ In St Mary's **Bury St Edmunds** there is a monument to Peter Gedge (died 1818) founder of the *Bury and Norwich Post* newspaper in 1782. The inscription reads:

Like a worn out type he is returned to the Founder,
In hopes of being recast in a better and more perfect mould.

❖ In St Mary's **Hadleigh** an epitaph reads:

To free me from domestic strife
Death called at my house and he spoke to my wife
Susan, wife of David Pattison, lies here October 19th, 1706.
It does not sound as though Mr Pattison was terribly upset!

❖ Robert and Mary Leman, on the other hand, were so devoted to each other that they died on the same day. On their memorial at St Stephen's **Ipswich** (used as the Tourist Information Office) is found:

Beneath this monument entombed lie
A rare remark of a conjugal tye.
Robert and Mary, who to show how neere
They did comply, How to each other deere,
One loath behind the other long to stay
(As married) Died together in one day,
3rd Sept 1637.

Their son and four daughters are beneath the kneeling couple and, we are told, 'the same sun that closed her eyes in the morning shutting up his in the evening'.

❖ There are many memorials to the several generations of the Young family in All Saints **Bradfield Combust** but one of the most arresting is for Martha Ann Young (born 1783), the 14-year-old daughter of the agriculturist, politician and writer, Arthur Young (1741–1820), whose last words are inscribed:

> Pray for me papa – Now! Amen.

Her tragic death plunged the Young household into deep mourning and her father, arriving back at the house the following day wrote 'I arrived at Bradfield, where every object is full of the dear deceased. On going into the library the window looks into the little garden in which I have so many times seen her happy'.

The Young family had been at Bradfield since 1620 but by the time Arthur's father inherited the estate it was very run down and unprofitable. Arthur wrote that while there had been good times in the past 'in these present times [Bradfield] just maintains the establishment of a wheelbarrow'. His father, though, had other advantages in being 'a remarkably handsome man and six feet high' and was much liked by the ladies.

Arthur himself had a long and adventurous career and travelled widely in France, where he witnessed the dawning of the French Revolution. He published a classic tome entitled *The Annals of Agriculture* for which he persuaded George III to write an article under the pseudonym of Ralph Robinson of Windsor. He was a well travelled and highly cultured man whose own epitaph recalls a man who loved his country:

> Let every real patriot shed a tear,
> For genius talents worth lies here.

❖ At St John the Baptist **Metfield** is an epitaph for a vicar who died in 1835 and which records that he died 'deeply deplored by his family and universally regretted by his parishioners'.

It is presumed that this meant it was his passing that was both deplored and regretted!

❖ In All Saints **Worlingham** are monuments to two families by the name of Sparrow and Wrenne. One is a pictorial brass of 1511, moved from its original site to the chancel wall, showing Nicholas and Mary Wrenne. The 18in figures show Nicholas with long hair and wearing a fur-trimmed gown, while Mary has an elaborate rosary and purse.

General Robert Sparrow died in Tobago in 1805 and his monument shows a sorrowing man resting his head against the epitaph tablet. This is believed to be the work of Sir Francis

Chantrey and is only one of two Suffolk pieces. General Robert's grandson Robert Sparrow is also commemorated.

In the same church is a wall monument to Mrs Parnell Duke with an epitaph that reads:

> A Rous by birth, by marriage made a Duke,
> Christened Parnell, she lived without rebuke.

Mrs Duke's daughter is remembered as 'the Dovelike Virgin Ms Anne Duke'.

❖ At St Mary's **Dalham** is found a pink-veined alabaster tablet for Colonel Francis (called Frank) Rhodes, brother of Cecil Rhodes (1853–1902), one-time prime minister of Cape Colony and founder of Rhodesia. Cecil Rhodes bought the Dalham estate in 1901 with the intention of retiring to England, but died the next year before ever having lived there. The estate was inherited first by his brother Ernest, to whom the east window is dedicated, and then by Francis in 1905 who restored the 15th-century church roof in memory of his brother Cecil.

The memorial for Colonel Rhodes reads:

> Long travel in this churchyard ends
> A gentleman who knew not fear,
> A soldier, sportsman, prince of friends,
> A man men could but love, lies here.

Colonel Rhodes was as adventurous as his brother and distinguished himself at the relief of Khartoum. He became war correspondent for *The Times* in Kitchener's Nile Expedition.

Also in the church is a series of 19th-century tablets for servants of the local squire – Francis Watts (dairy and poultry woman), Washington Andrews (the butler), John Keates and Joseph Brett. The last two were aged labourers and their epitaph concludes:

> Who change their places often change with loss,
> 'Tis not the Rolling Stone that gathers Moss.

FIVE – SUFFOLK FOLK

IN THE Suffolk vernacular, 'folk' are referred to as 'fook' (to rhyme with book) and is purely the result of the glorious Suffolk accent that is, unfortunately, heard less and less. An 's' is invariably added and Suffolk fooks can be taken to mean anyone so, while it is preferable that your forebears have lived in the county since the Norman Conquest, Suffolkers are much more tolerant of incomers than they used to be and happily refer to fooks in general, whether home bred or not. The county has had its fair share of eccentric, famous or infamous folk, one or two of whom are mentioned here.

❖ **'A Fool and His Money'**
The English poet and farmer, **Thomas Tusser** (1524–1580), farmed at **Cattawade**, a hamlet of **Brantham** on the north bank of the River Stour, where he wrote his famous poem *A Hundreth Good Pointes of Husbandrie*, a long poem in rhyming couplets recording the country year. Thomas is credited with the proverb 'A fool and his money are soon parted' and always preached the virtues of thrift. For his wife's health he moved to **Ipswich** but after her death he moved to Norfolk.

❖ **'Bishop John 'Bilious' Bale (1495–1563)**
Born in 1495 at **Covehithe**, **John Bale** was educated at a Carmelite convent where he learned to be an enthusiastic and zealous follower of Roman Catholicism, the national religion of all England at that time. He was so taken with the religious life that he took Holy Orders, only to discover that he was not, after all, cut out for the monastic life. He renounced his vows and, following Saint Paul's precept of 'it is better to marry than to burn', duly married a young woman named Dorothy (which is all we know about her other than the fact that she bore her husband many children). Bale described her as 'the faithful Dorothy' and she must, surely, have been the most long-suffering of wives.

Shortly after his marriage, Bale transferred his energies from championing the cause of Catholicism to that of the new Protestantism, an entirely fortuitous move since in the 1540s Henry VIII established the new Protestant Church of England. During the turbulent years of the Reformation, John Bale had to straddle the vagaries of the political and religious dictates of the time and seems to have been rather good at it.

Now a minister of the Protestant Church, he gained a reputation for outspoken sermons and unorthodox behaviour. He obtained the living of **Thorndon** but was summoned before the Archbishop of York to explain a sermon he had preached against the invocation of saints. One contemporary wrote of his 'rude vigour of expression, and his want of good taste and moderation'. He used his considerable wit and learning to ridicule the 'sentimental idolatry' of Catholicism that he had so enthusiastically embraced only a few years earlier. So vitriolic was his tongue in castigating the Old Religion that he was given the nickname of Bilious Bale and began to make enemies with his scurrilous sermons and unorthodox behaviour.

Bale wrote many plays, including *King John* in 1538 (performed in **Ipswich** in 1561), and he is regarded as writing the earliest historical drama in England, though much of his work is also considered profane, coarse and indecent. When, in 1540, his protector, Thomas Cromwell, fell from favour, he fled with Dorothy and the children to Flanders, where he continued writing parodies of Catholic beliefs and rites. He returned on the accession of Edward VI but was sent to Ireland, an uninspired choice since most of the clergy there remained faithful to Catholicism and, therefore, to clerical chastity. Having occasioned considerable scandal by advising his fellow priests to marry he finally left Ireland and returned to England amid controversy caused by his refusal of the Roman rite at his consecration.

When the Catholic Queen Mary came to the throne, Bale was again forced to leave the country. Over the next few years he, the faithful Dorothy and the children had a series of hair-raising adventures, one of which included Bale being arrested on suspicion of treason.

He returned to England when the Protestant Queen Elizabeth came to the throne and spent his last three years at Canterbury, where he died in 1563. Among his last work was a translation of Kirchmayer's 'Pamachius', which is said to be 'filled with coarse and incessant abuse of priests and popery'. He left behind a presentable amount of valuable and learned writing, although much of it was marred by misrepresentations and what might be called his 'earthy' turn of phrase.

❖ **The Elwes Family, Dedicated Misers**

In 1705, **Sir Hervey Elwes** inherited the historic Manor and Priory at **Stoke-by-Clare** from his grandfather, Gervase (created a baronet in 1660). On arrival at the family mansion, Stoke College, he found he was not as well off as he had thought and immediately set about reviving his fortunes. So successful was he that he was soon a rich man and the accumulation of wealth became his one and only passion throughout his long life. For the last 60 of his 80 years at Stoke he condemned himself to solitude, rarely indulged in the luxury of either fires or candles and set a high standard of solitary miserliness. Almost every window in the mansion was broken, rain came in through the roof, and his household consisted of one man and two maids. His only friends were Sir Cordell Firebrace and Sir John Barnardiston, with whom he met occasionally, but little was spent on entertainment as they were both as rich, and mean, as Sir Hervey.

Needless to say, Sir Hervey saw no reason to indulge himself in the needless expense of a wife and family and decided to make his nephew, **John Meggott**, his heir. John was the son of Sir Hervey's sister, Amy, who had married a rich brewer. Brewer Robert Meggott died young, leaving Amy a rich woman. In true family tradition, however, Amy became as miserly as her brother and starved herself to death, preferring that to buying food.

Once appraised of his expectations, young John Meggott grabbed the opportunity with both hands and on visits to Uncle Hervey always dressed down, so that his uncle would not think him profligate. In 1763 Sir Hervey died and in accordance with his will, John Meggott changed his name to Elwes and moved into Stoke College.

At first he gloried in his good fortune (and there was indeed a fortune, since Sir Hervey ran his household on a mere £110 a year) and set about restoring the house to something resembling its past glory. He even delighted his tenants by showing every intention of making amends for his uncle's years of dereliction of duty towards the maintenance of their farmsteads.

Alas, before long John Elwes succumbed to the family trait and became even more parsimonious than his uncle. In the words of one chronicler, 'in the annals of avarice, there is not a more celebrated name than that of Elwes'. He began in a small way, refusing to clean either his shoes or his clothes lest they wear out more quickly, and Stoke College began to fall into ruin once more, the broken windows 'mended' with brown paper. When he travelled he always went on horseback, avoiding all turnpikes and public houses, taking with him crusts of bread and hard-boiled eggs for sustenance and grazing his horse along the road fringes.

Although John Elwes became an MP, he claimed to have spent only one shilling and sixpence on election expenses (so he was not all bad, said some), once stole a scarecrow's hat and wore a wig that he had found on the road. On one occasion a neighbour found him pulling down a crow's nest so that he might use the sticks as kindling for the kitchen stove and on another he was known to have eaten a moorhen that had been brought out of the river by a rat.

Unlike his uncle he did not eschew company altogether and had two sons by his housekeeper, though he never married. When the lawyer who drew up his £800,000 will in 1789 attended him, he was forced to write by firelight as the dying man was too mean to provide a candle. His two illegitimate sons, John and George Timms, inherited everything and in 1793 John, like his father, changed his name to Elwes.

❖ **Samuel the Roundhead**
It was a Suffolk man who gave the Roundheads their name in the English Civil War. The story goes that Sir Samuel Barnardiston (1620–1707) of **Kedington** had a particularly handsome head. He was spotted by Charles Stuart's queen, who looked out of a window and noticed a shorthaired youth among a group of protesting Puritans. 'See what a handsome round head is there' she is reputed to have cried. Thereafter he was nicknamed Samuel the Roundhead and it quickly became a nickname for the Parliamentarians. As it happened, Samuel was a Royalist (though opposed to Charles I's arbitrary government) but he wisely did not draw attention to himself and spent most of the Civil War with his round head quietly below the parapet in Suffolk. However, he returned to London in 1660 to welcome Charles II back to the throne, was knighted for his trouble and afterwards awarded a baronetcy.

In spite of his low key approach to the Civil War, Samuel the Roundhead was something of rebel and was once made prisoner of Black Rod for criticising a judgement of the House of Lords. He also spent four years in jail for refusing to pay a £10,000 fine levied, unfairly as he saw it, by Judge Jeffreys. He enjoyed a successful career as a Member of Parliament for Suffolk from 1678 onwards and was in the forefront of national politics well into the reign of William III.

Sir Samuel married Thomasine Brand of **Edwardstone** and bought a large estate at **Brightwell** near Ipswich. On the roof of Brightwell Hall he built an enormous water reservoir, so large that it also served as a holding tank for fish so that the household could have a ready supply for the larder.

He retired from politics in 1702, at the age of 82, and died in London a few years later. He had no children and his nephew succeeded to his title and estate. Unfortunately his memorial in Kedington church consists only of an inscribed stone, very modest in comparison with other more grandiose tombs, so posterity does not get a glimpse of the famous head.

❖ **John Smith, Bare Knuckle Fighter**
If ever there was a man who showed a determined, if foolhardy, courage it must be **John Smith,** the bare knuckle champion of Suffolk in the 1740s. He challenged Jack Slack, champion of Norfolk, to an encounter in the grounds of **Framlingham Castle.** The fight lasted barely five minutes and Smith was roundly beaten by Slack. Not a man to accept defeat lightly, he immediately issued a notice to the effect that:

'At the Great Castle at Framlingham, Suffolk, on Monday, 12 November there will be a severe trial between the following champions [Smith and Slack]…for the sum of forty guineas and though I had the misfortune to be defeated by him before, I am much his superior in the art of boxing, and doubt not but I shall give him and the company entire satisfaction.'

What Smith should have been aware of was Slack's reputation within the game and that it was hardly a fair fight. Slack's favourite trick was a chop to the carotids, the two great arteries carrying blood to the head. Compression of these arteries caused stupor in his opponents with the inevitable result. Since Jack Slack was a rabbit butcher, this particular manoeuvre became known as the rabbit punch.

Alas, Smith succumbed to the rabbit punch and lost his 40 guineas but, ever the optimist, he challenged the London champion, John James. Having perhaps learned a thing or two from Slack, Smith later reported that he had given Mr James 'such a sharp blow or punch on the pit of his stomach as knocked him down for dead'.

❖ **Edward Fitzgerald (1809–1883)**

Famed for his 1859 translation of the great Persian poem, *The Rubaiyat of Omar Khayyam*, Edward Purcell was born at **Bredfield** near **Woodbridge** in 1809 and lived practically the whole of his life in the neighbourhood. He did not take the name Fitzgerald until 1818, when his father took his wife's name as a condition for inheriting a fortune from her Irish father. Fitzgerald attributed his various eccentricities to the fact that his was an ancient family where cousins had a tendency to marry and, while this had the advantage of keeping the money in the family, it resulted in certain peculiar manifestations from continued in-breeding. One of his proclaimed hates was 'respectability' and all that went with it.

After an education that included King Edward VI Grammar School at **Bury St Edmunds** and Cambridge University (where he befriended Thackeray and Tennyson), Fitzgerald returned to Suffolk and adopted an eccentric and Bohemian way of life. He walked the lanes with a handkerchief on his head, wearing his Inverness cape and a flowered-satin waistcoat. Although he married Lucy, daughter of the Quaker poet, Bernard Barton, Fitzgerald was not husband material. The couple were unsuited and parted quickly.

Fitzgerald kept a boat at **Lowestoft**, which he named *Scandal* since that was, he said, the 'staple commodity of Woodbridge'. He was also part owner of a herring lugger with a Lowestoft fisherman, Joseph 'Posh' Fletcher. Together they made an arresting sight: Fitzgerald in top hat and frock coat and Posh in his fisherman's gear. Eventually the two fell out when Posh broke his promise to abstain from alcohol, although Fitzgerald always maintained that his friend was 'a much nobler fellow' than he himself, in spite of his weakness for strong drink. In 1869 Fitzgerald published *Sea Words and Phrases along the Suffolk Coast*, mostly collected from Posh and the other Lowestoft fishermen.

'Old Fritz', as his friends knew him, had become interested in poetry at the age of 16, when his father took him to **Wherstead** near **Ipswich** to meet an Anglo-Indian major who filled the boy's mind with a love of the East and so laid the foundations for his eventual translation of the Persian poem by the 12th-century astronomer and poet, Omar Khayyam.

Fitzgerald was buried in **Boulge** churchyard but apart from the family mausoleum. Rose bushes grow beside the simple granite tomb that are said to have sprung from seeds brought back from the rose bush on the grave of Omar Khayyam in Persia.

❖ **A Whizz at Algebra!**
John Mole (1743–1827) was born at **Old Newton** the son of a bailiff to John Meadows and his wife, Sarah. With little opportunity for education, Sarah took the young John under her wing and taught him to read. He took a series of jobs on different farms ending up at **Nacton** where Mr Garrard, who ran a school in **Ipswich**, noted that John Mole had an extraordinary ability for mental calculation. Mr Garrard offered to teach John basic arithmetic, not suspecting that he would learn so quickly and thoroughly that by 1773 he would open a school of his own. John had an innate affinity with the elements of algebra, so much so that in 1788 he published a book on the subject, *Elements of Algebra,* and in 1809 *A Treatise on Algebra, Designed for use of Schools.* He also contributed to the *Ipswich Magazine* and in 1793 moved to **Witnesham** where he continued to teach. Although he married twice he had no children.

❖ **Bound for South Australia**
When **Colonel William Light** (1786–1839) of **Theberton** set sail for South Australia in May 1836 there was no such place as Adelaide. Instead, there were 1,500 miles of virgin coastline and, in his capacity as the newly-appointed government surveyor, his job was to select the best place for the first settlement. The task was formidable and nigh impossible since he had only two months in which to survey vast areas of uncharted territory.

William Light was born in Malaya, the second son of Captain Francis Light (died 1794), founder of the Colony of Penang and its first governor. Captain Light had been born in **Dallinghoo**, the illegitimate son of William Negus, a Suffolk landowner, and Mary Light, a serving girl, but had prospered and had become friends with Charles Doughty, a wealthy landowner of Theberton. Just two years before his death, when William was six, Captain Light asked Charles Doughty if he would educate his son William and provide a stable home for him in Suffolk. Charles agreed and William returned to England to spend his youth at Theberton Hall and **Martlesham Hall** (an estate of Mrs Doughty). The Doughtys honoured Charles' promise to Captain Light by educating William, treating him as one of their own.

William left Suffolk to join the navy and embarked on an adventurous and successful career, during which he survived more than 40 actions without a wound. He served with distinction in the Peninsular War and afterwards he and his wife travelled widely. He was said to be a man of extraordinary accomplishments, soldier, seaman, musician, and artist and good at whatever he did. In 1836 he accepted the appointment in South Australia. His ship, the *Rapid*, arrived off Kangaroo Island on 17 August of that year and sailed straight to Encounter Bay, which he rapidly rejected as unsafe and useless for a main harbour.

The eventual choice of a site for Adelaide (named for Queen Adelaide, wife of William IV) was made in haste and forced upon him when word came that settlers were on their way expecting to find a new colony already set up. Thanks to Colonel Light, the town of Adelaide was laid out with a belt of parklands, a feature of town planning ahead of its time. He said, 'I leave it to posterity ... to decide whether I am entitled to praise or to blame'.

Colonel Light was confirmed in his appointment as Surveyor General for South Australia, at £400 a year, but his last years were dogged by ill health and poverty. Shortly before he died, a fire destroyed his lifetime accumulation of papers, journals and sketches. With the aid of a few salvaged documents he wrote, and published at his own expense, *A Brief Journal of the Proceedings of William Light* (1839).

Colonel Light never forgot his formative years in Suffolk and named his house 'Thebarton' (spelling it the old fashioned way) and a suburb of Adelaide also bears the name Thebarton. Since the 1970s residents of Thebarton and Adelaide have contributed to repairs to the church in Suffolk and each year the names of many Australians are to be found in the Visitor's Book as they seek the origins of their founder.

❖ **Benjamin D'Urban**
Another Suffolk hero of the Peninsular War was **Sir Benjamin D'Urban** (1777–1849) who was born at **Halesworth**, the son of John D'Urban MD and his wife, Elizabeth. The family had come originally from France but for at least three generations they lived and owned land in Suffolk and South Norfolk. Benjamin's grandparents lived at Shotesham (Norfolk) where they and several of their children (who all died tragically young) are buried. The

D'Urbans also had land at **Framlingham** where there is still a D'Urbans Farm just west of the town.

At 16, Benjamin joined the Dragoon Guards and, when the Peninsular War broke out in 1808, he was sent as a Colonel to command a Brigade of Portuguese cavalry (under the command of the future Duke of Wellington). After the war ended he had a succession of governorships and in 1833 he was appointed first Governor of the Cape of Good Hope. He then moved to Natal, where the Boers had settled in 1837, and set about creating a new colony, the port of which was named Durban.

❖ **Eliza's English Bread Book**
Elizabeth 'Eliza' Acton (1799–1859) of **Ipswich** was the first writer to produce a cookbook aimed at the domestic reader and it was she who introduced the now-universal practice of listing the ingredients at the beginning of each recipe.

Eliza Acton was born in Hastings but her father moved to Ipswich when she was a child to take up a partnership in a firm of brewers, Trotman, Halliday, Studd and Company in College Street.

At 18, Eliza and a friend opened a boarding school offering 'a course of education combining elegance and utility with economy'. She also began writing poetry, some of which was published in Ipswich in 1826 with a subscribers' list containing all the names of the town's hierarchy, including the Cobbolds, Alexanders and Churchmans.

Due to ill health Eliza had a spell in France where she acquired a lifelong appreciation of French cuisine and began to consider the relationship between food and health.

It is thought that while in France she had an unfortunate love affair with an officer in the French army. There were rumours that she had a baby, who was brought up by her sister, but there is no record of the child. Eliza was unconventional in many ways, but living in Ipswich with an illegitimate baby would have been difficult and subscriptions to her books might have tailed off. Her love poems, however, would indicate that she had known what it was to have loved and lost, writing verses such as:

> I love thee, as I love the last
> Rich smile of fading day,
> Which lingereth, like the look we cast,
> On rapture pass'd away.

In 1830 Eliza approached Longmans publishers with an idea for another poetry book, but instead was asked to consider writing a cookery book. Either she was in no hurry to write it, or she was busy with her poetry, but *Modern Cookery in all its Branches* was not published until 1845. It was a great success and an expanded edition appeared in 1855, called *Modern Cookery for Private Families*. Her unorthodox method of presenting the ingredients followed by the method was a landmark in cookery writing and Isabella Beeton later imitated her style.

In *Modern Cookery for Private Families,* Eliza was the first to record a recipe for Mulligatawny Soup, a curried soup brought back to England from India by British colonists. Elizabeth David described the 1855 edition as 'the greatest cookery book in our language'.

Eliza's next book was *The English Bread Book*, published in 1857. Her health, though, had deteriorated again and she died two years later in London, due to 'premature old age'. On the title page of *The English Bread Book* she wrote, 'In no way, perhaps, is the progress of a nation in civilisation more unequivocally shown, than in the improvement it realises in the food of the community'.

She was, in so many ways, ahead of her time in her belief that processed food, especially store-bought bread (then heavily adulterated), contributed to Britain's poverty and malnutrition.

Eliza's father, John Acton, gave up his partnership in the brewers Trotman, Halliday, Studd and Company to set up his own business. However, he went bankrupt and had to go and live with his son, Edward, a surgeon who lived in **Grundisburgh**. In 1809 he wrote a small book about seed germination.

❖ The television cook **Delia Smith** lives near **Stowmarket**, and as a young cook spent hours in the British Museum reading room re-discovering traditional recipes, including those of Eliza Acton, which gave her an enduring respect for Eliza's work. Delia's first book was *How to Cheat at Cooking* (1971) and she has over 15 million book sales to her name. Many of the television programmes were filmed at her Suffolk home and she was married at the Church of Our Lady in Stowmarket.

❖ By coincidence, Mrs Isabella Beeton's in-laws came from the **Stowmarket** area. Isabella (the daughter of Benjamin and Elizabeth Mayson of Cheapside, London) married her husband, Samuel

Orchard Beeton, a wealthy publisher, in 1856. Her life was marred by tragedy and she died at the age of 28. Her famous cookery book *The Book of Household Management* used Eliza Acton's format for the recipes, of which there were nearly 100 for soup, 200 for sauces and 128 for fish.

❖ **Mrs Ricketts Ricketts of Yoxford**
One of the most colourful characters to live at Satis House **Yoxford** was Mrs Clarissa Ricketts Ricketts (as she styled herself on her calling cards), who had been briefly married to George Laurence Ricketts Ricketts in 1865. The marriage lasted only a short time and Mrs Ricketts Ricketts came to Yoxford with a private fortune of £36,000. The Yoxford historian Robert T.L. Parr described her as 'a fair, stoutest, middle-aged lady of good-natured aspect, who drove through the village in a brougham, with two little white Pomeranians or small dogs on the seat beside her, each placing its paws on the window ledge and gazing out, one on the off side and one on the near'.

Mrs Ricketts used some of her money to build stabling (she bred horses) and make improvements to the house (see also Chapter Eight, The Dickens Connection). She struck up a close friendship with the Honourable Morton William North (younger son of the 7th Earl of Guildford) and his wife at **Little Glemham,** who all enjoyed social gambling. One day the Norths received a telegram from Clarissa saying only 'Losing heavily', which distressed them greatly since they had entrusted her with their money. She had gone to Monte Carlo to work 'a system' and had failed. A few days later she arrived back in Yoxford and after a short interval her death was announced and a funeral arranged.

At the express wish of the 'deceased', the coffin was taken to the churchyard in her own carriage and 'at trotting pace'. The two little dogs were chloroformed and buried with their mistress. A 'Baron de Chaston' made the funeral arrangements though nothing was known of him, and the servants at Satis House were said to be pocketing jewellery and 'no one said anything'. Richard Vicary Garnham signed the death certificate and Andrew Shimmen, a local man who had done work for Mrs Ricketts, made the coffin and, supposedly, put Mrs Ricketts in it.

Rumours circulated that the 'death' was a fraud and that Mrs Ricketts herself looked through the window of the church at her 'funeral'. Shortly after the service 'a stout, short gentleman' was seen leaving on a train from **Darsham**, never to be seen again.

A sign appeared on the churchyard gate, presumably with reference to the two little dogs:

Mrs Ricketts is not dead,

But two fat pigs were buried instead.

Sir John Blois tackled Andrew Shimmen about the matter but he would never answer any questions and would blank anyone who asked.

❖ The Weather Prophet

The tombstone of **Orlando Whistlecraft** (1810–1887) records that he was a 'poet and weather prophet' but he was also a smallholder, grocer and teacher. Born at **Thwaite,** he suffered childhood illness and at seven was severely disabled. He was, though, able to attend school, which he did as a boarder at an academy in **Ipswich**. When he was 17, he came under the influence of Dr Robert Hamilton and began writing poetry. After winning a drawing prize in 1826, Orlando began illustrating the seasons of the year and developing his interest in the weather. He married Elizabeth Rush of **Stonham Parva** and they set up home at Mimosa Cottage, Thwaite.

From 1857 until 1878 he published a series of *Weather Almanacs*. He made what turned out to be very accurate weather predictions and soon he was a household name throughout Suffolk. But fame is fickle and eventually Orlando had trouble making ends meet. After a fall he became bedridden and died in February 1887. There is a cast iron memorial to Orlando Whistlecraft in Thwaite churchyard.

❖ Mary Anne's Children of God

Mary Anne Girling (1827–1886) was born at Tinker Brook, **Little Glemham,** the daughter of William Clouting, a local carter. Aged 16 and with no formal education she married George Girling of **Ipswich,** a seaman and later a general dealer in the town. Mary became a wife and mother and, so far as anyone knew or cared, she had settled down to an ordinary, humdrum life. But on Christmas Day 1858, when Mary was 31 years old, she announced that she had had a vision (in her Ipswich bedroom). Christ appeared to her and told her that she had been granted a mission to lead the

Children of God to the Promised Land. Furthermore, she had been given the startling news that the Second Coming was imminent and that anyone who believed in her, Mary Anne Girling, would live forever.

The Victorians were very prone to occurrences of this nature but what persuaded an ordinary, ill-educated woman from Ipswich to leave her husband and family to devote the rest of her life to the Children of God will never be known. The Promised Land was not to be in Suffolk, however, and Mary began gathering together the 'Children' and preparing them for a move to Hampshire (why Hampshire, no one knows). Nearly 40 men, women and children rallied to her cause, coming from **Letheringham, Easton, Peasenhall, Parham, Kelsale** and other villages thereabouts to become 'the sons and daughters of Mary Anne'. The group set out for the New Forest, stopping off in London to pick up a few more converts, which swelled the number of followers to 164. The locals did not quite know what to make of this seemingly crazed woman from Suffolk and her fanatical followers, who performed frenetic dances and shook with religious fervour. Mary Anne was both feared and revered, and was at one stage threatened with being tarred, feathered and burned as a witch

In the 1881 census, the Children of God declare no occupation other than 'Prefers to Live by Faith' and inhabit 'The Shakers House and Tents' in the New Forest, so the census collector did very well to obtain all the detailed information he did. There is no mention of Mary's husband, although she had her son William with her, so perhaps Mr Girling was less convinced of his wife's vision and stayed in Ipswich.

The Children were called Shakers, as a result of their public displays of religious passion. Such activities attracted huge press coverage, not least because of Mary's repeated assertions that she was a new incarnation of the Deity. These sons and daughters of God thought they would live forever, and that Mary Anne would ultimately rule the world, but alas for all concerned the dream came to an end with Mary's death on 18 September 1886.

❖ **Fowl Play!**

Poor **Catherine Foster** of **Acton** must have been very cross indeed when, on a fateful day in 1846, her next-door neighbour's chickens wandered into her garden and ate some discarded dumplings. She had been married for only three weeks, but it was long enough for her to decide that she did not much like her husband or her new life and wished to return to her former life as a domestic servant. Aged only 17, she saw widowhood as the only way out. She procured some arsenic, which she duly sprinkled onto a plate of dumplings and served up to her husband.

Mr Foster's sudden death was diagnosed as being the result of English cholera and all would have been well had the chickens not found their way into the garden and eaten the rest of the dumplings. Their sudden death alerted the neighbours and the authorities were summoned. A post-mortem confirmed that Mr Foster had died from an overdose of arsenic.

Catherine was arrested and at her trial her younger brother was coerced into giving evidence that he had seen his sister sprinkle some powder onto the dumplings. The defence did not query if this was, in fact, the poison or whether the child had merely witnessed the baking process. But it was enough for the court to find Catherine guilty and sentence her to hang.

On 27 March 1847, before a crowd of more than 10,000 on-lookers, Catherine Foster was hanged on Market Hill in **Bury St Edmunds**. She was the last woman to be publicly executed in Suffolk. Before she died, Catherine exhorted other young women not to follow her example but to accept their lot in the marriage stakes.

By coincidence, Catherine's father had once been suspected of murdering a man during a robbery in 1838. William Morley, it was said, had killed William Kilpatrick and had attempted to cover it up by hanging the man from a signpost at **Lavenham**, where he was said to have committed suicide. The case was never proved.

❖ **Alice Was Her Name, Poker Was Her Game!**
One of the most colourful women in the early days of the American Wild West was **Poker Alice Tubbs** (1851–1930) who was born Alice Ivers in **Sudbury** on 17 February 1851. Her father was a schoolmaster and blessed not only with a sense of adventure, but also with the courage to travel to the unknown lands of the New World. Like many Suffolk men of the second half of the 19th century, Mr Ivers wanted to realise the dream of a new and bright future for his family, so he emigrated to Virginia in around 1867, taking his only daughter with him.

Alice was sent to a fashionable women's seminary and brought up as a respectable and religious young lady in Virginian society. Soon after she left the seminary the family moved to Colorado, where they encountered an altogether different culture. Here they found life dominated by the miners, loggers and cowboys of the American frontier, along with the men who had gone west at the height of the gold rush, most of them destitute and desperate. Gambling was their chief occupation, a subject not taught at the seminary. Colorado was as different as it could be from Virginia.

Into this male-dominated world came Alice Ivers, a young woman who liked frilly, feminine clothes and who spoke with a soft English accent. She quickly married Frank Duffield, a mining engineer with both means and education, and moved to Leadville, the largest mining town in Colorado and the most lawless. Alice is described at this time as 'a petite 5ft 4in beauty with blue eyes and long, lush brown hair'. Frank was an enthusiastic gambler and she sat behind him at the tables night after night, learning all there was to know about poker and the men who played it. By now this petite young woman carried a .38 pistol and smoked cigars, but as yet had never sat at the gambling tables in her own right.

Her married life was cut short when Frank Duffield was killed in a mining accident and Alice was left to fend for herself in less than hospitable circumstances. She took to the gaming tables and almost overnight became one of the most successful female professional gamblers in the south. During the 1890s she travelled by stagecoach through all the most notorious frontier towns, playing poker. In Creede (Colorado) she worked in a saloon owned by Bob Ford, the man who shot Jesse James, and at Silver City, New Mexico, she broke the house bank and walked away with 6,000 dollars.

In Deadwood, South Dakota, Alice shot a man who had pulled a knife on a fellow gambler. The latter was Warren G. Tubbs and when they married, Alice became known as 'Poker Alice Tubbs'. Mr Tubbs died only a year or two after their marriage, and although she married for a third time (to George Huckert, whom she first employed to run her farm and then decided it was cheaper to marry him) she was always known as Poker Alice Tubbs. Widowed again she took to the road but, always quick on the draw, shot and killed a 4th Cavalry trooper in a brawl. Alice was acquitted on grounds of self-defence but her luck had turned. The saloon she had opened was closed down and the years of tough living caught up with her.

Alice's name has gone down in the annals as the most famous woman gambler of the American West. She always said, 'I would rather play poker with five or six experts than eat'. She had abnormal luck with the cards, though she would never work on a Sunday. She was also an accomplished tarot dealer, and a fair shot with her ever-present .38 gun. She was famous for her spending sprees in New York City and, in her youth, for her beauty and gentility.

When she died, ill, penniless and alone, Poker Alice Tubbs had travelled a long way from her cultured upbringing in more ways than one. She took an unusual path but was one of many pioneering women who left behind a comfortable existence in Suffolk for the hazards, and rewards, of the New World.

❖ **Flora Sandes, a Soldier in the Serbian Army**
Flora Sandes (1876–1956) was the daughter of the Revd Samuel Dickson Sandes. She was born in Ireland but in 1880 came to Suffolk with her family, where her father was first curate at **Monewden** and then Rector at **Marlesford**. Flora did not marry but became a nurse and when war broke out in 1914, at the age of 40, was among the first to volunteer for service with a Serbian ambulance unit. When the Serbian Army was overrun by invading Austro-Germany-Bulgarian forces in November 1915, Flora travelled with the Army during the Great Retreat to Corfu via the Albanian mountains. For practical reasons she enlisted with the Army – the Iron Regiment – and achieved a remarkable promotion to Sergeant-Major. She was the first woman to hold a commission in the Serbian Army.

To help raise funds for the Serbian cause she wrote and published *An English Woman-Sergeant in the Serbian Army* (1916) but in the same year sustained a serious wound caused by an enemy grenade during hand-to-hand fighting. Unable to fight, she reverted to a nursing role.

Ishobel Ross of the Scottish Women's Hospital Unit recorded in her diary the day she met Flora:

'Colonel Vassovitch came into the camp with an English woman dressed in the uniform of the Serbian army. Her name is Flora Sandes. She is quite tall with brown eyes and a strong, yet pretty face. She is a sergeant in the 4th company and talked to us for a long time about her experiences, and the fierce fighting she and the men of her company had to face. We felt so proud of her and her bravery.'

At the end of the war Flora chose to remain with the Serbian Army and eventually retired with the rank of Captain and Serbia's highest decoration, the King George Star.

In 1927 she met and married Yuri Yudenitch. Flora Sandes Yudenitch had led a truly extraordinary life but when her husband died she swapped Belgrade for England and returned to Suffolk. She died in **Wickham Market** aged 80, a commendable age for a woman who had endured the rigours of army life in World War One and sustained a debilitating wound on the field of battle.

❖ **No Votes Means War!**
During the first decade of the 20th century the cause of women's suffrage was one of the hottest, and most passionately fought, issues of the day. Suffolk was a hotbed of dissent and the climax of a two-woman campaign came at four o'clock in the morning of 28 April 1914 when the Bath Hotel, **Felixstowe**, was set on fire by an incendiary device planted in the East Wing. The coastguards at the wireless station alerted the Fire Brigade, but by the time they arrived the fire had secured a firm hold. In two hours the building was gutted. Attached to the trees at the corner of the hotel were found a number of ordinary tie-on labels bearing inscriptions such as 'No Peace Until Women Get the Vote', 'Votes for Women', and 'No Votes means War'. Not without reason, the incident was attributed to the Militant Suffragettes known to be at work in East Suffolk causing mayhem wherever they went. Fortunately there was no one at the hotel at the time, as it had recently been refurbished for the new season at a cost of £30,000.

The chief suspect was Hilda Birkett (alias Byron) who was already wanted in connection with the burning down of a football stadium. She and her protégé, Florence Tunks, were arrested and on 22 May arrived at Felixstowe Town Hall to answer the charge of 'setting fire to the Bath Hotel, two wheatstacks at Bucklesham Farm, and a stack at Stratton Hall'. While the suffragette movement had many supporters, they were not in evidence as the women arrived. Instead they received a hostile reception from the crowd, several hundred in number, who jeered their arrival.

The final trial took place on 5 June 1914 at the Suffolk assizes when Hilda Burkett protested 'I don't recognise the judge or any of these men – I object to all these men on the jury'.

They were both found guilty. Burkett was handed a two2-year sentence but Tunks, called 'the fool of the other', got only nine months. Both were sent to Holloway Prison but soon afterwards war broke out with Germany and all suffragette prisoners were released.

The bare and blackened walls of the Bath Hotel were demolished soon afterwards and its destruction was the last 'outrage' of the suffragette movement in Suffolk.

❖ **The Misses Thompson**
The 17th-century Linden House in Eye was for 30 years the home of the Misses Thompson, six unmarried sisters – all of them career women –who lived there from the 1920s until the late 1950s. Two of the sisters, Margaret and Mary, were involved with the suffragist movement. Margaret Thompson was a militant suffragette and she had three spells of imprisonment with Mrs Pankhurst and Mrs Pethick-Lawrence between 1909 and 1912. She had a facial disability caused by a car accident and in 1912 was examined and declared fit for force feeding, although by the cup not the tube. When the doctor asked Margaret in Holloway if she was a vegetarian she said 'Here, I am'. The liquid used for force feeding was particularly disgusting and made from fatty meat and Bovril. Mary and Margaret published their memoirs in 1957 in a small book entitled *They Couldn't Stop Us!*

❖ **Get Yourself a Dog!**
In May 1911, Constance Emily Andrews of **Ipswich** was sent to prison for refusing to pay her dog licence. Constance was secretary of the Ipswich branch of the National Union for Women's Suffrage Societies and said that, although she was very fond of her dog, she resented having to pay a dog tax when she had no say in parliamentary elections. After her refusal to pay the fine the magistrate sentenced her to a week in Ipswich gaol.

On her release Constance said that Ipswich prison was 'as good as a prison could be' and urged her supporters that no woman should pay the dog licence and that if they did not have a dog they should buy one so that the prisons would be full.

❖ **Mr Diesel's Untimely Death**

During 1912 and 1913 there was great excitement surrounding a new factory being built at a 46-acre site on Hadleigh Road, **Ipswich**, by Consolidated Diesel Engine Manufacturers Limited (CDEM). Such manufacturing giants as Ransomes of Ipswich had put the town at the forefront of the march of industrial development and another factory would bring new employment and kudos. Indeed, so many jobs did the new factory promise that the Borough Council was under pressure to consider constructing more council houses to accommodate them.

What was particularly exciting was the word 'diesel', which at the beginning of the 20th century still meant very little in terms of fuel and engine manufacture. The diesel engine had run for the first time in Augsburg, southern Germany, and was originally called the 'oil engine', ignition relying on combustion inside a cylinder instead of a spark to ignite the fuel. In 1897 the compression ignition engine prototype was named after its inventor, **Rudolph Diesel** (1858–1913). Dr Diesel applied for a patent for the 'internal combustion engine' and continued his research into the possibilities of using vegetable oils to fuel the new device. With farsighted vision that was a hundred years ahead of its time, Diesel stated in 1912: 'The diesel engine can be fed with vegetable oils and would help considerably in the development of agriculture of the countries which use it'. He added that 'The use of vegetable oils for engine fuels may seem insignificant today. But such oils may become in course of time as important as petroleum and the coal tar products of the present time.'

Through Diesel's Belgian consortium Carels, and with some help from a group of London financiers, building of the CDEM premises was commenced and in September 1913 Dr Rudolph Diesel was invited to open the new factory. He embarked on the SS *Dresden* cross-Channel ferry on 29 September but never reached Suffolk alive. When the ferry docked at Harwich Mr Diesel was not on board. A coastguard boat found his body two days later. As was usual at the time personal effects were removed from the body before it was thrown back into the sea. His sons later identified the items.

There are three main theories as to why Dr Diesel drowned, the first being that he simply fell overboard, and the second that he had committed suicide as his finances were later found to be in a poor state. His family categorically refuted the second allegation. They argued that he had been on his way to open a factory that was manufacturing his engines and that the financial situation was likely to improve. As one of the master engineering inventors of his age, he had everything to live for and there had been no hint that he was at all depressed or downhearted. Quite the contrary, as George Carel (director of the Diesel company in Belgium) said that Dr Diesel had been looking forward to opening the new factory and having talks with his backers in London. Sidney Whitman, director of CDEM, told the *East Anglian Daily Times* that he had been in regular correspondence with Dr Diesel and that he knew he was keen to visit Ipswich. However, 'We can hardly hope to see him again' he added.

In addition to the new Ipswich factory there was one being opened in St Louis, America, by the American Diesel Engine Company. The newspaper reported that on board ship, Dr Diesel had dined with George Carel and colleagues then they strolled on deck for a time as the evening was warm. He was in excellent spirits, 'quite jolly, in the best of humour' said Dr Carel. They separated for the night at 10 o'clock. Dr Diesel shook Dr Carel's hand and said he would see him in the morning. That was the last that was heard or seen of him.

Dr Carel also said that Dr Diesel's night shirt had been laid ready for him on his bed, 'but the bed had not been slept in. His bunch of keys hung from the lock on his hand bag in his cabin and his watch was placed in such a position that he could see it if he was lying down'.

The third, and most likely, theory is that Dr Diesel was murdered and thrown overboard, but who the perpetrators were is unknown. Being a German by nationality but born in Paris, Diesel was known as an internationalist who wanted his inventions to be available to all countries. But in 1913 it is likely that there were those in Germany who did not want a potential weapon of war to fall into the hands of their likely adversaries. Also, Diesel was very outspoken in his hopes for self-sufficiency in terms of renewable fuels like peanut oil, which threatened the dominance of the mineral oil engine. Since the petroleum industry was already highly consolidated globally, those whose profits were tied up in petrol oil monopolies were unlikely to welcome the advent of bio-oils.

At the start of World War One the CDEM factory was taken over by Vickers, who were instructed to manufacture engines for submarines. From 1915 onwards a number of submarines based at Harwich were regularly towed up the Orwell to Ipswich docks, where men from the old CDEM factory worked on them under top secret conditions. So secret was the operation that no records whatsoever survive anywhere that tell what happened during the war years. After the war Vickers continued operating from the factory and teamed up with Petters to manufacture diesel engines, though curiously no records of those days survive either.

This lack of documentary evidence has led to it being dubbed 'the factory that vanished without a trace' and greater mystery arises from its eventual demise. It seems to have disappeared sometime during 1926 and possibly had something to do with the General Strike of that year. The Vickers-Petter partnership clearly closed the factory, though it is strange that, for what would obviously have been a far-reaching event for the local workforce, nothing appeared in the local press.

Although Dr Diesel never reached Suffolk, his invention led to the CDEM factory in Ipswich, which gave employment to hundreds of local men. The conundrum of his death, and the peculiar lack of evidence for the works and its overnight demise, remains to be solved. The site of the old Diesel works is now the Hadleigh Road Industrial Estate.

❖ **The Dream of Mrs Pretty's Friend**
For centuries a group of ancient mounds on an expanse of sandy heathland at **Sutton Hoo** presided over the comings and goings on the River **Deben** relatively undisturbed and entirely overlooked by archaeologists. It had been thought that there might be 'something' there but no one knew quite what, and there seemed little or no impetus from anyone to find out. It was left to **Edith May Pretty** (1883–1942) to initiate an excavation of the site in 1938 and, in doing so, uncover the Anglo-Saxon secrets of Sutton Hoo. It is said that the result of Mrs Pretty's excavations at Sutton Hoo is 'page one of the history of England' and it was a friend's dream that encouraged her to do it.

Edith (née Dempster) Pretty was born into a prosperous manufacturing family and her father had a penchant for world travel. The family visited just about every country that it was possible to reach going by boat, as far as South America, Japan and Australia. She was educated at Roedean (in its early incarnation as

Wimbledon House School in Brighton) where one of her friends was Florence Sayce, the niece of Professor Sayce, the Egyptologist. The Dempsters travelled to Cairo, where Edith climbed one of the pyramids.

Edith had known Frank Pretty for most of her adult life but while he proposed to her annually, marriage was not on the cards. They were apart during World War One and, due to her mother's death in 1919, Edith continued to travel with her father until his death in 1925. She finally married Colonel Frank Pretty (1878–1934) in 1926 and they bought **Sutton Hoo House** near **Woodbridge** with its accompanying 526-acre estate. The Pretty family had a successful retailing company in **Ipswich**, William Pretty and Sons, and while Frank had served with the Suffolk Regiment during the war, he was also a director of the family company. Their deliriously happy but short marriage was brought to a cruel end with Frank's death from cancer in 1934.

Life for Mrs Pretty was never the same again and it was a visit from a friend in 1937 that led her to wonder again at the mounds on part of the estate, marked as 'Roman Tumuli' on the map. Her friend had a dream in which she saw the ghostly figure of a warrior beside one of the mounds. Edith contacted Guy Maynard of the Ipswich Museum, who put her in touch with Basil Brown, a retired farmer who had done a certain amount of archaeological excavation and was known for his thorough and careful work. No one had any idea at this stage what, if anything, was in the mounds that were still covered with bracken and gorse. During 1938, Basil Brown opened three mounds and found they had been robbed out in earlier centuries, although there were some finds in the form of cremation urns, traces of a buried boat and ornaments of glass, bone and metal.

In May 1939, with Europe on the brink of war, Basil Brown made a startling discovery in one of the largest mounds. Iron ship rivets began to appear and gradually the outline of a huge ship emerged in the sandy soil. It was almost 90ft long and 15ft wide, with places for 38 oarsmen, and was definitely not Roman (or Viking, as was first surmised). It must have been hauled up from the river and lowered into a rectangular pit. But there was more to come. A burial chamber emerged, unlike anything that had been seen before, with artefacts that were of unprecedented importance to British archaeology. During July the discoveries were overwhelming and 'gold jewellery, coins, silver plate, weapons and bowls, the remains of cauldrons, buckets and dishes of bronze and iron, textiles, leather, cups, drinking-horns and miscellaneous other objects' were recovered from the seventh-century burial chamber in the central part of the buried ship. There was antique silver from Eastern Europe and 'late classical spoons and magnificent gold work by East Anglian craftsmen'. This was an important, and probably royal, Anglo-Saxon burial of unparalleled proportions that was missed by earlier grave robbers and had lain undisturbed for 1,300 years.

A coroner's inquest was held to decide whether or not the objects were Treasure Trove, but the coroner found that such was not the case and the finds were, therefore, the property of Mrs Edith Pretty. In haste, with the war clouds gathering, the objects were taken to the British Museum laboratory and, after cursory cataloguing, deposited in its underground vaults for the duration. On Wednesday 23 August, it was announced that Mrs Pretty had given the contents of the Sutton Hoo funerary ship to the nation.

The reconstructed Sutton Hoo helmet is now an icon of Anglo-Saxon Suffolk and of England. Both it and the fabulous grave probably belonged to King **Redwald** of the **Wuffinga** dynasty, whose great hall was at **Rendlesham**. Redwald ruled the East Angles from about 600 to 626 and for the last few years of his reign was also supreme ruler of the English kingdoms. Putting 'Mrs Pretty' into an Internet search engine results in over half a million sites, but add 'Sutton Hoo' and it more than doubles. Edith Pretty put Suffolk on the archaeological map in a big way and her generosity in gifting it to the nation is immeasurable.

❖ **Suffolk's Human Arrow**

In 1969 Mrs Pansy Chinery, aged 90, died in an Ipswich retirement home. She was old, childless and, it has to be said, bad tempered and reclusive. Few people mourned her passing, but after her death her family made the most amazing discovery. A trunk in the attic was found to contain evidence that Pansy Chinery had once been an internationally famous trapeze artist and one of only a handful of women who performed the act of being shot from a giant crossbow, fired into a huge paper target and caught by her sister swinging from a trapeze. Pansy had kept photographs, programmes, posters, newspaper cuttings and props relating to her career; even the hook and leather strap she used as the mouthpiece in her speciality act, teeth-spinning while suspended from the bar of the trapeze. There were also wigs, and hand-made silk costumes (complete with their patterns), which showed that she performed in tights, corset and skimpy shorts – not what every Victorian girl was wearing!

Frances Elizabeth Mary Murphy (always called Pansy) was born in Liverpool in 1879, the daughter of an Irish tailor. Her mother was from **Hadleigh** and in 1881 Pansy and her sister Adele were living with their parents and other siblings in **Ipswich.** Mrs Murphy encouraged her daughters from a very early age to go on the stage and arranged for them to have dancing, singing and recitation lessons. But she could not know that both Pansy and her sister would pursue a career that would take them to circuses and theatres all over the world.

By 1891 both Pansy's parents were dead and her sister had already run away to join the circus. Barnham and Bailey's 'Greatest Show on Earth' circus visited Ipswich several times during the 1890s and it would have been easy for Adele to join them on one such visit. Soon afterwards Adele met and married John Zedora, a member of a troupe known as The Flying Zedoras. Adele being her only family, Pansy joined her on the high trapeze and became Pansy Zedora.

Her career developed from there and she joined The Uniques, a ladder-balancing act. Then Pansy learned to perform as Alar, The Human Arrow shot from a crossbow, the star attraction of Barnum and Bailey's Circus 'from St Petersburg to St Louis'. She performed her spectacular feats of daring in New York's Madison Square Garden, where the American newspapers hailed her as 'The crowning miracle of physical and mechanical sensation, surpassing adequate description...the bravest of all living artists'. It was in New York during 1897 that Pansy had a near-fatal accident on the high trapeze in which she broke her arm and was 'knocked senseless'. The newspapers screamed 'Stunned – the Human Arrow...the string was pulled too soon, and Alar was knocked senseless on her lofty perch'.

Pansy returned to Ipswich over the years and in 1904 she married Horace Osborne, an Ipswich hosier, but before long he, too, had joined the circus and they were performing a clownish Ritz and Ritz routine together. In 1916 she was still performing her teeth-spinning act but World War One brought her career to an end. After the war, circus and music hall entertainment gave way to early cinema and Pansy's adventurous life drew to a close. She was widowed and remarried, this time to a sailor named Hugh Chinery who was a distant cousin. Pansy and Hugh settled in Ipswich and although it was well known that she had worked in a circus, she never spoke of her one-time fame to anyone. It was only after her death that the family made the astounding discovery in the attic.

Quite how Pansy had managed to amass her astonishing archive, most of it in pristine condition, will never be known, as she was constantly on the move. The fact that she collected all the posters and programmes shows how much she cherished her adventures. She had had two husbands but no children and in her old age never talked about her life or vouchsafed any confidences to any of the Chinery family. The only clue to her former life that anyone had seen was the metal hook (and its leather strap, complete with teeth marks) that she kept in a jar in the bathroom. She lived the rest of her life with her husband's family in Ipswich and was known as a 'loner'. She would sit in her room and slam the door shut if anyone came to the house. Ralph Chinery, Hugh Chinery's grandson, donated the collection to the London Theatre Museum.

❖ Suffolk has always had a strong and enduring affection for both the theatre and its players. In the early 16th century there were many open-air theatres, or Game Places, where a visit from a London troupe was a welcome diversion from country life. It is thought that William Shakespeare himself performed in **Ipswich**, **Hadleigh** and **Sudbury** on several occasions as a young travelling player.

The famous actor and theatre manager, **David Garrick** (1717–79) made his stage debut at **Ipswich** in 1741 before a crowded audience in the new Playhouse in Tacket Street. He had joined a company of comedians in London and, as a raw and nervous tyro, was eager to try his luck in the theatre. His Ipswich audience gave him such confidence-boosting applause that his future was assured and he returned to London where, by the end of the year, he was the talk of the theatrical world for his performance in Shakespeare's *Richard III*.

❖ **The Fishers**
During the 1820s and 1830s the itinerant singer and actor **David Fisher** (1760–1823) toured East Anglia with his family playing to

packed audiences. In 1812 Fisher founded the Norfolk and Suffolk Company of Comedians, which visited all the theatres on their circuit in turn, the company taking to the road for two years at a time. The company, which ran for four generations, was particularly popular because it had strong links with the London stage and meeting the players was the closest that many rural communities got to theatrical celebrities. For the two years, the Fishers travelled with three large wagons drawn by six horses and would stay in one of the major towns of the area for several weeks, visiting outlying villages to put on plays and revues.

Fisher erected or adapted 13 theatres in Suffolk and Norfolk including those at **Beccles**, **Sudbury**, **Woodbridge**, **Lowestoft** and **Newmarket**. The **Bungay** theatre (founded 1828) is one of the few still standing and maintains its original façade. Since it closed in the 1840s the Fisher Theatre was used as a Corn Hall, laundry, cinema and a textile warehouse until the Bungay Arts and Theatre Society bought it in 2001 and reopened it as a theatre in 2006. David Fisher's wife Elizabeth died just after the opening of the Woodbridge theatre and she is buried in the local churchyard.

The **Eye** Theatre was built as a result of David Fisher's regular performances in the town. In 1793 a petition was signed by a number of residents to support Fisher's application to set up a theatre in Eye, which suggests that there had been some opposition to the project. It was eventually opened on 18 June 1815.

The **Halesworth** theatre was opened in 1808, but only after defeating vociferous opposition from the Methodist minister, who preached against plays involving 'love intrigues, blasphemous passions, profane discourses, lewd descriptions and filthy jests'. A pamphlet war ensued between those who supported the theatre and those against it. Those in favour won the day and the hall was used by the Fisher family troupe from 1812–44. It is now the Rifle Hall, so called because at one time it was used as a drill hall by the local rifle corps.

SIX – WHY IS IT CALLED THAT?

HAVE you ever wondered why places, streets and houses are called what they are? Sometimes, we are so familiar with names that they are just accepted unless, perhaps, the novelty of one attracts attention, such as **Kettleburgh** – a place where kettles were made, maybe? No, the word is made from '*Ketil*' and '*berg*' (Old Norse) or '*cetel*' and '*beorge*' (Old English) which meant Ketil's hill, or hill by a narrow valley (Ketil being an Old Norseman who lived there). Or how about **Sweffling**, commonly said to be the place where swifts congregate but which appears as '*Sueflinga*' in the Domesday Book and means (the place of) Swiftel's people. Nearby **Bruisyard** is invariably interpreted as 'brewers yard' and said to be where the Romans had a brewery, but it appears as *Buresiart* in the Domesday Book and is an evolution of two Old English words *(ge)bur* and *geard* meaning peasant's enclosure.

Everywhere you look there are names that contain clues to the local history, or a street name that tells a story. Not every place name can be explained with any certainty, but here are a few whose origins are either modern enough to be safely documented or have stood the test of history.

❖ **The Three Bradfields**
Bradfield St Clare is one of the three Bradfields situated just south of **Bury St Edmunds**. Originally the three hamlets were known collectively as Bradfield, which comes from the Old English 'brad' and 'feld', which meant 'a broad stretch of open land'. It appears as 'Bradefelda' in the 1086 Domesday Book. **St Clare** was added to that part where the Seyncler (or St Clair-sur-Epte) family owned the land, and **Bradfield St George** takes its name from the church dedication.

In 1333, **Bradfield Combust** was called Little Bradfield, but by 1353 had assumed its present name, Combust being a Middle English addition meaning 'burnt'. It is an enduring reminder of the eruption of violent rebellion against the Abbot of the all-powerful Benedictine Abbey at Bury St Edmunds, which owned Bradfield. Those who worked the land did so as serfs and not as free men, and in 1327 Abbot Richard of Draughton angered the people of Bury St

Edmunds by reneging on a new charter of liberties. 3,000 men stormed the abbey, breaking down the gates and destroying parts of the monastery. Resentment overflowed from the town into the lands owned or administered by the abbey and at Bradfield the men burned down the grange where the monks kept their corn stores, before joining the rioters in Bury.

Order was restored both in Bury and in the surrounding villages but the village name became Bradfield Combust so that the events of the rebellion against the monks should not be forgotten.

❖ **Plague Free Market**
The name **Newmarket** comes, literally, from the Latin *Novum Forum*, which means new market place. During one of the many outbreaks of the plague, the market at **Exning** was closed and a new one sprung up a few miles away. In the 13th century this became *Novum Mercatum* (New Market) and by the early 15th century the two words took the English form of Newmarket.

❖ **Chainhouse and Chainbridge**
From 1663 to 1665, **Needham Market** was isolated because of a particularly virulent outbreak of the plaque. No one was allowed in or out, and chains were put up to mark the parish boundaries. **Chainbridge** on the west of the town, **Chain House Farm** to the east and **Chainhouse** (Road) to the south, are reminders of the points at which those inside the chains would put out money (soaked in vinegar) in return for food, provided by those outside. It was thought that vinegar would kill germs on the coins and so contain the disease.

During the two years of confinement, the area around the town became overgrown and many inside the chains succumbed to the disease, so that fewer and fewer coins appeared in the vinegar. The gradual impoverishment of those inside gave people little hope that anyone would survive. However, after 1665, the danger had abated and, to the astonishment of many, a number of villagers emerged into the wider world. Due in part to better policing of ships using the eastern ports, this was the last serious outbreak of the plague in Suffolk.

The name Needham Market is said to derive from the Old English '*nied*' (needy) plus '*ham*' (homestead). Those living in the town in the 1660s might well have thought it an appropriate name.

❖ **Knights Templar**

The word Temple crops up in road and house names and is a clue to the long-forgotten houses or lands of the **Knights Templar** or **Hospitaller** in Suffolk. Together, the Knights Templar, the Teutonic Knights and the Hospitallers were the three most powerful orders of chivalry that lived under the vows of religion. They played a significant role in the defence of Christian settlements in Palestine and Syria and are most closely associated with the Crusades, fighting alongside crusading forces in the wars against Egypt and Turkey. The houses were founded in the 12th century or before and in Suffolk the most famous and oldest Knights Templar foundation, known as a preceptory or commandery, was at **Dunwich**. King John supported the house with lands and liberties, and in 1227 was confirmed in strength by Henry III.

At the suppression of the Knights Templar in 1312, after their failure to prevent the fall of Acre, the last Christian stronghold in the Holy Land, the Dunwich property was transferred to the Knights Hospitaller, who held it until the Reformation. Their manor extended into **Middleton** and **Westleton** and their church was called the Temple of Our Lady in Dunwich. At the dissolution of the Hospitallers in 1540 the Temple revenues fell to the Crown.

The preceptory of the Knights Hospitaller at **Battisford** was the largest house in Suffolk and founded in around 1150. They received the support of Henry II and Henry III and during the 12th and 13th century amassed lands and assets including the right to a free warren, plus houses with gardens in **Coddenham** and **Mellis** and the rectory at **Badley**. At the Dissolution, the Battisford preceptory was granted to Andrew Judde, alderman of London.

There is a Temple Street in **Ipswich** and **Stowmarket**, a Temple Bar at **Edwardstone**, a Templars Court in **Haverhill** and a Temple Bar and Temple Bar house in Earsham (near **Bungay**).

The village sign at **Ashley** near **Newmarket** depicts the eight-pronged star of the Knights Hospitaller of St John in commemoration of their association with the village.

❖ **Sandy Downham**

The village of **Santon Downham** is sometimes called Sandy Downham, to commemorate the years when the village was continually in danger of being submerged by sand storms. In 1668, after years of strong winds continually blowing tons of the light sandy soil across the Breckland from the **Lakenheath** hills, a huge gale brought yet more sand, almost burying the village.

The 1668 drift covered almost 2,000 acres and choked part of the Little Ouse River, which became almost unnavigable beneath 'an inundation of sand'. *White's Directory* of 1844 tells the story of Mr Wright, who owned the largest farm house in the parish and fought for years to stop it being engulfed by sand. He tried planting hedges but they were submerged more quickly than they grew. Eventually he let a wall of sand build up and made a gap through it, which he managed to keep open with the help of his neighbours.

The breck, called the Suffolk Brecklands, means a tract of sandy heathland cultivated and then allowed to revert to wasteland, which is what happened at Santon Downham in the 17th century. In the 1920s the area was taken over by the Forestry Commission and the remains of the village are more or less in the middle of **Thetford Forest**.

❖ **Bloody Marsh**
In his *Historical Account of Dunwich, Blythburgh and Southwold* (1745), Thomas Gardner recorded an incident that appeared in the **Walberswick** churchwardens' account books. The event took place in April 1644, during the Civil War, when a man came to Walberswick and was killed in a fight with three local men over some grazing rights. The local Justice of the Peace and Lord of the Manor, Sir Robert Brooke, sentenced the men to hang. There ensued a long battle on behalf of the condemned, principally because they thought Sir Robert prejudiced against them in view of the fact that the murdered man was his henchman. The two sides of the argument were recorded in the churchwardens' account books (now preserved in the Suffolk Record Office at **Ipswich**).

The arguments centred round the complexity of the rights and wrongs of enclosure of common land, in this case the salt marshes and heathlands of Walberswick. 1644 was a very fraught time in English history and fuses were short, especially when it came to villagers losing their livelihoods through the high-handed actions of the ruling classes. The issues were not to be resolved for many years.

Here, as elsewhere, the fight for commoners' rights was often a bloody one. The men were hanged and the marshland thereafter was afterwards known as the Bloody Marsh.

❖ In 1648 **Bury St Edmunds** once again lived up to its long-standing reputation for riotous behaviour in an incident that became known as the **Maypole Riots**. In 1647 Cromwell's Commonwealth Government prohibited the celebration of Christmas by anything other than a church service. This was followed by an edict banning all May Day Celebrations – especially the erection of a maypole and traditional dancing, which, in Puritan eyes, was sin incarnate. Undeterred, on 12 May 1648 the townspeople erected their maypole in Market Square as usual, whereupon the ruling Puritans ordered that it be taken down. Riots ensued, culminating in the storming of the town magazine.

The New Model Army quelled the insurrection and the rebellious maypole rioters gave in, but not before an amnesty was demanded and granted.

At the Restoration of Charles II in 1660 a 134ft-high maypole was erected at St Mary-le-Strand in London. There is a **Maypole Green** near **Bradfield St George** and another near **Dennington**.

❖ **The Tattingstone Wonder**
In 1790, in the days when the local squire could build whatever folly he might desire, Thomas White of **Tattingstone Place** decided that he wanted a view of a church from his house. His was a large and neat mansion surrounded by a well-wooded park and extensive fish ponds, but unfortunately no view of a church and no houses for his employees. So he solved two problems in one by building his workers' cottages to look like a church, complete with a flint tower and a traceried east window.

It quickly became known locally as the Wonder since, as Edward himself observed, his neighbours were always wondering what he was up to and he intended to give them something to wonder at.

Another example of a church that is not a church is found at **Euston Hall** where the water mill is disguised as one. It has a tower that was built onto the existing mill in 1731.

❖ **Mockbeggars Hall**
At **Claydon** a Jacobean Manor House, built in 1621, stands in a conspicuous place about a mile from the village and built on the site of an older building. It is called **Mockbeggars Hall** and was once owned by Richard Corder, father of the Suffolk historian and heraldic expert, the late Joan Corder. Its unusual name has given

rise to much speculation over the years but the general consensus finds the answer in its apparently hospitable aspect. For many years the Hall stood empty, although lights were often seen in the windows, luring travellers from the road in search of food and shelter.

The origins of the legend undoubtedly go further back than the present house, to a time in mediaeval England when many travellers were likely to be mendicants, or those seeking alms. They would knock on doors and beg for money and food, which might have annoyed a one-time owner, who purposely put a light in a window but would not open the door and admit that he was at home. In the days when it was incumbent on the homeowner to offer assistance to passing pilgrims (or vagrants), it no doubt became rather expensive when your house stood on a prominent part of a popular route. Unfortunately for the travellers, their search proved fruitless as they were met with an empty house and the door was not opened to them, thus the beggars were mocked.

In A.O.D. Claxton's *Suffolk Dialect* it is described as 'a house with an inviting external aspect, but within poor, bare, dirty and disorderly, and disappointing those who beg for alms at the door'.

Mockbeggars Hall featured in *Lord of the Harvest* (1899) a novel by the Suffolk writer, **Matilda Bethan-Edwards** (1836–1919) of **Westerfield**, author of a series of novels about Suffolk rural life. In 1902 she wrote another title and called it *Mock Beggars Hall*, which drew on her experience of agricultural life and farming communities. A character asks: 'What is life but a Mock Beggar's Hall, each of us getting a snub in turn?'

❖ **Anyone For a Game of Camp?**

There are many places and field names in Suffolk that have the word 'camping' or 'campen' in them, such as Camping Close (**Eye**), Camping Pightle (**Hawstead**), and Campen Close (**Stoke by Nayland**). A small green beside the wall encircling Abbot's Hall (**Stowmarket**) was known as Camping Land and indicates the place where the ancient game of 'camp' was played.

Camping is said to derive from the Anglo-Saxon word *cempan* (to fight) and the term 'Camping Pightle' occurs in a document dated 1486. A modern reader could be forgiven for misinterpreting an entry in the court records of 1644 for **Eyke** which censured the Rector, Nicholas Stoneham: 'That he hath been present with such of his parish as have been at the same tyme camping on the Lord's Day and showed no dislike thereof.'

Camping took place from at least early mediaeval times right up to the 19th century and was a game of football played throughout East Anglia, although it was particularly popular in Suffolk and, even more specifically, in the area between the rivers Orwell and Alde. It could loosely be described as the forerunner of today's soccer, though it had certain characteristics of rugby in that the ball could be either kicked or thrown. Some commentators have likened it to the Eton Wall Game. Both teams took full advantage of the fact that there were no rules to prevent rough play and pretty well any tactics were allowable. An Elizabethan writer described camping as 'a friendly kind of fight, a bloody and murdering practice with everyone lying in wait for his adversary to pick him on the nose and dash him against the heart with his elbows'. James I forbade the game as too many of his men were injured on the field of play and he considered archery far less dangerous.

Although there were officially 12 in each team, there were frequently many more and it was said that 'a combatant required to be a good boxer, runner and wrestler' since one or all three could be useful on the field.

At **Burgh Castle** there is a field that was used for camping matches and, because Burgh Castle is on the border between Norfolk and Suffolk, there were several inter-county matches held there on the field inside the old castle walls. Indeed, many such matches took place along the county border, including the epic one between Norfolk and Suffolk which took place on Diss Common in the middle of the 18th century, when there were no less than 300 men on each side, and was described as 'a savage camp'. The Norfolk side taunted the Suffolk men, asking whether they had brought coffins with them, and 'play' continued for 14 hours during which time the field and players were reduced to a gory shambles. The Suffolk team were eventually declared the winners though nine combatants died of their injuries within a fortnight.

The pitch could be anything from a fenced-off piece of land to the village common and was slightly larger than a modern football pitch. Two goals were placed at either end and to score the players, stripped to the waist, had to convey the ball between them by any means at their disposal in what one commentator described as a 'very animating' spectacle. The size of the ball could vary between that of a present day football (when it was called a 'kicking camp') and a cricket ball (which qualified as a 'free for all').

If no land was available the village street was used and games rarely ended 'without black eyes, bloody noses, broken heads or shin, and other serious mischiefs'. Hundreds and sometimes thousands of spectators would turn up to cheer their teams on to victory achieved by whatever means possible. The game was so popular in **Debenham** that the Camping Ground is reputed to have had stands and tiered seating.

The game fell out of favour at about the time that the East Suffolk professional police force was established in 1840 (see also Chapter One, This and That) and following two deaths that occurred during a 'savage camp' at **Easton**. Only the field and place names now survive as a reminder of a former long standing pursuit.

❖ **The Douglas Bader Public House**
Between 17 December 1940 and 18 March 1941 the famous fighter pilot and World War Two hero, **Sir Douglas Bader** (1910–1982), flew from **Martlesham Heath** as a member of 242 Squadron. Sir Douglas became a legend in his own lifetime. A double amputee (caused by an aeroplane accident in 1931) he served as an aviator and fighter ace during the war and made several escapes from prisoner of war camps after he was shot down and captured.

Although Sir Douglas was a teetotaller, he opened the public house named after him in 1979. Parts of the forecourt and car park are actually pieces of runway covered over.

Dating from 1917, Martlesham was Suffolk's earliest airfield and during the 1939–1945 war other famous pilots flew from there on raids across Germany. In 1940 a Rhodesian squadron was stationed there, one of whose pilots was Ian Smith, later Prime Minister of Rhodesia. When the No. 85 Squadron arrived, it was led by Squadron Leader Peter Townsend (later Group Captain) who was to become the fiancé of Princess Margaret.

❖ **The Case is Altered**
The **Ipswich** public house, the Case is Altered, is said to be the original that gave its well-known name to public houses all over England. During the Napoleonic wars, when troops were housed in temporary barracks at the top of Woodbridge Road, an inn was built to accommodate the soldiers. After the barracks were removed

and the soldiers disbanded, 'the case was altered' as far as the profit of the publican was concerned.

There is a rhyme that is said to have been displayed over the bar:

The Brewer doth crave

His money to have

The distiller say have it I must

So good people you see

How the case is with me

In this tap-room I never can trust.

There is also a Case is Altered at **Bentley**. However, the Case is Altered at **Woodbridge** was said to have stood on a site formerly occupied by a nunnery, which a Father Casey used to visit for confessions. After the Reformation, part of the old nunnery was converted into an inn and 'Casey's Altar' became the Case is Altered.

❖ An old inn sign at the Palomino in **Newmarket** depicted a palomino pony being ridden by a lady on one side and a horse in a circus ring on the other. It is thought to be the only inn with that name in the whole of Great Britain.

❖ The **Elephant and Castle** public house at **Eyke** has been an inn for at least 700 years, as there is a record of Margaret Wright building a house on the opposite corner to where stood 'a common Inn for all comers' in the 14th century.

The first mention of it being named is in 1627, when Thomas Studd (a carrier) became the landlord and called it the Castle. It is thought there was some connection between Thomas and Sir Michael Stanhope of Orford Castle, who in 1619 bequeathed land in **Blaxhall** to provide money for the poor of the parish.

The pub was called the Castle for some years but in 1707 is referred to as the Old Castle and as situated 'at the corner of a lane and abutting the highway'. It is likely that the old premises were destroyed, perhaps by fire, and rebuilt. At about this time two brothers, John and Thomas Fuller, took it over and set about converting a nearby property into a second establishment, which they considered 'a more suitable site for an Inn', calling it the Elephant and Castle to distinguish it from its neighbour. Both inns appear to have thrived since and in 1742 Thomas Fuller's son inherited the Old Castle and in 1748 Samuel (another Fuller son) inherited the Elephant and Castle.

No one is quite sure why the Elephant and Castle is so named, but the rumour is that Charles I was at one time engaged to marry the Infanta of Castille, a Spanish princess. Although the marriage never took place, the people of London thought 'Infanta of Castille' sounded like 'Elephant and Castle' and because they liked the sound of the name it became popular in London and gradually throughout the country. 1707 is a little late for it to have been topical, since Charles I was beheaded in 1649, but by then the name had become widely accepted.

Eyke has ancient connection with the Manor of Staveton, under which name it appears in the Domesday Book, and there are records to show that it was at one time part of the Manor of Eyke Rectory. An elephant carrying a castle on its back is found in heraldry (as a representation of the Cutlers' crest) and it may be that there is another connection with Orford Castle, or the ancient Manor of Staveton, yet to be discovered.

❖ **Old Grogram**

Vernon Street in **Ipswich** is named in honour of **Admiral Edward Vernon** (1684–1757), Member of Parliament for Ipswich 1741–1754. He joined the Navy in 1700 and served in the vessels *Ipswich* (1700) and *Barfleur* (1709) and saw action at Chagres, Portobello and Cartagena. He was promoted to Admiral in 1739 and quite soon acquired the nickname 'Old Grogram' (because he wore grogram breeches and cloak, grogram being a mixture of silk and wool or mohair). He was famous for being the first to introduce the practice of watered rum into the Navy. On 21 August 1740 he ordered that the quarter pint of neat rum, issued daily to each sailor, be diluted to 1 gill of rum to 3 gills of water, to prevent drunkenness. The mixture was called 'grog' after Old Grogram.

Despite his heroic status, Admiral Vernon's fiery and sharp temper lead to difficult relations with his naval superiors and he was eventually cashiered in 1746 for exposing abuses within the Navy in Parliament. Thereafter he lived on his estate at **Nacton.** His portrait, by Thomas Hudson in around 1750, is in Christchurch Mansion. The 1739 attack on Portobello is depicted in the picture's background. To commemorate the Admiral's famous engagement in Spain, there was a pub in Lower Orwell Street (Ipswich) called the Portobello.

❖ Mausoleum House, **Felsham**, owes its name to a long lasting disagreement between the rector and a former owner, Mr Reynolds, who was determined that the church should not profit from his funeral expenses. In 1755 he built a mausoleum in the grounds of his house for his only child and both he and his wife were also buried there. Succeeding members of the family later resolved the feud by removing the bodies to the churchyard. Today only a few courses of the yellow and red brickwork of the mausoleum remain, the rest having been recycled over the years.

❖ **Sweet Shade**
The boundary between **Rushmere** (once part of the parish of Rushmere St Andrew) and **Ipswich** is called Humber Doucy Lane. It is said to owe its name to the days when a camp was set up on the heath in the 19th century for French prisoners of war, taken during the Napoleonic Wars. These prisoners were said to enjoy the '*ombre douce*', or 'sweet shade' of the lane that gradually became Humber Doucy.

Rushmere Heath was an ancient battleground that saw fierce fights between the Danes and Saxons and over the centuries saw clashes between the lords of the manor and the Rushmere Commoners. The common was also the site of the Ipswich gibbet, which stood just beyond the borough boundary. It was here that Margery Bedingfield of **Sternfield** was publicly strangled and her body burnt at the stake for the murder of her husband in 1763. She and her lover, Richard Ringe, were taken to Rushmere where Richard was hanged and Margery's became the last recorded instance of execution by burning in the borough.

❖ **Ice Pits**
At **Great Barton** is found Icepits Woods and Icepits Farm, so named because here was once a granary store for the mediaeval Benedictine Abbey of **Bury St Edmunds**. The pits were dug for the abbey's ice store.

❖ **White Woman**
The naming of White Woman's Lane in **Eyke** is thought to belong to a time when colour was not only a significant factor in society but white in particular denoted wealth and status. Over the centuries, sumptuary laws have regulated and reinforced social

hierarchies and morals through restrictions on clothing and food. These fashion regulations decreed that people should dress according to their station in life, so in 1337 the wearing of white fur was restricted by statute to those with an income of over £100 a year, while those in lower income brackets were allowed to wear the furs of humbler creatures, such as the cat, rabbit or fox. In Elizabethan times the colour white held great significance because of the difficulty and expense of producing white clothing and the subsequent problems in keeping it clean.

The name of the Eyke lane is found on a map dated 1601, where an isolated cottage is marked on its west side, close to a watermill, where the Widow Alchard lived. She might well have been one of the privileged few allowed to wear white.

White Ladies was a term used for Cistercian nuns, but there was only one house of that order in Suffolk, at **Sibton.**

Another theory is that the White Woman was a white witch, or wise woman, who procured herbal remedies for the villagers. Witches could be seen as vessels for good or evil, white witches being those on the side of good. Perhaps this White Woman worked at the watermill and went home each night covered in flour. Lanes have been named for less!

❖ **The Cat House**

At **Woolverstone** on the south bank of the **River Orwell** is Cat House, which owes its name to the activities of the smugglers in the 18th century (see also Chapter Two, The Coast). The cottage was built in 1793 by the Berners family, who built Woolverstone Hall, and is distinguished by its step-gabled, red-brick walls and by the incongruous Gothic windows. The window on the end wall has intersected tracery painted on it, plus a white cat on its sill. It overlooks the estuary and is easily seen from the river. This is the famous Cat Window in which the owner of the house would place a white porcelain cat as a danger signal to the smugglers that the Customs and Excise officers were about. Pevsner described the cottage as an uninhabitable folly, and so it is.

SEVEN – WRITERS
AND ARTISTS

IT WOULD be impossible to record the numerous writers and artists who have visited Suffolk, or to list the many who were born here and used the wide open skies, the wild and unpredictable North Sea, and the picturesque towns and villages as their inspiration. But, choices have to be made so here are a few of the men and women who have recorded Suffolk in their writing or art.

❖ **Agnes Meets George**

Agnes Strickland (1796 or 1806–1874), the third daughter of Thomas Strickland of Reydon Hall, **Wangford**, was an historian and poet and is famous for her *Lives of the Queens of England* (from Matilda of Flanders to Queen Anne), begun in 1840 and finished in 1848. There were also eight laborious and conscientious volumes about the Queens of Scotland and English Princesses. Agnes had a 'refined nature', having been 'well brought up' by her wealthy father, and she was often observed driving into **Southwold** in her gig, wearing gold rings on the outside of her gloved fingers. Her father, unhappily, lost much of his fortune and, after his untimely death, Agnes and her sister were obliged to earn a living. They both chose to write.

On one occasion Agnes met the morose and irritable author and traveller, **George Borrow** (1803–1881), who lived at **Oulton Broad**. Borrow's works and lifestyle could hardly have been more different from those of Agnes Strickland. He was an advocate of the open road and lived the life of a vagrant, invariably in the company of the gypsies, with whom he had an abiding affiliation. His most lasting works are his two autobiographical books, *Lavengro* (1851) and *Romany Rye* (1857).

At their meeting, Agnes graciously offered to present George with a set of her works, upon which he replied 'For God's sake, don't Madam! I should not know where to put them or what to do with them!'

❖ **Suffolk's Own Gainsborough**

If asked to name one of England's best-known landscape and

portrait painters, **Thomas Gainsborough** (1727–88) would surely be top of the list. He was born in **Sudbury**, the son of John Gainsborough, and spent seven crucial years of his professional life in **Ipswich**. John Gainsborough was engaged in Sudbury's millinery and clothing manufacture, but his business failed and he became the town's Postmaster. Gainsborough's mother was an amateur artist and it was clear in his early teenage years that her son had a prodigious talent. At 13 he was already drawing landscapes and took much of his inspiration for the paintings from the wooded banks of Suffolk's rivers and the countryside of the Stour valley.

He left for London to pursue his career and in 1746 married Margaret Burr, 'hastily' it was said, suggesting that Margaret was already pregnant. Visits to his Suffolk relations (ultra Non-Conformist on his father's side) without a marriage licence were not likely to have gone down very well.

In 1752 he returned to Suffolk with his wife and two small daughters and lived in Ipswich. For the next seven years he established his artistic reputation and made many friends, joining in the cultural life of the town. Wanting to spread his wings, he then moved to Bath, where he was more likely to pick up lucrative portrait commissions. He developed a business-like attitude to portraiture and would not waste time talking to 'gentlemen' who called in to pass the time of day if he thought their conversation was unlikely to end in a commission. On those occasions he instructed his manservant to tell such people that he was out, although if the caller was an attractive woman that was an altogether different matter!

His success grew and by working as an independent artist, rather than for a patron, he was able to support his family (albeit grateful for his wife's income of £200 a year). Luckily for Gainsborough his wife kept hold of the purse strings, which prevented him from succumbing completely to the worst excesses that contemporary artists were prone to. Towards the end of his life he wrote of his 'dissipated life', but 'they must take me altogether – liberal, thoughtless and dissipated'. However, he enjoyed royal patronage and became much sought-after by anyone who was anyone in society. Among others he was a contemporary, and great rival, of Joshua Reynolds. On his deathbed, Gainsborough wrote to Reynolds asking him to visit. He whispered to him, 'We are all going to heaven, and Van Dyck is of the company'. Reynolds wrote afterwards, 'If any little jealousies had subsisted between us, they were forgotten, in those moments of sincerity'.

Gainsborough is not forgotten in Sudbury where his birthplace, now an exhibition gallery and education centre, is a Mecca for art lovers from across the world. In the centre of **Sudbury** stands a bronze statue of Gainsborough wearing breeches and a long coat.

❖ **Constable Country**
On a par with Gainsborough is **John Constable** (1776–1837), a painter ranked with Turner as one of the greatest English landscape artists, who always acknowledged his admiration of Gainsborough's art. Two of his best-known paintings, *The Haywain* (1821) and *Flatford Mill* (1816–17), depict the **East Bergholt** area and the River Stour now known as 'Constable Country'.

Constable was born at East Bergholt and after schooling, which included a spell in a school at **Lavenham** where a tyrannical usher flogged him and the other boys, he worked in his father's water mills at **Flatford** and Dedham (Essex). He knew the area intimately: Willy Lott's white cottage, the timbered house, the wooden bridge and the mill were all everyday scenes to him. Though he worked at the mill, he was constantly sketching and drawing and when he was 20 he attracted the patronage of Sir George Beaumont, who used his influence to allow him to be sent to London for formal study. His father gave up hope of him ever taking over the mill or, as he had preferred, going into the church.

Constable's original style of landscape was not appreciated by the contemporary art world, which was still obsessed with paintings of melodrama and myth, but he continued working and recording his view of the English countryside without, as he put it, the 'fal-de-lals' of formal composition. He did, however, paint formal portraits as a means of earning a living, but his heart was always with landscape. It was over 20 years before he exhibited at the Royal Academy and when he did it was with a view of the Stour, *The White Horse*, but it did not bring him instant fame or, indeed, acclaim. That came a few years later when *The Haywain*, returned unsold from the Royal Academy, was exhibited in Paris. The Paris Salon awarded him the gold medal and the French painters acclaimed him 'the new master', one critic writing 'Look at these landscapes by an Englishman – the ground appears to be covered with dew'.

In 1816 he married his childhood sweetheart, Maria Bicknell, and the marriage was a happy one until Maria's death in 1828. Luckily, Maria had a small income and they were able to survive financially, which was just as well since Constable sold only 20 paintings in England in his lifetime.

Although Constable is now hailed as the foremost artistic exponent of 19th-century English countryside, success only came after his death. Critics ridiculed his trickling sunlight, filtered through leaves onto shimmering water, which they called 'Constable's snow'. They did not like the very thing that lent his work genius, the true reproduction of the appearance of the countryside, including horses and their horsemen, boat builders and bending gleaners. He wrote, 'These scenes made me a painter, and I am grateful'. By acute observation of every detail he was able to record its constantly changing aspects. Constable thought that 'No two days are alike, nor even two hours; neither were there ever two leaves of a tree alike since the creation of the world'. No previous artist had painted in such a way and it seemed beyond the comprehension of contemporary critics.

In 2002 an exhibition of Constable's work was mounted in Paris for the first time in 200 years and *The Times* said, 'Constable's works have become so familiar that it is easy to forget how profound and far-reaching were his innovations and to take him for granted as the portrayer of a cosy rural England'. Instead, he must be admired as the man whose vision broke the established rules and whose work was poetry in paint.

No description of Suffolk can better bring to life the Stour Valley as it was in the 19th century than Constable's: 'The beauty of the surrounding scenery, its gentle declivities, its luxuriant meadow flats sprinkled with flocks and herds, its well-cultivated uplands, its woods and rivers, with numerous scattered villages and churches, farms and picturesque cottages, all impart to this particular spot an amenity and elegance hardly anywhere else to be found.'

❖ **A Sotting Life!**

The satirical artist, **Henry William Bunbury** (1750–1811) was the younger son of the Revd William Bunbury, 5th Baronet, who had estates at **Mildenhall** and **Barton Mills**. Bunbury preferred social to political satire and spent much of his time in fashionable London circles or observing the antics of local society in **Bury St Edmunds**, where he was described 'a bit of a lad'. The diarist Joseph Farington wrote of Bunbury as 'living most of his time a sotting life in Suffolk'.

He caricatured local tradespeople and among his most amusing pictures are those involving contemporary university life, horsemen and episodes from his time as a captain in the West Suffolk Militia. He was later appointed equerry to the Duke of York in 1787, which gave him both the opportunity and the leisure to pursue his humorous drawing. He was a contemporary of Thomas Rowlandson and James Gillray but, unlike other caricaturists, Bunbury never offended anyone by his satire and was, by all accounts, a popular character of the day. His series of 25 engravings concentrating on the comic and ridiculous scenes of Shakespeare's plays was commissioned by John Boydell, who had embarked on an exhaustive publishing venture, namely over 100 large engravings detailing Shakespearean themes. Bunbury's interpretation of the comedies is best remembered in his portrayal of Shakespeare's greatest comic creation, Falstaff, which shows him being reproved by Henry V.

St Mary's Mildenhall has many monuments to the Bunbury family including Sir Charles, who owned the winner of the first Derby (a horse named Diomed) in 1780 and sat in Parliament for 43 years.

❖ **At Her Majesty's Pleasure**

Two famous but very different writers have spent time at the **Hollesley Bay Colony** open prison, which began life in 1887 as a Colonial College training those intending to emigrate (hence the word 'colony'). In 1938 the college was acquired by the Prison Commission to train young offenders in the Borstal system and until 2002 was the largest prison farm within the national Prison Service.

One of the first inmates of the new borstal was the Irish playwright, **Brendan Behan** (1923–1964), who was arrested in Liverpool when he was 16 on suspicion of IRA terrorist activities. He was sent to Hollesley Bay in 1939.

Although the new borstal had a relatively tolerant regime it was, nevertheless, not a place that Behan would ever have visited voluntarily. However, in later years he wrote almost affectionately of his time there in his autobiographical novel, *Borstal Boy* (1958).

He worked on the farm, in the vegetable gardens, and on the maintenance gangs that repaired the sea defences. Among his autumn and winter descriptions he wrote of 'the freezing marshes, the dirty grey shore, the gunmetal sea, and over us the sky, lead coloured'.

In *Borstal Boy* he describes a trip to **Shingle Street** where the hard stones reminded him of the 'people of the place'.

The second most famous writer to serve time at Hollesley Bay was the novelist, politician, and Lord of the Realm, **Jeffrey Archer**, who was convicted of perjury and perverting the course of justice at the Old Bailey in 2001. A senior Conservative party politician when Margaret Thatcher was Prime Minister, Archer made his fortune from best selling novels, such as *Not a Penny More, Not a Penny Less, Kane and Abel* and *First Among Equals.*

After sentencing he went first to Belmarsh Prison, then Wayland, and in October 2002, after serving just three weeks in Lincoln's high security jail, was moved to Hollesley Bay. Only months before, it had been opened to adult Category D offenders and life sentence prisoners nearing the end of their custodial time.

There was much press criticism about the 'soft option' of Hollesley Bay, dubbed a 'holiday camp', and the prison authorities were accused of giving special treatment to the former politician, both charges being strongly refuted by the governor. Archer left Hollesley Bay in July 2003.

❖ **Enid Blyton (1897–1968)**
In 1916, one of the most famous and enduring of children's authors, **Enid Blyton**, came to Seckford Hall (now a hotel) near **Woodbridge** to stay with friends. Taking a liking to the county she then moved to Christchurch Street, **Ipswich** and trained as a kindergarten teacher at Ipswich High School. She was already writing stories at this time, although none were published until the 1920s. When she left Ipswich she was a fully-fledged Froebel teacher, which stood her in good stead as a children's writer.

❖ **Beatrix Potter's Puddleduck**
Another children's writer who often visited Suffolk was **Beatrix Potter** (1866–1943) who stayed at **Melford Hall** with her cousins the Hyde Parkers. She always brought with her a collection of small animals to draw and there is a dedicated Beatrix Potter room at the

Hall, housing a display of paintings and documents relating to her relationship with the family. The Jeremy Fisher illustrations were drawings of the ducks that congregated round the Melford Hall fishponds and the original Jemima Puddleduck, with bonnet and paisley shawl, is on display. Beatrix gave the Puddle duck toy to Lady Ulla Hyde Parker, who later wrote a memoir about her friendship with Beatrix, entitled *Cousin Beattie*. She recalled that when at Melford, 'Cousin Beattie had not spoken a great deal to the children, though she read her stories to them to find out their reactions'.

❖ **The Science of Sex**
The essayist, psychologist, and pioneer in establishing a modern, scientific approach to the study of sexual behaviour, **Henry Havelock Ellis** (1859–1939), was born in Surrey but came to live at Cherry Ground, **Hintlesham**, in the county of his ancestors. He wrote over 50 books and edited several more, many of them of a controversial nature. He married the English writer, Edith Lees, but theirs was a stormy relationship and they soon parted.

In 1883 Ellis met the South African writer, Olive Schreiner, author of *The Story of an African Farm* (1883) and they embarked on an intense, long-term relationship, but he had many other women in his life.

Ellis's titles include *Erotic Symbolism* (1906), *Sex in Relation to Society* (1910) and *Psychology of Sex: A Manual for Students* (1933). He is credited with paving the way for the work of Alfred Kinsey and other modern writers. Much of his work was published in Germany, although he disagreed with many of Freud's theories.

He died at Hintlesham in 1939 and his library was purchased by Yale University.

❖ **Never, Never Land**
There are many thousands of people who have fond and abiding memories of childhood holidays at **Thorpeness** holiday village, some of which is down to Sir James Matthew Barrie, 1st Baronet, better known as the playwright **J.M. Barrie** (1860–1937), who visited the Ogilvies of **Leiston** in the early 1900s and left Suffolk with its own corner of the fictional Never, Never Land.

The Ogilvies had come down from Scotland in 1859 and eventually established an estate of some six thousand acres. The fantasy holiday village was the brainchild of the playwright, barrister and landowner, Glencairn Stuart Ogilvie (died 1932), who inherited the family estate in 1903, part of which was the tiny fishing hamlet of Thorpeness. In 1911 Ogilvie embarked on a long-held ambition to create a holiday village, influenced by the Garden City Movement that promised a new direction in town planning to create an environment that combined the best aspects of town and country life for healthy living. He built mock-Tudor holiday homes, all with servants' quarters, a ballroom and Palm Court, five acres of ornamental grounds plus 'Juvenalia', an eating place for 40 children with a supervising Matron. Chief among his creations was the Meare, a 64-acre lake that is one metre deep and was dug by hand between 1910 and 1912. The River Hundred feeds it and a water bore pump controls the level. The spelling originated because the marsh area used to be saline and the word meare distinguishes it from a freshwater lake.

Barrie's play *Peter Pan* was an instant success in 1904 and had enormous appeal across the country. The *Peter Pan* characters were a perfect match for Ogilvie's dream of a fantasy world and he created islands and waterways in the Meare named after the characters, calling it the Home of Peter Pan. There are huts, caves and upturned boats for children to seek out and Crocodile Island (complete with crocodile) and The Fort can be reached by one of the punts or rowing boats for hire. The perimeter path is called Barrie's Walk.

Barrie's mother was Margaret Ogilvy and was the inspiration for a book *Margaret Ogilvy* by her son. He made frequent visits to Suffolk, not only to Leiston, but also to **Aldeburgh**, where he joined the stream of *literati* who sought out the rationalist agnostic Edward Clodd. His other connections with the county are forgotten but thanks to Barrie's association with the Ogilvie family there is a piece of Suffolk that is still a Never, Never Land.

❖ Among the other famous literary figures to visit Edward Clodd at **Aldeburgh** were George Meredith, H.G. Wells and the novelist and poet, **Thomas Hardy** (1840–1928). Hardy made a great secret of what are described as his 'clandestine visits' to Aldeburgh between 1909 and 1912, where he enjoyed the company of his secretary, Florence Dugdale (whom he married in 1914, two years after his wife died).

❖ Edward Clodd lived at Stratford House on Crag Path, **Aldeburgh**, and was responsible for founding the Omar Khayyam Club in London in 1892, as a tribute to Edward Fitzgerald (see also Chapter Five, Suffolk Folk).

❖ **A Writer's Garden**
One of the most popular gardens in the annual Hidden Gardens Scheme in **Bury St Edmunds** once belonged to the novelist **Norah Lofts** (1904–1983).

Norah Lofts was a best-selling historical novelist who was born and brought up in Suffolk. She lived most of her life and died in the elegant Northgate House (Georgian at the front and Queen Anne at the back) in Northgate Street. Norah wrote more than 50 bestsellers, and was renowned for her meticulous research. Her books were very popular in the United States.

❖ **The Days That We Have Seen**
George Ewart Evans (1909–88) was born in Wales, where his father was a grocer. He went to Cardiff University and by the 1930s had decided that he wanted to become a writer. He saw no prospects in his native Abercynon so moved to Cambridge, where he met and married his wife, Florence (called Ellen), in 1938. After five years in the RAF, George moved to Suffolk where his wife acquired the post of headmistress at **Blaxhall** School. She had seen it advertised in a newspaper and it appeared to have several things going for it. Firstly there was a house that went with the job, albeit with no electricity, sanitation or running water, and secondly she knew Suffolk, having visited her great-grandfather in **Woodbridge** as a child. For the interview, Florence took the train from London to **Campsea Ash** and walked the three miles to Blaxhall and then back again. She was offered the position and the family left London for Suffolk.

At first George had no success with his writing. Much of his work was rejected and, while his wife became the breadwinner, George looked after their children, wrote and continued to study the work of the Suffolk poet, **George Crabbe** (1754–1832), in particular *The Village*. He also read all of Beatrix Potter's books, copies of which 'became battered and dog-eared through constant use' he later recalled. This inspired him to start writing children's stories and he at last began to have some success on the BBC's *Listen With Mother* radio programme. Crabbe's work continued to inspire him and slowly it began to dawn on him that under his nose was the material that could, to some extent, allow him to emulate his hero in chronicling the everyday events and culture of the ordinary farm worker, and the fast declining Suffolk dialect and vocabulary, which he later called a 'Prior Culture'.

In 1952 he bought a recording machine and set about collecting, by means of interviews with local men and women, events and people as far back as the 1880s. The Suffolk countryside was recalled and documented, from the pre-mechanisation of farming to the years following the World War Two, during which time the face of the countryside and farming changed forever.

The classic *Ask The Fellows Who Cut The Hay* (1956) was the first of a series of books that documented a unique social portrait of rural Suffolk. This was followed by *Where Beards Wag All* (1970), *The Days That We Have Seen* (1975) and *Horse Power and Magic* (1979).

The family left Blaxhall for Florence's new job at **Needham Market** where George wrote *The Horse in the Furrow* (1960), which explores the customs associated with horsepower. The book was illustrated by **C.F. Tunnicliffe** and was dedicated to the old horsemen whose personal recollections were the lifeblood of his work. While at Needham, he discovered the existence of a secret society of horsemen in **Stowmarket,** whose members passed down their knowledge only to those who were proven trustworthy.

Florence then got a new teaching post at the village school in **Helmingham,** where he wrote what is considered to be his finest book, *The Pattern under the Plough* (1966). Here he discovered many pre-Christian beliefs and traditions, including the use of the hagstone (a flint with a hole through it) that is said to ward off the 'hag', a devil who would ride the horse at night and leave it 'hagridden' by the morning. The hagstone was hung over the stable door and, indeed, many can still be found today hanging in old farm buildings, invariably covered with a layer of ancient cobwebs.

Although he always dreamed of returning to Wales, he never did. He moved to Norfolk shortly before his death in 1988. His pioneering techniques of oral history are now commonplace but in the 1950s, George Ewart Evans drew his inspiration from the everyday life of Suffolk farm workers and made sure that both its beauty and brawn were not lost to posterity.

❖ **Down and Out in Suffolk**

The writer **George Orwell** (1903–50) was a regular visitor to Suffolk and took the name of its main river as his pseudonym. The village of **Burstall** is credited with the inspiration for his last novel, *Nineteen Eighty-Four* (1945) when, as a 17-year-old schoolboy, he visited cousins of his father there. He is said to have picked up a large cage rat-trap, which biographers have suggested was the prototype of that which finally broke Winston Smith's resistance to torture.

The son of Richard and Ida Blair, Eric Arthur Blair moved with his family to **Southwold** in 1921. After a spell in Burma in the Indian Imperial Police, Orwell returned to live with his parents for a few years, all the time trying, without any great success at first, to obtain work as a freelance writer. Stifled by life in Southwold he moved to **Walberswick**, where he took a job tutoring what he called 'an imbecile boy'.

Between 1930 and 1931, Orwell took several journeys dressed as a tramp and so began the research for what was to become his most famous work, *Down and Out in Paris and London* (1933). Although he had a dislike for the genteel Southwold life, Eric (who became George Orwell in 1932) nevertheless had some regard for the rugged countryside and for the seashore. He often walked to the partly ruined church at Walberswick, where he sat amid the crumbling stonework and read.

Orwell's sister Avril kept a tea shop in the High Street and his parents were very much part of the social life of Southwold, his father golfing and his mother participating in bridge parties, but he was always at odds with it all. Eventually he moved to London, returning to Southwold for the last time in 1939 for his father's funeral.

❖ **Bloomsbury Meeting House**

In the 1920s and 1930s the elite of the **Bloomsbury Group** gathered in the home of the artist and critic **Roger Fry** (1866–1934) at Rodwell House, **Baylham**. The Bloomsbury Group was the name given to a clique of artistic friends who originally met at 46 Gordon Square, Bloomsbury, which in 1904 became the home of sisters Virginia (later Woolf) and Vanessa (later Bell) Stephens. Both Virginia and Vanessa visited Baylham in the company of Augustus John, Lytton Strachey, Henry Lamb and Carrington (called Dora, though her first name was never used). Fry's companion, Helen Anrep, had been married to Count Boris von Anrep (descended from a line of Baltic barons who, in their turn, were descended from an Abyssinian prince) and the couple entertained not only a rarefied collection of the prevailing *literati* but also former lovers.

Roger Fry first came to Suffolk in 1892 on a bicycling trip to see the tomb of Edward Fitzgerald at **Boulge**. His most famous work is *Blythborough, the Estuary* (1893), with Blythburgh spelt incorrectly, which is a stylised study of the upper reaches of the River Blyth seen from Walberswick heronry.

❖ Wissett Lodge

In 1916, **Wissett Lodge** near **Halesworth** was also a meeting place for the various members of the Bloomsbury Group, including Virginia Woolf and Lytton Strachey. It was briefly the home of novelist and critic David Garnett, who had hoped to gain exemption from military service on the strength of being employed in horticulture. Although he and Duncan Grant made a reasonable, but uninformed, stab at reclaiming the neglected orchard at Wissett, the local Blything tribunal hearing in Halesworth refused exemption to both men. However, they both appealed to an **Ipswich** tribunal and were persuaded to go to Sussex, where they both found employment on a farm and were, therefore, excused military service.

In his biography of Virginia Woolf, Quentin Bell quotes her as saying, 'Wissett seems to lull asleep all ambition. Don't you think they have discovered the secret of life? I thought it wonderfully harmonious.'

❖ R.L.S. at Cockfield

In the 1870s, **Cockfield Rectory** was home to the notable professor of archaeology **Churchill Babington** (1821–89) whose wife was a cousin of **Robert Louis Stevenson** (1850–94), author of the enduring classic *Treasure Island* (1883) and *The Strange Case of Dr Jekyll and Mr Hyde* (1886). R.L.S., as Stevenson signed his letters, made visits to the Babingtons early in his career where he met influential writers and academicians, including Sidney Colvin, who gave R.L.S. his first introduction to a London editor. (Colvin was later the biographer of R.L.S. and there is a memorial to him in **Little Bealing's** church.)

Writing to his mother from Cockfield Rectory in 1873, Stevenson said, 'I am too happy to be much of a correspondent. Yesterday we were away to Melford and Lavenham, both exceptionally placid, beautiful old English towns'.

Although frequently homesick for Scotland, he nevertheless made the most of his time in Suffolk and found that 'on the whole there are too many amusements' that distracted him from his studies. It is said that Stevenson based the character 'Long John Silver' on a local man, Peg Leg Brinkley.

Another strong influence on R.L.S. was Mrs Fanny Sitwell, whom he met at Cockfield rectory and fell hopelessly in love with. He referred to her as 'Madonna' and 'the mother of my soul'. They had a mutual interest in literature but Fanny was 12 years older than him and recently separated from her husband. She had many admirers and, although their love never developed as the young man might have wished, they remained friends and biographers have since concluded that their relationship may have been of an intellectual nature rather than one of passion.

❖ **The Pastoral Poet**
In 1800 the so-called ploughman poet, Robert Bloomfield (1761–1823) of **Honington** wrote the extraordinarily successful poem, *The Farmer's Boy*.

He was born in a wattle and daub cottage just across from the church where his mother brought up six children in extreme poverty. His father had died of smallpox and Robert's mother turned her hand to spinning and teaching in a local dame school. As a result, Robert was able to receive an elementary education but had to leave school at 11 and go to work on his uncle's farm in the neighbouring parish of **Sapiston**. Here he became the farmer's boy, all the while observing with affection the life that he was to write about so movingly.

After a few years his uncle saw that Robert was unfit for arduous farm work and sent him to London to be apprenticed in the shoe trade. There he married and some years later began writing poetry, but looked in vain for a publisher. Eventually he met Capel Lofft (1751–1824), an influential patron who lived at **Troston Hall**, near Honingham, who read Robert's poetry and, with the help of the Duke of Grafton, arranged for it to be published (for which he earned the scorn of Byron, who called him 'the Mycaenas of shoemakers', Bloomfield by then being a shoemaker).

The Farmer's Boy was an overnight success and within three years it had run to seven editions, been translated into several languages, and sold 26,000 copies. Although the work paints a rosy picture of a rural idyll, ignoring the harsh realities of farm life, he nevertheless wrote a sincere celebration of the countryside. He later wrote *The Horkey*, a poem in dialect that was equally a labour of love.

Although Robert had a few years in which to enjoy his success, allowing him to move in society as a man of letters, his health declined and, in spite of earning the praise of Wordsworth, his fortunes waned, returning him to poverty. He died at Shefford in Bedfordshire after an acrimonious split with his Suffolk family. His attendance at his mother's funeral in 1805 was his last trip to the village of his birth.

There is a memorial plaque to Bloomfield at **Euston Park**, home of the Duke of Grafton, and in the church at Honington a plaque was erected in 1916 at the 150th anniversary of Bloomfield's birth.

❖ **Artist Arrested as Wartime Spy**
In 1914 the usually sleepy village of **Walberswick** was put on high alert when a newly arrived stranger was observed walking along the seashore at night, carrying a lantern. War had been declared and while most of the visiting artists had left for their permanent homes, this one had not. The solitary, black-coated figure of the architect, designer and water colourist **Charles Rennie Mackintosh** (1868–1928) became an object of close scrutiny and, it was firmly believed, his nocturnal wanderings could only mean one thing. He was signalling to the Germans.

Matters became worse when it was noticed that Mackintosh's wife was often absent for several days at a time and, in the climate of fear and suspicion, the local police and military authorities were prevailed upon to search his room. There they found letters written in German which, combined with his almost impenetrable Glaswegian accent (thought by the villagers to be 'possibly German'), confirmed their worst suspicions. In a vain attempt to convince them of his innocence, he said the letters were from an artist friend in Austria and thus written in German, but this did not make him a German. No, he could not account for his wife's absence, and he had not been signalling with his lamp to a boat out at sea, merely keeping it alight so that he could see to walk along the beach. Mackintosh was arrested and thrown in gaol, but not before he had flown into a tremendous rage and uttered a string of Scottish obscenities. Unfortunately this only served to exaggerate his outlandish accent, which to the police sounded remarkably Germanic and further convinced them of his guilt.

Margaret Mackintosh arrived back in Walberswick a week later and was able to convince those concerned that her husband was not a spy but a well-regarded and successful artist and architect. Shortly afterwards they left Walberswick and went to London.

❖ *Twinkle, Twinkle, Little Star*
One of the most enduring traditional lullabies, *Twinkle, Twinkle, Little Star*, was written by **Jane Taylor** (1783–1824) whose family moved to **Lavenham** in 1786. Jane and her sister Ann (1782–1866) were the daughters of the Revd Isaac Taylor, an artist, engraver and minister at the local meeting house for Independents. The sisters both wrote poetry from an early age and frequently collaborated in their writing. Jane also wrote novels, plays and short stories. The girls were brought up in an atmosphere of culture and learning, which included the study of astronomy. Their mother also wrote, as did their brothers.

The Star was a poem first published in an anthology, *Rhymes for the Nursery*, in 1806. Where Jane actually wrote *The Star* is the subject of some discussion (as the family later moved to Essex), but the inspiration for it belongs to her formative years in Lavenham.

The Star had five verses but only the first is remembered. Although Jane and Ann wrote many more poems, it is *The Star* that is their single claim on posterity.

❖ **Classic Words and Phrases**
Edward Moor (1771–1848) was born in **Alderton,** the son of John, steward to the Marquis of Hertford. (It was John who planted most of **Hollesley Heath** with oak trees, resulting in a plantation known as Moor's Folly.)

At the age of 12, Edward went as a cadet in the East Indies Company and travelled extensively, not returning for any length of time to Suffolk until he retired. He bought **Great Bealings Hall** and published several books, including *Suffolk Words and Phrases* in 1823, which is considered a classic of its type and which spawned similar (and, it has to be said, better researched) volumes.

❖ **We Didn't Mean to Go to Sea**

It is not every writer who can appeal to different age groups at different levels, but **Arthur Ransome** (1884–1967) is one of them. Although he wrote for adults, it was his children's books that became phenomenally successful and one of the most famous, *We Didn't Mean to Go to Sea* (1937), is widely recognised as a classic in children's seafaring literature. It was one of the books written while Arthur and his Russian wife Evgenia lived at Broke Farm, **Levington** (1934–39) and at Harkstead Hall on the **Shotley** peninsula (1939–40).

Although Ransome was born in Yorkshire he was a member of the engineering Ransome family of **Ipswich** and regarded Suffolk with affection. Having made his name with *Swallows and Amazons*, set in the Lake District, he and Evgenia decided to move here in the hope that the sea air would improve Arthur's health. He would not only have a rich source of material for his books, but he could also indulge his love of sailing.

The description of Pin Mill in *We Didn't Mean to Go to Sea* is very evocative of the 1940s as the Walker children and their mother arrive to wait for the return of Commander Walker:

'Only the evening before they had come down the deep green lane that ended in the river itself, with its crowds of yachts, and its big brown-sailed barges and steamers going up to Ipswich or down to the sea.'

The barges and steamers have largely gone but the lane still ends at the river.

❖ Ransome named his favourite yacht *Nancy Blackett* after the adventurous leader of the Amazon Pirates, who first appeared in *Swallows and Amazons*. She was built in 1931 but was reluctantly sold six years later in deference to Evgenia's request for a larger galley.

❖ Alma Cottage, not far from the Butt and Oyster at **Pin Mill,** is where the fictional Walker family took lodgings in *We Didn't Mean to Go to Sea*. The children's landlady was based on Annie Powell, who lived in the pub, and she appears as herself as the children 'waked for the first time to look out through Miss Powell's climbing roses at this happy place where almost everybody wore sea-boots.'

❖ Down the coast from **Pin Mill** is **Hamford Water**, where Ransome set *Secret Water,* the sequel to *We Didn't Mean to Go to Sea*.

❖ *Peter Duck*, Arthur Ransome's boat (named after an imaginary friend of Titty in *Swallowdale)* can still be seen sailing on the River Deben. Known as PD, the character was an old **Lowestoft** sailor who longed for 'one last blue water voyage'. He, in turn, was based on Captain Sehmel, the old Baltic seaman who had sailed with Ransome on his first Baltic cruise in the ketch *Racundra* in 1922.

PD was restored in 1999 by the writer Francis Wheen, whose biography of Karl Marx enabled him and his partner, Julia Jones, to buy her. The tenders to PD are named *Karl Marx* and *Jenny Marx*. Ransome's own association with Russia began when he first visited in 1913 and developed sympathy for the cause of Leon Trotsky and the Russian Revolution. His wife Evgenia had been Trotsky's secretary.

❖ Another writer associated with Pin Mill is Eileen Arbuthnot Robertson, writing as **E. Arnot Robertson** (1903–1961), who saw things from a very different perspective to the one portrayed by Arthur Ransome. Instead of writing sympathetically, or with celebration, of the yachting fraternity, she ridiculed it. Having spent her childhood on the East Coast she came to loathe messing about in boats, preferring to go bird-watching. Her novel *Ordinary Families* (1933) was set in **Pin Mill** and parodied the 'antics' of the nautical family and their 'insufferable middle-class friends'.

❖ **Jack Freeman**
The writer H.W. 'Jack' Freeman (1899–1994) was the son of a schoolmaster who, in his early school years, was shown to have both promise and academic ability. He won a scholarship to Oxford University where he read classics. World War One interrupted his studies but after surviving service with the Light Infantry in France, he embarked on European travel and started writing. He was in Italy when he heard that his first novel *Joseph and His Brethren* (1928) had been accepted for publication.

The novel is set in **Bruisyard** and tells of the 'Geaiter' family of Crakenhill Farm and the trials and tribulations of two generations working the land. Jack had worked on a farm at Bruisyard and, like George Ewart Evans, liked to listen to tales of the countryside as told by the villagers and farm workers. The book describes the backbreaking hours of stone picking in the fields, the long days of harvest and carting corn to the local mill.

Down in the Valley (1930) is considered a classic work. It is a tale of several love stories, woven together into an unsentimental but evocative narrative that concerns one Everard Mulliver, a grocer from **Bury St Edmunds**, who is released from the constraints of life as a 'gentleman' by the death of his mother. Everard was prevented by his upbringing from answering the call of the land – the countryside being his first and most deeply rooted love, all the more impassioned for being thwarted. However, Everard soon discovers new and undreamed of loves, one in the shape of Ruthie, with her long hair and 'exquisitely soft and petal-like throat', and another called Laura, whose sad story touches the heart of the young man not yet acquainted with the pitfalls of involving himself in the lives of the gentler sex.

Freeman's characters are real: the men in the bar of the Olive Leaf pub are able to argue and speak roughly to each other, confident in their friendship and the intimate relationships that were, in the 1920s and 1930s, the bedrock of country life.

In 1941 Jack married Elisabeth 'Betty' Bodecker, a German theatrical costume designer, and they settled in **Offton**. Here the local landmarks found their way into print, the Limeburners public house becoming the Roses. He and Betty were a popular couple and Jack, described as a tall sinewy man with a friendly face furrowed with laugh lines, would always stop and chat with villagers.

Jack died in 1994 at the age of 94. He and Betty died within three months of each other.

EIGHT – THE DICKENS CONNECTION

CHARLES DICKENS (1812–1870) was a frequent visitor to Suffolk and many villages, towns, events and characters in his novels were based on those he observed or heard about during the several sojourns he made in the county. In 1848, for instance, he took a walking holiday in the **Lowestoft**–Great Yarmouth area and later, after he had achieved national acclaim, made exhausting tours of Suffolk reading his work to appreciative audiences. In his celebrity capacity he opened the lecture hall for the **Ipswich** Mechanics' Institute in 1851 and he always held a special affection for **Bury St Edmunds** that was entirely reciprocated.

It is known that he purchased a copy of Edward Moor's *Suffolk Words and Phrases* (1823), which gave him a good purchase on the language and dialect of Suffolk.

It is also thought that like many a writer before and since, Dickens read the works of **George Crabbe** (1755–1832) that describe so vividly the essentials of the coastal villages and villagers of 19th-century Suffolk. Indeed, the description of old Mr Peggotty's beach house (in *David Copperfield*) echoes Crabbe's own fisherman's shed, 'with the low paling, form'd of wreck, around'. The storms that caused the shipwreck of a Spanish schooner that leads to the heroic death of Ham is not unlike Crabbe's own masterly description of a drowned man found on the beach after his ship had run aground, 'Tis a sorry sight! A seaman's body: there'll be more tonight!'

Due to Dickens's habit of drawing on real places and persons for his work, it has become a national sport to claim a person or a place for a particular location. Suffolk has more claims than most since it was Suffolk that inspired the characters and atmospheres of arguably his most successful novels.

❖ *David Copperfield*
David Copperfield (1849–50) is the novel about which Dickens said 'Of all my books, I like this the best', and is a thinly disguised autobiography (the initial CD in reverse). The book opens with Davy Copperfield being born at the Rookery (the Rectory) in Blunderstone (**Blunderston**) where he lives with his mother and the

devoted Peggotty for the first few years of his life, before his mother marries the infamous Mr Murdstone. It was at Blunderstone that the elms bent to one another and 'some weather-beaten old rooks nests burdening the higher branches, swung like wrecks upon a stormy sea'.

Dickens often passed along the Blunderston road to **Lowestoft** and in 1848 he went that way to visit his friend, Sir Morton Peto, at **Somerleyton Hall** (who was Lord of the Manor at Blunderston). He was in the company of his illustrator, the *Punch* artist John Leech, and might possibly have stayed at Blunderston Hall, as descriptions of the interior of the Hall suggest that he had been inside.

❖ **The Plough Inn** at **Blunderston** is an old coaching house dating from 1701, where Barkis made the acquaintance of Davy's old nurse, Peggotty. A sign above the door proclaims that 'Barkis (The Carrier) from the novel David Copperfield by Charles Dickens started from here'. Dickens might well have seen a carrier's horse standing dejectedly in front of the inn, giving rise to Barkis's horse being 'the laziest horse in the world', which 'shuffled along, with his head down, as if he liked to keep the people waiting to whom the packages were directed'.

Dickens often walked along the coast when he was staying in **Somerleyton** and would have known the Plough, as indeed did anyone who travelled by road in the pre-railway age when the coaching inns became familiar to regular passengers. Dickens would have alighted here on his way to Yarmouth but by the time he wrote *David Copperfield* the railways had already put the coachmen out of business in many places. However, he deliberately set the novel in the coach age in order to recall his earlier experiences. He once remarked that it was 'a mistake to fancy that children ever forgot anything' and he often sent his characters journeying back into his own childhood.

❖ The Village Maid public house at **Lound** was built in 1834 and is reputedly where Davy complained, 'We made so many deviations up and down lanes, and were such a long time delivering a bedstead at a public-house, and calling at other places, that I was quite tired.'

❖ Dickens mentions a Suffolk speciality in *David Copperfield*, namely batter pudding, which was traditionally served as a starter with gravy so that when the meat course was served you ate less of it. When Mr Murdstone sends Davy away from Blunderstone he stops for a meal and a greedy waiter takes an interest in the child's food, asking if he is eating a pie.

'It's a pudding' I made answer.

'Pudding!' he exclaimed. 'Why, bless me, so it is! What!' looking at it nearer, 'you don't mean to say it's a batter-pudding?'

'Yes, it is indeed.'

'Why, a batter-pudding' he said, taking up a tablespoon, 'is my favourite pudding! Ain't that lucky? Come on little 'un, and let's see who'll get the most.'

Unfortunately the waiter had a tablespoon and Davy had only a teaspoon so he got very little of the batter pudding.

❖ The Feathers public house in **Gorleston** is mentioned in *David Copperfield*. Dickens would have travelled through Gorleston on his way up to Great Yarmouth and seen the many hundreds of fishing boats that landed their herring catches there. It was said that at one time there were so many boats that you could walk across the river using them as stepping-stones.

❖ Among the islands and waterways of the Meare at **Thorpeness** is 'Peggoty's House' in tribute to Charles Dickens (see also Chapter Seven, Writers and Artists).

❖ *The Pickwick Papers*
As a young reporter for the *Morning Chronicle*, Dickens visited Suffolk in 1835 to report on the General Election. The corruption and bribery he witnessed at **Sudbury** and **Bury St Edmunds** was later used in *The Posthumous Papers of the Pickwick Club*, known as *The Pickwick Papers*, which was published in monthly instalments during 1836 and 1837.

❖ The real Eatanswill of *The Pickwick Papers* is **Sudbury**, where chaotic scenes of electioneering took place and 'never had such a commotion agitated the town before'. There are no lengths to which the prospective members for Eatanswill will not go in order to gain votes. Mr Pickwick was so anxious not to give offence to anyone that he disguised Eatanswill even from the fictional members of the Pickwick Club, who claimed they 'had never heard of Eatanswill'. They searched in vain for proof of its actual existence although it was clear from Mr Pickwick's notes that the people of Eatanswill 'considered themselves of the utmost and most mighty importance'.

Amid a noisy reception, the results of the Eatanswill election were read from what was clearly recognisable as Sudbury Town Hall and the Peacock, where Mr Thompson and Mr Snodgrass stayed, represented the Swan (since demolished, but it stood near the Corn Exchange).

❖ The Black Boy public house at **Sudbury** also appeared in *The Pickwick Papers* and is where the participants in the 'corrupt election' stayed.

❖ Mauldon's Black Adder Brewery at **Sudbury** has celebrated Dickens over the years by naming its beers after characters in his books. Peggotty's Porter is a traditional dark porter brewed with roasted rye malt and fuggle hops (hops originally propagated by Richard Fuggle). Dickens is a light coloured bitter and Micawber's Mild is brewed with pale, roasted barley and crystal malts with Amarillo hops.

Anna Maria Mauldon opened the brewery in 1795, so it is not inconceivable that the young Charles Dickens, who first visited Sudbury in 1835, may have drunk Sudbury beer in the the Swan.

❖ After leaving Eatanswill, Mr Pickwick proceeded to **Bury St Edmunds** where he famously stayed at the Angel on Angel Hill. Mr Pickwick and Sam Weller arrived in the coach that 'rattled through the well-paved streets of a handsome little town, of thriving and cleanly appearance'.

Dickens first visited Bury in 1834 and returned several times, always staying at the Angel. In 1859 he gave readings of his work at the Athenaeum (named after a literary institution of that name formed in 1854) and then again in 1861. He wrote to his sister that he was staying in Room 15, 'a lovely room' that overlooked the ruined Abbey, now called the Dickens Room. He was received with unreserved enthusiasm and wrote to Wilkie Collins, 'Last night I read "Copperfield" at Bury St Edmunds to a very fine audience. I don't think a word – not to say an idea – was lost!'

Nicholas Nickleby (1838–39) was also much appreciated at Bury, and in 1861 Dickens was again staying at the Angel, writing to a friend, 'I think Nickleby tops all the Readings! Somehow it seems to have got in it, by accident, exactly the qualities best suited to the purpose; and it went last night, not only with roars, but with a general hilarity and pleasure that I have never seen surpassed'.

❖ South Hill House in **Bury St Edmunds** forms part of the property once owned by the Gage family. In the mid-1800s it was an Academy for Young Ladies and lays claim to be the fictitious

Westgate House girls' school in *The Pickwick Papers* to where Pickwick is lured on false pretences, ending in his getting entangled in a rose tree, several gooseberry bushes and eventually being helped over a wall by Sam Weller. He gets thoroughly soaked in a rainstorm and eventually realises he has been tricked by the fraudulent Alfred Jingle and Job Trotter. Dickens is known to have visited the school to read to the students. It afterwards became a boys' boarding school and is now run as a bed and breakfast establishment.

❖ Members of the Pickwick Club still meet at the Angel Hotel in **Bury St Edmunds** every Tuesday for a lunchtime drink. Started as a social gathering for ex-army officers it was traditionally men-only, though their President is currently Mary Gough, whose family have owned and run the Angel for over 30 years.

❖ The Great White Horse Inn at **Ipswich** is immortalised as the setting for Mr Pickwick's inadvertent intrusion into the bedroom of 'a middle-aged lady, in yellow curl-papers, busily engaged in brushing what ladies call their "back-hair"'. Having extricated himself from the bedroom he finds himself 'alone, in an open passage, in a strange house, in the middle of the night, half dressed'. Sam Weller comes to the rescue and returns a befuddled Pickwick to his own room.

Although Dickens liked Ipswich he felt ambivalent towards 'this overgrown tavern' which he said was famous in the neighbourhood for its size, 'in the same degree as a prize ox, or county paper-chronicled turnip, or unwieldy pig'. He criticised its 'labyrinths of uncarpeted passages' and 'clusters of mouldy, ill-lighted rooms' in which Mr Pickwick loses himself so hopelessly that he has to be rescued by his manservant, Weller.

On Dickens's subsequent trips to Ipswich he did not stay at the Great White Horse and the landlord did not attend his readings!

❖ Another man who was perhaps not quite so pleased for **Ipswich** to be immortalised in a Dickens novel was William Brooks, proprietor of the *Ipswich Journal*. He sued the novelist for what he considered his libellous description of the Great White Horse in *The Pickwick Papers*.

❖ The character of Mrs Leo Hunter in *The Pickwick Papers* was based on **Mrs Elizabeth Cobbold** of **Ipswich**. Born in London, she had first married William Clarke in 1790 (a Portman of the borough and Comptroller of the Customs of Ipswich) but after his death, Elizabeth became the second wife of John Cobbold of the Cliff Brewery, Ipswich. She was 20 years his junior. He already had 14 children under 17 years old and Elizabeth gave him a further six sons and another daughter. It was rumoured that she had been an actress in her youth and she later wrote poetry, dedicating a volume of verse entitled *Six Narrative Poems* to the artist Sir Joshua Reynolds. Mrs Cobbold was famous for her Valentine parties (for which she wrote appropriate verses) and later published two volumes of *Cliff Valentines*. Mrs Leo Hunter also doted on poetry and gave literary breakfasts 'to a great number of those who have rendered themselves celebrated by their works and talents'. Dickens composes an extraordinary poem for Mrs Hunter, *Ode to an Expiring Frog*, written in the style of Mrs Cobbold. Mr Pickwick is persuaded to join in the fancy dress *dejeune* and is treated to a rendition of the Ode, which began:

> Can I view thee panting, lying
> On thy stomach, without sighing;
> Can I unmoved see thee dying
> On a log,
> Expiring frog!

❖ The St Clement's area of **Ipswich** featured in *The Pickwick Papers* when Sam Weller sits deep in thought staring at 'the old brick houses' and 'bestowing a wink upon some healthy-looking servant girl as she drew up a blind, or threw open a bed-room window'.

He had walked there from the Great White Horse and 'strolled among its ancient precincts'.

❖ Stagecoaches took at best some six hours to reach **Ipswich** from Yarmouth. John Cole was the original for Tony Weller in *The Pickwick Papers* and was the last coachman to try and compete with the railways. He gave up in October 1859, shortly after the **Beccles** to **Lowestoft** line was opened.

❖ *Great Expectations*

It is by no means clear if Satis House in **Yoxford** was the house where the eternally bitter, jilted Miss Havisham lived as a recluse in *Great Expectations* (1859) but the house has strong connections with Dickens. A Satis House is mentioned by name in the novel, 'Is Manor House the name of this house, Miss?' asks Pip, to be told by Estella that the house has more than one name, 'Its other name was Satis, which is Greek, Latin or Hebrew, or all three' she replies. 'It meant…that whoever had this house could want nothing else'. *Satis* is the Latin word for sufficiency.

Although there had been a dwelling house on the site since at least 1471, the Georgian aspects came in 1802 and in 1813 George Wilson (a tenant of Mrs Hulkes) gave it the name Satis House, well before Dickens was writing *Great Expectations*. The Hulkes family also had property in Notting Hill and Dickens lived at nearby Gadshill Place, which he bought in 1856 (three years before *Great Expectations* was published). Mr Hulkes is mentioned in John Forster's *Life of Dickens* as one of the 'two nearest country neighbours with whom the family had become very intimate'.

Mr and Mrs Hulkes were invited to the wedding of Dickens's youngest daughter Kate to Charles Alston Collins, brother of William Wilkie Collins (the novelist), in 1860.

Mrs Hulkes later sold Satis House to another member of the Collins family, William Anthony Collins of Lincoln's Inn, a barrister at law. Yet another coincidence is that Mrs Hulkes had relatives living at Rochester in Kent (where there is another Satis House).

❖ **Bleak House**

Bleak House, the ninth novel by Dickens, was published in 20 monthly instalments between March 1852 and September 1853. The plot concerns a long-running legal dispute over inheritance, Jarndyce v Jarndyce, that reflects two such cases which occurred in Suffolk. Drawing on his time as a legal clerk, Dickens takes a dig at the protracted and laborious way in which the law worked, saying 'no two chancery lawyers can talk about it for five minutes without coming to a total disagreement as to all the premises'. When pronounced Jarndyce and Jarndyce sounded similar to Jaundice and Jaundice and *Bleak House* is credited as being one of the factors in the change in trust law that prevented such complex trusts being drawn up ever again.

❖ The first was that of William Jennens of **Acton Hall** near **Long Melford** who died on 27 June 1798 at the age of 99. When he died, William was dubbed 'the richest commoner in the land' and the value of his estate exceeded £2 million. He had barely touched the inheritance from his father, instead living in self-imposed poverty. He was known as the Acton Miser. In the newspaper account of his death it was said that William was 'more given to penuriousness than hospitality' and 'his accumulations magnified even beyond his power of computation'. He was reputed to have kept £50,000 in cash for 'sudden emergencies' and thousands of pounds were found under his bed. The only instruction he left was that, after his death, the Hall was to be burned down. However, William Jennens, a lifelong bachelor, died intestate and no one was prepared to burn down what might be their inheritance.

No sooner had he departed this life than relations began arriving from all directions with claims to his fortune, many with forged documents. Someone even tried to tamper with an inscription on a Jennens tomb in the church. To complicate matters, the Jennens family had taken different sides at the time of the Civil War, and the two branches of the family carried on as though the other did not exist. It also transpired that William's grandfather had married twice. He had had several children by both wives and two of the sons (one from each wife) were called Robert. No one knew which one was William's father.

Lord Curzon was expecting to inherit the estate and descended on Acton to arrange the funeral before setting off for the lawyers to stake his claim and, he hoped, take up residence in William's house in London's Grosvenor Square. It soon became apparent that he was not alone but competing with numerous nieces and nephews from the two families. A will of sorts was produced but was not of sufficient legality to be considered safe and so began a legal case that lasted for a magnificent 80 years, during which time the money accumulated interest but not enough to keep pace with the bills from uncountable lawyers.

In 1805 it was announced in the local newspaper that three soldiers in the East Suffolk Militia had come into large fortunes, 'proved to be legal by the representatives of the late William Jennens'. The soldiers are unlikely to have got their money and no doubt their descendants were among those still fighting for their share of the inheritance many years later.

As late as 1875 a female descendant of one of William's brothers, who lived in America, was still petitioning the English courts to recover her fortune. She was not alone, since by then there were even more descendants of the original claimants who were trying their luck.

The inevitable result of all the petitioning and the claiming, so poignantly observed by Dickens in Jarndyce v Jarndyce, was that the money went mostly to the lawyers. Very little was left for any heirs who might be pronounced 'rightful', many of whom were dead by the time the judgement was handed down.

❖ The second case of a protracted legal wrangle over inheritance was that of **Peter Thellusson** of **Aldeburgh** who died in 1797. He had set up a vastly complicated trust fund for his heirs that, at his death, was contested by his widow, sons and grandsons. Thellusson's plan was to leave a modest amount to his wife but the bulk of his considerable estate was to be held in trust and allowed to accumulate for 100 years, to benefit the third generation of his descendants, his grandsons, thereby disinheriting his sons. If no such descendants survived then the whole trust was to be put towards paying off the national debt. Thellusson computed that by the time the trust, tied up in Government funds, was paid out the final recipient would be the richest person in the world (he appears not to have taken inflation into account). He estimated his £500,000 estate would yield £4,500 per annum (with an interest rate of seven and a half percent) producing a final value of £19,000,000, 30 times the original legacy.

Thellusson's will was immediately contested and found its way into a court of Chancery. So convoluted did the case become that it lasted for 61 years and it is no wonder that Dickens found plenty of material for his novel. However, lawyers could find no fault with the legality of the will, nor could the House of Lords, when it was referred to them.

Matters were complicated in that Thellusson's wife was pregnant (with twins) and a court case ensued as to whether, or not, the twins could inherit, were the will to be overturned. Thellusson's daughters-in-law both obligingly produced sons to ensure whatever inheritance their husbands might gain.

During the case the trustees of the will availed themselves of the many Thellusson properties. Brodsworth Hall near Doncaster was listed in the early 1800s as being 'the residence of the Trustees of the late Peter Thellusson'.

It was estimated that had the trust been allowed to accumulate it might have eventually have reached £140 million, which could have destabilised the nation. A law was passed in 1800, known as the Thellusson Act, under which no property bequeathed by a will would be allowed to accumulate for more than 21 years.

At least one of Peter Thellusson's sons finally inherited a sizeable proportion of the trust in 1858. Another of his sons, Peter Isaac, was created the first **Lord Rendlesham** in 1806.

❖ A character in *Bleak House* is Krook the rag and bottle merchant and collector of papers, who smells of brimstone and eventually dies of spontaneous human combustion, attributed to his evil nature. When the book was published, Dickens was castigated for including the 'impossibility' of spontaneous combustion but he said he knew of at least 30 such cases, one of them no doubt a famous **Ipswich** story of just such an event.

In April 1744, Grace Pett, a fisherman's wife who lived in the parish of St Clement's, was said to be a witch and to have died from spontaneous combustion. Her daughter found her 'like a log of wood consumed by fire, without apparent flame'. Nearby clothing and furniture was undamaged. The coroner discovered that Grace had been drinking 'plentifully of gin' the previous evening and had gone downstairs in the night, where she apparently burnt to ashes. No other cause of death was discovered and the only conclusion was spontaneous combustion.

Dickens set several events in the parish of St Clement's and the story of Grace Pett would not have escaped his notice.

❖ *A Tale of Two Cities*
It was the **Thellusson Bank** that Dickens used as the template for the Tellson bank in *A Tale of Two Cities*, where the action takes place in both France and England during the French Revolution. Peter Thellusson (of the trust case) was a Huguenot whose family settled in England in the middle of the 18th century. Thellusson had at one time been a business partner of the famous Jacques Necker, Louis XVI's Director General of Finance.

The Thellussons became successful merchants and bankers in London and acquired property all over England, including Suffolk. When Dickens needed a bank for the novel, an English institution run by a Frenchmen could hardly have been bettered. He did not attempt to conceal the model for the fictional bank, calling it Tellson's.

During the French Revolution Thellusson's bank did considerable business with French refugees and great fortunes were placed in their vaults for safekeeping.

❖ **The Peasenhall Murder**
In one of the most famous unsolved murders in Suffolk, concerning Rose Harsent of **Peasenhall**, the prosecution was led by Henry (later

Sir Henry) Fielding Dickens, KC, son of Charles Dickens. In 1902 a local man, William Gardiner, was accused of the brutal murder of a young girl, Rose Harsent, at Providence House where she worked as a live-in maid. Gardiner was known to have had an association with Rose and when her body was found he was immediately arrested.

Although he was tried twice, he was never convicted and the murder remains a mystery. Gardiner died in London without making any deathbed confessions although he maintained his innocence throughout.

Henry Dickens was considered to be a fair prosecutor, praised for his 'moderate and balanced prosecution' although he did have a tendency to make long, dramatic speeches. However, at the first trial he was unable to prosecute successfully, although the local newspapers could not believe their luck in not only having one of the most notorious murders of the century to cover, but also an opportunity to write about Henry Dickens and his famous father. Although the jury brought in a hung verdict, Gardiner was not acquitted but told he was to be tried a second time. When the new trial began in January 1903, Henry Dickens was again prosecuting but his father's notability was referred to by the defence, who on one occasion called the court's attention to 'the histrionic ability my friend possessed from heredity and personality. It is the sort of thing that would do in a novel, but not a murder case'.

At the end of the second trial the jury was again undecided by a margin of 11-to-one in favour of the prisoner, the complete opposite of the first trial, where it had been eleven-to-one against. Henry Dickens went on to higher and greater things, but his failure to win the case rankled with him. He always maintained that the opposition had 'intrigued' against him and he held a personal grudge against Ernest Wild for the rest of his life.

The murder of Rose Harsent was never solved. The Peasenhall Murder case was the first in English law where fingerprint evidence was admitted.

❖ **Wilkie Collins**

The novelist **Wilkie Collins** (1824–1889) was a great admirer of Dickens and came to Suffolk in search of the places that had served as the inspiration for *David Copperfield*. He was one of the first writers to avail himself of the new transport opportunities, arriving by train rather than in a coach. He already knew Suffolk, his brother having lived at Satis House (see above).

Collins set a section of his novel *No Name* in Aldeburgh, calling it 'this curious little seaside snuggery', and described the fashionable promenading along the seafront where 'Magdalen Vanstone' engineers a meeting with Noel Vanstone, the sickly heir to her father's estate. Together with her accomplice, the scheming Captain Wragge, she walks towards **Slaughden** and sits on the grassy bank below the Martello Tower. Like Dickens, Collins could not fail to be influenced by Crabbe and, indeed, Magdalen Vanstone walks past the very place where Crabbe had worked in his father's shop.

NINE – PARTICULAR TO SUFFOLK

THERE are some things that are particular, some might say peculiar, to the county of Suffolk and as such are cherished by those acquainted with them. There is a colour named after it, Suffolk Pink, which in its turn has inspired the name of a wine and an apple variety. Being primarily an agricultural county, Suffolk people could not be prouder of the **Suffolk Trinity**, made up of the **Suffolk Punch horse**, the **Red Poll cattle** and the **Suffolk Sheep**. Sculptures of all three have recently been commissioned and stand at the entrance to Trinity Park, home to the Suffolk Agricultural Show.

❖ **The Suffolk Punch**
One of the first references to Suffolk's iconic 'Punch' horse is in Camden's *Britannia* where he refers to a 'Suffolk Horse' that existed in 1506. This was the ancestor of the famous Sam Crisp's Horse of **Ufford,** a stallion foaled in 1768, from which almost all Suffolk horses in existence now trace descent. The stallion's services were advertised at five shillings a time and in his prime he was said to be a 'five-year-old bright stallion, standing a full 15 and a half hands'. He was never named but was known as 'horse 404'.

The Suffolk is the oldest pure heavy horse breed in the British Isles and has one of the best documented histories of all. The first volume of the Suffolk Stud Book (1880) contains 712 pages of extended pedigrees and as much material about each breeding line as it was possible to record at the time, a retrospective register of genuine Suffolk stallions. The compiler was **Herman Biddell** of **Playford** and his name is synonymous with the history and development of the Suffolk Punch. The Punch nickname came about after an observation by the diarist and Master of the Guild of Trinity House, Samuel Pepys, on one of his many visits to **Lowestoft** in the 1680s to oversee the Guild's lighthouse. There he heard the parents of fat children with short legs address them as 'punches'. The Suffolk horse is also stocky, with relatively short legs, and so the name Punch was coined.

The characteristic of the Suffolk horse, wrote Herman Biddell, is 'the uniformity of colour, the short leg, the rounded carcass, the longevity with vitality, frequently reaching nearly 30 years of age'. There are seven shades of colour, all variations on 'chesnut', which is always spelt without the central 't'. A stallion can weigh up to a ton.

The suitability of the Punch to work Suffolk's heavy clay soil lies in its enormous strength and was one of the reasons the breed thrived here. Farmers moving to the area and bringing with them some of the other heavy breeds, the Percheron, Shire or Clydesdale, found them inadequate for the task. These all had varying degrees of 'feathers' (hair growing on the lower legs). A horse whose feet are weighed down by clay-impacted 'feathers' is a less efficient worker and the Suffolk is feather-free, an important characteristic.

Until the 20th century farming had relied solely on horse power to work the land, but the advent of the mechanical age, and the often parlous state of British agriculture, witnessed a decline in Suffolk horse numbers. World War One saw some clawing back in importance and the similarities between the Suffolk and the old war horses were sufficient to make it a prime target for the army looking for horses to take to France. World War Two also offered a brief respite for the breed but as tractors became more common and farming fortunes steadily improved the Suffolk Punch became redundant. In the late 1940s and early 1950s numbers plummeted and by the 1960s the breed had almost died out. Today there are only 396 Suffolks in the United Kingdom. It is still counted as Category 1 Critically Endangered by the Rare Breeds Survival Trust.

❖ The Suffolk Horse Society was founded in 1877 and its headquarters is at the Suffolk Punch Heavy Horse Museum on Market Hill, **Woodbridge**. Patron of the Society is HRH The Princess Royal.

The Museum opened in 1994 and also houses records and exhibitions relating to **Red Poll** cattle, **Suffolk Sheep** and **Black Pigs** (the Large Black and the Suffolk Small Black are the oldest and were, until the 20th century, the most common pigs in the county).

❖ In 2002 a registered charity named 'The Suffolk Punch Trust' was formed to purchase the Suffolk stud belonging to the **Hollesley Bay Colony** prison (see also Chapter Seven, Writers and Artists).

Between the years 1759 and 1803 the Barthorp family acquired land in the Wilford Hundred, of which Hollesley was a part. The Barthorps farmed the Red House Estate, where they became breeders and exhibitors of the Suffolk Horse. Over the years the farm changed hands but in 1938 there were still 72 Suffolks on the farm and 23 foals were born that season. When, in June of that year, it was taken over by the Prison Commissioners, they agreed to retain the Suffolks.

For many years the horses were given names reflecting the association of the old Colonial College, such as Rhodesia, Winnipeg, Alberta and Calgary. In 1914 the prefix 'Colony' was adopted and all horses foaled at Hollesley Bay since then have been registered with the same prefix.

When it was announced that the Prison Service (who had farmed the land since 1938) could no longer keep the stud going, a feasibility study was carried out to assess the potential effect on the Suffolk breed. In 2001 the study warned that without the Hollesley Bay Stud the Suffolk Punch could become extinct within 15 years. The *East Anglian Daily Times* launched a Save the Suffolk Punch petition and by April 2002, 30,000 people had signed it. The Prison Service announced that it had pledged to ensure that the stud was given a new home as close as possible to the existing farm.

❖ The Suffolk Punch horse is not only esteemed by agriculturists but also by supporters of **Ipswich Town Football Club**, on whose club badge the 'Punch' appears. It also became the trade emblem for lawnmowers manufactured by Ransomes of Ipswich in the 19th century and is retained to the present day.

❖ The Suffolk Horse emblem is seen throughout the county. The village sign at **Ufford** shows a Suffolk Punch stallion to commemorate Sam Crisp's famous Horse of Ufford. The **Hepworth** village sign shows a Suffolk Horse, led by a farm worker, pulling a tumbril of hay. Those at **Pettaugh** and **Blaxhall** also depict working horses. **Laxfield** has two horses at plough.

❖ In **Newbourn** church there is a wooden roundel containing a Suffolk Punch, carved by H. Brown.

❖ **Suffolk Red Poll Cattle**
The **Red Poll** cattle take their name from the blood red colour of the

old Norfolk cow which was crossed with the polled (or hornless) Suffolk bull to produce the ideal dual-purpose breed. The polled gene in the Suffolk suppressed the Norfolk horn and in 1863 the name Norfolk and Suffolk Red Polled cattle was adopted. In 1883 the breed became known as the Red Polled and in 1888 the Red Poll Cattle Society was formed. It is, therefore, one of the original native dual-purpose breeds and in the early years of the 20th century was one of the dominant breeds in English dairy farming.

The breed society headquarters are at **Wickham Market** and Her Majesty the Queen is its Patron. Exhibitions concerning the Red Poll are mounted at the Suffolk Horse Society Museum in **Woodbridge**.

❖ **The Suffolk Sheep**

The **Suffolk** Sheep breed originated by mating Norfolk horned ewes with Southdown rams in the late 1700s. In 1810 it was recognised as a pure breed and it has a very distinctive look, with a black face and (down-turned) ears and a prominent Roman nose. Originally they were known as Southdown Norfolks, or just 'black faces', but in his first recording of the new breed in *General View of Agriculture in the County of Suffolk* (1797), Arthur Young stated 'These ought to be called the Suffolk breed' and from then on they were. The first classes to exhibit the sheep were at the Suffolk Show in 1859 and the first flock book was published in 1887. The Suffolk Sheep Society was formed in 1886 at a meeting in **Stowmarket** and is now the largest sheep breed society in Great Britain.

The Suffolk sheep thrived and developed around the rotational system of farming that was prevalent in East Anglia in the 19th century, grazing on grass or clover in the summer and in the winter on swedes, turnips or mangolds. The latter was very labour intensive and involved fencing off a fresh area each day, often in very inclement weather in open, arable fields, where the penetrating east winds do their worst, giving both the sheep and the shepherd a well-earned reputation for hardiness and endurance.

The Suffolk was so successful that very soon it was being exported to almost every corner of the world, to most countries in Europe, Russia, North and South America and the colonies. They are now found throughout the world's sheep-producing countries and there is even a Suffolk Sheep Society in Australia.

❖ **The Ixworth**
During the 1930s, in the village of **Ixworth**, Reginald Appleyard began developing a new breed of chicken. He set out to produce a quick maturing table bird that would also give reasonable egg production. In his search for the new breed he used the White Sussex, Indian Game, White Old English Game, White Minorca and White Orpington and finally, in 1939, the Ixworth chicken bred 'true', or 'pure', and the breed was a reality. He named it after his home village.

There is only one colour of Ixworth, which is an all-white plumage with pinkish legs and beak. Once Mr Appleyard's original aims were realised, the Ixworth's characteristics were accepted into the Poultry Club's Standards, which set out the uniformity in type and colouration of the various breeds.

By the 1970s numbers of the Ixworth had dropped to a low level, putting it on the rare breeds register. While it is still not quite out of the doldrums, Ixworth numbers are gradually increasing, their prospects being all the better for it being an active, hardy bird that does well under free-range conditions.

Reginald Appleyard also bred the Silver Appleyard duck. He wanted to produce the ideal duck for both egg and meat purposes and for exhibition and he succeeded in breeding the Silver Appleyard, which is still a firm favourite of the 'Fancy'. Reginald was a much-regarded writer and breeder of domestic fowl.

❖ **Hard Cheese!**
In the 19th century, when brewing in the county was at its peak, there were many popular sayings that referred to the county's cheese, one of which ran 'Suffolk cheeses are hard as stones, but Suffolk ales are sharp enough to cut them with.' The renowned poet, Robert Bloomfield (1761–1823) of **Honington** said that even in the hog trough, the cheese was 'too big to swallow, and too hard to bite'. In *The Farmer's Boy* he wrote that the very name Suffolk cheese engendered smiles:

> Hence Suffolk dairy-wives run mad for cream,
> And leave their milk with nothing but its name;
> Its name derision and reproach pursue,
> And strangers tell of 'three times skimm'd Sky-blue'
> To cheese converted, and what can be its boast?
> What, but the common virtues of a post!

One Suffolk farmer is recorded as having reproved his wife for her purchase of an iron chest in which to guard her cheese from mice, on the grounds that when the mice had made their way through the metal it would be impossible for them to produce any effect upon its contents.

The diarist, Samuel Pepys (1633–1703), recorded his wife as 'vexed' at people for 'grumbling to eat Suffolk cheese'. There was a saying 'Hunger will break through stone walls and anything but Suffolk cheese' and in his capacity as secretary to the Admiralty, Pepys witnessed at first hand the navy's opposition to it. Suffolk cheese was so bad that in 1750 even the Admiralty condemned it as 'totally unfit for our warships' and it was a standing joke that it needed buttering on both sides to make it edible. One commentator wrote: 'The Navy has always issued Suffolk Cheese, a thin, hard and durable variety, but practically inedible'. There were sustained complaints against it and in 1758 the decision was taken to switch to Cheshire and Gloucester cheese, even though they were considerably more expensive and probably did not keep so well.

Locally, the cheese was called Suffolk 'bang', or 'thump', and known as a coarse 'flet' cheese made not from whole milk but from 'flet, the watery skimmed liquid left over after the cream has been taken for butter and the milk twice, and sometimes thrice, skimmed. The Revd Alfred Sucking (1796–1856) noted that Suffolk cheese was 'proverbially execrable' while an anonymous poet wrote of it:

> 'Those that made me were uncivil:
> They made me harder than the devil:
> Knives won't cut me, fire won't sweat me,
> Dogs bark at me, but cannot eat me.'

Daniel Defoe, in his *Tour through the Eastern Counties* in the 1720s, reported that **Woodbridge** 'is a considerable market for butter and corn to be exported to London...they are famous for the best butter, and perhaps the worst cheese, in England'.

❖ Crinkle-Crankle Wall

Also called a crinkum-crankum, ribbon or serpentine wall, the **crinkle-crankle garden wall** is associated mostly with Suffolk, which has around 50, almost twice as many as the rest of the country. Its curvy design gives it its strength and, being only one brick thick, was cheap to erect. It is usually aligned east to west so that one side faces south on a plan of elongated S-shaped curves, which continuous serpentine shape stiffens the wall so that no buttresses are required. They were first built in the mid-1700s during the heyday of the new fashion for landscape architecture so successfully advanced by the likes of 'Capability' Brown (1716–83) and Humphry Repton (1752–1818). They were popular in Suffolk because of their low cost, which appealed to the natural propensity in the county towards value for money!

The crinkle-crankle wall at **Easton** was said to be the longest in the world (until it was breached a few years ago) and goes right up to the base of the church tower. Other examples can be seen at **Eye, Bildeston, Bramfield, Cavendish, Halesworth, Needham Market, Redisham** and **Saxmundham**, among other places. Capability Brown himself designed the one at **Heveningham** in 1781.

There were two parallel walls at **Lowestoft** running along Maltster's Score and another along Spurgeon Score (see below, The Maltster's Score).

At **Long Melford** there are two within the gardens of Melford Hall, which are dated 1793, and there were once six others in the village. One can still be found near Westgate Terrace and another in Cock and Bell Lane, which is the smaller and runs alongside the cemetery behind the United Reformed Church.

❖ **The Maltster's Score**
The remains of unusual crinkle-crankle walls are to be found along one side of **Maltster's Score**, leading down from **Lowestoft** High Street. Until recently the Score went down between two crinkle-crankle walls, but only part of one survives. The Lowestoft scores are ancient thoroughfares that led down to the beach families living on the shoreline and are notches, cuts or furrows in the cliff face. Edward Fitzgerald described a score as 'a cut down a declevity' connecting the beach villages to the town, and the town with the sea. These declivities were tracks trodden by those who found the safest way down the cliffs in ancient times, some of which have survived while others have gone into the sea. Most of the surviving scores now have steps and each has a name, although names, too, have changed over the centuries. Admiralty charts of the 19th century show a number of Scores nearer the sea, now lost to coastal erosion.

Maltster's Score is unusual in that it has abrupt turnings and in the 19th century had a bad reputation for robberies. It was said that the Score was constructed in this way as a trap to waylay seamen returning to shore but it is more likely to have been a simple means of reducing the downward slope by zigzagging the path.

There are over 12 main scores including **Cart Score**, formerly known as Gallows Score, and **Mariners Score**, originally known as Swan Score. **Crown Score** was known as Lion Score, so named because the Lion Inn stood at its head. Maltsters Score, with its crinkle-crankle walls, was at one time large enough to have shops along its length, as well as three taverns on its west side. The top of **Martin's Score** (known as Gowing's Score until 1850) is famous as being the spot where the Methodist, John Wesley (1703–1791), preached in the open air on 11 October 1764. He noted afterwards 'A wilder congregation I have not seen'. He must have thought he could make a difference though, as he subsequently returned to Lowestoft 14 times to preach the virtues of Methodism, the last occasion in 1790 when he was 87 years old.

Frost's Alley Score is reckoned to be the most intriguing track as it is said to have formed the seaward end of an ancient alley that led from **Mutford** (now Mutford Bridge) at **Oulton Broad** along the north shore of **Lake Lothing**.

❖ **Ipswich Window**

Some early 19th-century houses in **Ipswich** still sport examples of the bow-fronted 'Ipswich' oriel windows, which sit on corbels projecting from wall faces. The corbels are blocks built into the wall that supports the window. These were replicas of the original 17th-century Ancient House windows and were copied and widely paraphrased by several Victorian architects and used on buildings around the town. The 'Ipswich' window became fashionable and was taken up by architects in other towns across the country. It was the inspiration for the architect, R.N. Shaw (1831–1912) who used it at New Zealand Chambers in London (demolished in 1871) and elsewhere.

❖ **Ipswich Pudding**

The **Ipswich Almond Pudding** is made with cream, eggs, ground almonds, sugar and breadcrumbs, with a few drops of rosewater added in just before cooking. The recipe first appeared around the 1740s and is occasionally found in old cookery books. However, the 'true' proportions of each ingredient were a closely guarded secret within families and no definitive version exists.

❖ **Tye**

This is the term for a green or common pasture and only occurs in place names in west Suffolk and a small area in Essex where the two counties meet. It occurs particularly in the **Hadleigh** and **Sudbury** areas.

Barking Tye is particularly large in that it consists of 50 acres of common land, the grazing rights belonging to the surrounding farms. The Tye was cultivated during World War Two and revenue from the cereal crops provided funds for the parish council to erect street lamps and keep the grass areas maintained. Three windmills once stood on the Tye but they are long gone. **Nedging Tye** is, like Barking, one of the largest.

There are several Tyes nearby, among them **Battisford Tye, Charles Tye, Kersey Tye, Lindsey Tye** and **Bower House Tye. Tye Green** at Glemsford is, according to local legend, where village meetings (tithings) were held.

❖ **The Pashford Pot Beetle**

Little is known about the rare **Pashford pot beetle** (*Cryptocephalus exiguous*) other than its habit of fashioning 'pots' in the mud for its home and its existence in only a small area at Pashford Poors Fen near **Lakenheath**. When the mud pots dry out they form perfect houses so that, when it feels threatened, the beetle can scurry into its pot and close itself in.

The beetle is the smallest of the British *Cryptocephalus* species and is shiny black in colour with yellow legs. The male's head is also yellow with a black line down the centre. Since the 1950s the Pashford pot beetle was thought to be extinct until, in 1980, a single male was found at Pashford Poors Fen, since when several more have been discovered at the same site. It appears to be particularly fond of the common sorrel growing at the edge of the fen but is barely clinging to existence in this small area of Suffolk. Unfortunately, this tiny beetle is threatened by drainage of nearby land and by water abstraction, which is lowering the water table, and there are fears for its survival. It is beginning to look as though the pot beetle might be on the verge of extinction from its final stronghold in a single Suffolk fen.

❖ **Westhorpe's Rarities**

Not only is **Westhorpe** home to some rare barberry plants, but it will also, it is hoped, be the habitat of the rare barberry carpet moth that feeds exclusively off them. According to the Suffolk Rare Plant Register, there are less than 40 records of the wild barberry (*Berberis vulgaris*) across the county. It is native to the dry, chalky soils of West Suffolk but planting in mediaeval times confuses distribution.

The Westhorpe barberry became even more precious by the destruction of some of the bushes that used to grow in Shaker's Lane, **Bury St Edmunds**, when the A45 was constructed. Some plants survived the building work, but a later fire in an adjoining field burnt a lot of the bushes on one side of the lane. Although a few bushes remained untouched on the other side of the lane, the carpet moths that fed there appear to have died out. However, the Suffolk Wildlife Trust took a hand and moved a new colony of the moth to the surviving Westhorpe barberry bushes and now awaits developments.

The Suffolk Moth Group keeps a close eye on the barberry moth and while introductions to new sites were tried in the 1980s and 1990s, none were successful and the moth remains a very rare creature in the county.

Westhorpe is also one of only three sites of the rare Bladder sedge (*Carex vulgaris*), the other two being **Laxfield** and **Culford**.

❖ **The White Bricks of Woolpit**

For at least two centuries, the brick kilns of **Woolpit** were celebrated for their white bricks. Woolpit Museum has records going back over 400 years which show that the distinctive Woolpit white bricks were exported worldwide. It is even thought that the first White House in America was constructed of Woolpit bricks. Soon after the railways reached Suffolk in the mid-19th century, Woolpit and **Elmswell** were linked by a tramway used to transport bricks from the Woolpit brick kilns to Elmswell station for onward transportation to the rest of Suffolk and beyond.

The Woolpit bricks (made from Ice Age calcareous lake clay) had a reputation for being harder and more durable than the red brick (made from non-calcareous London clays). This obviously gave them a sought-after exclusivity, with Woolpit bricks costing nearly twice as much as red brick. When, in the early 19th century, many timber framed buildings were re-faced in **Bury St Edmunds**, the white bricks were frequently used. In *The Suffolk Guide* Norman Scarfe wrote of the white brick façades in Bury that they resemble building in the local stone, 'that is to say, in some lights and weather conditions, it has something of the look of good flintwork'. However, here as in **Ipswich**, they were often used only on the front of the building, which could be seen from the street, so as to create the outward appearance of wealth for a much reduced cost!

The Great White Horse Inn in **Ipswich** is faced with Woolpit bricks, as is Hengrave Hall, which also used stones from **Ixworth Priory** (dissolved in 1536).

Not everyone, however, thought well of the white bricks. Frederick Hervey, Earl of Bristol and Bishop of Derry, wrote to his daughter in 1796 after she had asked him about the bricks for his new building project at **Ixworth**. He wrote: 'You beg me on your knees that Ickworth may be built of white stone brick...What, child, build my house of a brick that looks like a sick, pale jaundiced red brick that would be red if it could! And to which I am certain our posterity will give a little rouge as essential to its health and beauty?'

He thought that white bricks always looked as if the bricklayers had not burnt them sufficiently ('had been niggardly of the fuel') and that they looked like 'all dough and no crust'.

Although not all white bricks were from the chalky clay of Woolpit, some being made nearby, anyone paying to have their house re-fronted in the fashionable and expensive brick to impress the neighbourhood would certainly have claimed them as such. During World War Two production was halted, as it was thought sparks from the giant open kilns could have exposed the village to enemy raids.

❖ **Suffolk Pink**
Suffolk is famous for its pink washed houses and cottages, the colour and shade of which can be anything from deep red ochre to a bright, pastel pink.

The reasons for the pinkness are several and varied, though most of them were valid at one time or another. Traditionally the distemper was mixed with buttermilk and pig's blood and then painted on to the 'wattle and daub' cottages.

Colours in limewash are achieved by using alkali-resistant (lime fast) pigments, particularly metal oxides from natural earths, which is why the 'pink' differs greatly from one part of the county to another. Around the **Sudbury** and **Hadleigh** areas, for instance, the pink is almost brown. The juice of the blackthorn, or sloe, was also added to the brew to produce a deeper, redder pink.

Esther Freud, in her novel *The Sea House*, writes that 'Gertrude's house was pink. That stone-ground Suffolk pink that managed to be manly'.

Suffolk pink is also used to describe an apple, a type of Laxton's Fortune, which was found growing in orchards at **Braiseworth** near **Eye** in about 1900. It has a pale yellow skin with a delicate pinkish blush and is now enjoying some commercial success locally as a crisp and juicy early season dessert apple.

Even more recently, the vineyard at **Ickworth House** has produced a Suffolk Pink rosé wine from Auxerrois and Pinot Noir grapes. The first Suffolk Pink vintage was 1999.

❖ **Pargetting**

Pargetting is the art of external decorated plasterwork and although it is not exclusive to Suffolk it was practised here with enthusiasm from the late-Tudor period right up until World War One. With the 'wattle and daub' method of construction (pargetting being suitable only for a lathed and timbered backing) the craft became an important and integral part of the building trade until bricks became more freely available. The pargetter would press the moulds of wet plaster (usually a mixture of slaked lime, sand, hair and the inevitable 'secret ingredient', known only to individual craftsmen) to the house exterior until it was fixed. Pargetting patterns came in a variety of forms including friezes (using ribbons of chevrons, scallops, fantails or dots), overall frames enclosing motifs, geometrical or floral designs, and coats of arms. The popularity for pargetting in Suffolk is often attributed to the plasterers who arrived here from the Low Countries and many of the parget themes are similar to those fashioned by Flemish craftsmen.

The most famous example of 17th-century pargetting is seen on the Ancient House in **Ipswich**, described by Pevsner as 'the most spectacular house in Ipswich'. Among the numerous motifs are a large coat of arms of Charles II, nymphs, a pelican, and an entire scene containing a traveller, shepherdess and grazing sheep. A domed structure, a crocodile, a Gothic church and a tobacco pipe represent the continents of Asia, Africa, Europe and America respectively. (Australia is missing for the simple reason that it had not, then, been discovered.)

The art of pargetting proliferated in West Suffolk, particularly **Clare**, where the 15th-century Ancient House is notable for its superb plasterwork, **Lavenham** and **Hadleigh**.

In the village of **Yoxford** there is a cottage bearing trails of honeysuckle ending in dragons' heads and in **Walpole** is found a pineapple motif.

A cottage or two can be seen in almost any Suffolk village, bearing a single horizontal foliate frieze that was added to give extra protection to joins between the timber framing and the wattle and daub filling.

❖ **Kersey and Lindsey**

The place names **Kersey** and **Lindsey** are particular to Suffolk in more ways than one. Firstly they are contiguous villages and secondly they gave their names to a type of fabric woven in Suffolk in the 14th century. 'Kerseymere' and 'linsey-woolsey' were two locally woven clothes that took the name of the villages where most of the weavers lived. Kerseymere originated in Suffolk but in 1475 it was being produced in the West Riding of Yorkshire. Traders needed to be able to refer specifically to that category of cloth and so it became known by its Suffolk name.

Early in the 14th century large numbers of Dutch and Flemish weavers descended on the **Sudbury, Hadleigh** and **Lavenham** areas. Outlying villages rapidly became hives of the new weaving industry and home working became a boon to many a rural community. Kersey became renowned for its coarse woollen cloth and in the 15th century English 'kerseys' were exported to central Europe. At the end of the 16th century kerseys were being exchanged for wine in the Canary Islands. During the 1540s Kersey woollens were mentioned in an Act of Parliament during the reign of Edward VI, which sought to fix the standard for the cloth.

Linsey-woolsey was not as successful as the Kersey but was of sufficient importance to have sustained the village and gained it a place in Suffolk's industrial history.

Although weaving died out in the 16th century, its place taken by spinning, the name lives on in the form of equestrian accessories, such as the Kersey wool dress rug and the Kersey saddle cloth.

❖ **Apples and Pears**

As a result of the East of England Apples and Orchards Project, several apple varieties have emerged as being unique to Suffolk. The Lord Stradbroke apple was discovered by the Earl of Stradbroke's head gardener, Mr Fenn, at **Henham Hall**, in about 1900. Another long-keeping cooking apple originated in the garden of the Live and Let Live public house in **Combs**, near **Stowmarket**. Villagers called it the Catherine.

St Edmund's Russett was raised by Richard Harvey of **Bury St Edmunds** and received a Royal Horticultural Society award in 1875.

Other unique varieties were found at **Clopton Hall, Assington** and **Sudbury**.

❖ **How the Greengage got its Name**

In the 18th century, **Sir Thomas Gage** of **Bury St Edmunds** received a shipment of fruit from France that included the plum, Reine-Claude, which originated in Armenia. Mr Gage's gardener forgot its proper name so renamed it the Green Gage, which quickly became greengage. Most of the greengages grown in Suffolk, and elsewhere, were bred from Sir Thomas's original fruit.

❖ **The Suffolk Shroff**

The 'shroff hut', a cart or multi-purpose shed of unique construction, was once a building particular to Suffolk. It consists of a flat roof of horizontal beams that are supported by uprights of undressed trunks. On top is piled brushwood, enough to form an A shape, over which thatch is laid. It could be related to the Suffolk word 'shruff', which is light, dry kindling for fuel, and could refer to the roofing material or to the place in which it was kept.

❖ **Flonking the Dwile!**

The Suffolk game of 'dwile flonking' sounds as though it should have its roots in the Middle Ages or before, but only began in the 1960s. The idea is that a 'dwile' (the Suffolk word for a floor cloth or house flannel) is soaked in beer ('flonk' is reputedly an old word for 'ale') and mounted on a pole about two or three feet long (called the 'driveller'). Teams form a circle (the 'girter') in the middle of which stands a member of the opposing team holding the driveller and the dwile, which he (or she) then attempts to throw at those in the circle as they move in an anti-clockwise direction. As the penalty for failing to hit a moving target is more beer the 'game' is likely to take its own course. Theoretically the winner is the team with the most points, or hits, with points deducted for any member of the team still sober at the end!

The story goes that in 1966, George High of **Bungay** found an old parchment in his grandfather's attic entitled *Ye Olde Booke of Suffolk Harvest Rituels,* one of which, more or less, resembled dwile flonking. George and a few colleagues at the printers, Richard Clay of Bungay, decided to revitalise this ritual but update it by using a Suffolk 'dwile'. It took off as a pub game not only across the county but also in neighbouring Norfolk, where its popularity reached a par with Welly Throwing (the throwing of a Wellington boot for the longest distance), which is similarly 'played' at open air events.

In 1967 the Three Tuns pub in Bungay applied for a licence extension for the dinner dance of the Waveney Valley Dwile Flonking Association but had to wait for an answer while the magistrate demanded an explanation of exactly what dwile flonking entailed. This was followed by an appearance on a television programme hosted by Eamonn Andrews, which resulted in letters from Australia, Hong King and America, some asking for copies of the rule book, alas yet to be written!

❖ **Molly Dancing**

Another very curious county peculiarity is the Suffolk version of Morris Dancing, **Molly Dancing**, traditionally performed on Plough Monday, the first Monday following 6 January (or the first Monday after Twelfth Night, which signified the end of Christmas). In the 1800s it was ostensibly an occasion to raise money for the local parish church by dragging a plough around the streets, accompanied by players enacting a play involving song, dance and verse. The exact origins of when the players became the Molly dancers is vague but it is thought that it originated from the all-male Morris dancers with one man dressed as a woman, the Molly.

Those dragging the plough would cry out 'Penny for the Plough Boys' and anyone who did not oblige them was likely to find a furrow drawn across their lawn the following morning.

Molly dancers gloried in looking disreputable in tasselled hats and wearing hob-nailed boots, as worn by the farm workers, and acted in a riotous (and eventually drunken) manner while making a series of dubious 'dance' steps. They would also blacken their faces with soot for anonymity, to prevent anyone from being recognised by the farmers and land owners who did not take kindly to their workers ploughing up their neighbour's lawns.

Plough Monday has survived into the 21st century (though not as a public holiday) and is celebrated in several parishes including **Rumburgh** where the plough is decorated with white ribbons and dragged to the Buck Inn, accompanied by a display of Molly dances, the toasting of the plough and the ceremonial burning of greenery.

❖ **Lowestoft Porcelain**
The venture of Lowestoft Porcelain lasted from 1756 to 1803 and tradition has it that it began after a shipwreck, when a Dutch vessel founded off the coast. All hands were lost, except one – Van Der Huvel – who was given refuge by Hewlin Lusson at **Gunton Hall**, bought by Lusson in 1749. Lusson's 804-acre estate included farmland, cliffs, springs, watercourses and woods, all of which Van Der Huvel roamed in complete freedom. On his walks he observed the white clay that stuck to his boots and brought it to his host's attention. Lusson sent a clay sample off to a London porcelain firm for analysis and the report came back that it was 'somewhat finer than that called the Delftware'. Almost immediately, he set up an experimental kiln and began to make porcelain, which he hoped would make him his fortune. Tea drinking was becoming fashionable and those who drank it liked to do so out of porcelain teacups. Unfortunately it did not, and in spite of having farming and fishing interests Lusson was declared bankrupt in 1761. He had made the mistake of employing men from the same London firm who had analysed his clay, and production 'was so far tampered with by his workmen that they spoilt the ware and thereby frustrated Mr Lusson's design'. The London firm saw Lusson's porcelain as competition of the highest order and decided to sabotage his efforts.

However, the secret of the white clay was out and a tenant of Lusson, Philip Walker, who was already in business producing glazed and red pantiles, had seen the porcelain experiments on the estate. Since porcelain firing required a different process to that of earthenware tiles and bricks new skills and techniques were required. Walker and Obed Aldred (a local bricklayer) formed a partnership and set up business in **Lowestoft**. Since Walker had access to the clay, his role was key as 'without the raw material that he alone could provide there would be no factory'.

A third partner in the business was Robert Browne, who noted from the first that the enterprise was lacking expertise in how to obtain the right mixture of clay, bone ash and pigmentation. He managed to persuade a workman at the London factory to let him hide in the workshops close to the mixing table, where he spied on the proprietor working alone at night.

Browne returned to Lowestoft with the mixing secrets and production began. The Lowestoft China factory began advertising its wares, 'a great variety of neat Blue and White china', encouraging the local shopkeepers to 'give encouragement to this laudable undertaking, by reserving their spring orders'.

In 1763 they were confident enough to advertise in a London directory using the local dialect style of spelling for the town's name, 'Loestoffe China Warehouse'.

They also produced 'Trifles from Lowestoft', and inscribed birth tablets, which were sold to the fisher folk for a few shillings. The Lowestoft colour and design became a trademark and the porcelain, as well as common household items, such as mugs, sauceboats, jugs and bowls, were all hand painted in under-glaze cobalt oxide blue. Transfer printing came in at the beginning of the 1770s and different colours were introduced.

The demise of Lowestoft porcelain came in the early 1800s and by a stroke of irony its end was hastened by the loss of crate loads of merchandise in a shipwreck off Rotterdam. It had been a Dutchman that had set the whole thing off and it was Holland that hastened its end. As there are no factory records to back up the value of the cargo it is difficult to assess the effects of the disaster, but that, and competition from real bone china, heralded the finish. There is also the possibility that the white clay was running out and there was disagreement between the then partners. Factories in Derby and Worcester continued to produce fine porcelain but the London rivals of the 1760s ceased some 12 years before Lowestoft's demise. In 2000 a new Lowestoft Porcelain factory was established in the town.

❖ **Suffolk Dollies**

The making of a straw **corn dolly** was part of the ritual associated with the last sheaf of corn (in pre-combine harvester days) and was originally a cage woven in wheat straw, about the height of an average hand, which symbolised the capturing of the corn spirit. Most counties had their own particular form of dolly. In Suffolk they were sometimes shaped as a bell, but were generally woven in the shape of a **horseshoe** with either a single straw bunch placed diagonally or two criss-crossed. The plaited dollies were usually hung in the farmhouse until the spring when it was returned to the field so that the corn spirit lived on.

❖ **Trains Run Late to Suffolk**
The age of the train arrived late in Suffolk chiefly because of the vested interests of those who had relied on traditional water and road systems of transport to serve the county's commercial needs. Not only did the estate owners not want their land dissected by the new-fangled rail lines, but the coach drivers, stables and coaching inns were also hostile. The barge owners saw the railways as a threat and it was not until the 1840s that some of the more entrepreneurial men of the county got together to raise some venture capital. The coming of the railways changed the entire structure of Suffolk irrevocably and by the 1840s the county was poised to produce several of the greatest rail engineers and entrepreneurs of the age.

One of the first lines to be opened was at **Lowestoft** due to the industrialist Sir Morton Peto (1809–1889), who was a keen supporter of the railways. Peto used rail to great advantage and was among the first to see its commercial potential. Bricks from the **Somerleyton Brickworks** were used in the building of London's Liverpool Street railway station (1875), the Great Eastern Hotel, Covent Garden Opera House and the Royal Albert Hall. The **Lucas Brothers,** Charles (1820–1895) and Thomas (1822–1902), had the brickworks on a 21-year lease from Sir Morton Peto and with his contacts, and the general surge of Victorian building, the works saw its greatest period of prosperity. In addition to the many London hotels, railways and dock projects, Lucas Brothers built hundreds of properties in the Somerleyton and Lowestoft area including Peto's own residence, Somerleyton Hall, as well as Lowestoft's Esplanade, St John's Church and the railway station.

Once the businessmen of **Ipswich** had seen the possibilities of the new rail links, several banded together to form the Eastern Union

Railway Company and complete the Ipswich to Colchester line, which had faltered due to lack of finance. In 1846 the new line was opened. The Ipswich engineer Peter Bruff, called 'the Brunel of the Eastern Counties', became the man of the hour by undertaking complicated and ambitious engineering projects. Ransomes and Rapier was formed in 1869 as a specialist railway-engineering branch of the mighty Ransomes company and its manufacturing arm soon assumed a superbly successful international role.

The main rail link to **Bury St Edmunds** was opened in 1846 but only after much resistance from the local landowners. Northgate Station was built in 1847 and the line extended to Norwich in 1849.

At **Wickham Market** the railway encountered opposition from a local landowner, as a result of which the rails were laid a mile east of the town and the station built at **Campsea Ashe**. It was not until 2005 that the station finally got a new sign advising passengers that it is Campsea Ashe *for* Wickham Market.

The railway arrived at **Halesworth** in 1854 but the platform was very short and as the trains became longer passengers could only alight from the train at certain points. In 1888 a moveable platform was installed and it is one of only a handful left in England.

The Eastern Union Railway Company set about persuading **Eye** to accommodate the main line through from Stowmarket. The land was staked out for many years but landowners consistently opposed the project. Eventually Eye was connected to **Mellis** by a branch line in 1867. It was the shortest branch line in England and was taken over by the Great Eastern Railway at the end of the 19th century.

❖ **Ipswich Time**

In the 18th century coachmen carried timepieces, which they adjusted as they travelled from east to west. From about the 1790s most towns used local mean time, but with the advent of the railways and, subsequently, telegrams it was found necessary to introduce a 'standard' time into Britain for the first time and **Ipswich Time** ceased. In 1840 the Great Western Railway ordered that London time should be used on all the timetables and Rail Time was instituted.

In 1880 the Statutes (Definition of Time) Bill received the Royal Assent and a standard time was imposed across the whole of Britain.

❖ Before the invention of timepieces in the late 14th century, people told the time by means of public **sundials** that were usually sited on the south wall or buttress of the building at the centre of all community life, the church. H. Munro Cautley writes that there are no fewer than 126 churches in Suffolk that have one or more dials on their walls.

Later, scratch dials became more widely used and were usually circular and inscribed with the divisions of the day shown as radial lines cut at intervals of 15 degrees. A wooden or metal peg was put in a central hole and its shadow marked the time of day. There is a Saxon scratch dial on St Mary and St Laurence **Great Briscett**, which is said to be the oldest timepiece in Suffolk. Above an original Norman door the scratch dial can be seen cut in a large circular stone. It has four deeply incised lines, one of which is marked with a cross, probably to indicate the hour of the parochial mass.

❖ One of the most unusual sundials in the county is found on a gravestone at St John the Baptist **Saxmundham**. The stone of John Noller (died 1725) has small, oblong recesses on the east and west faces. A shadow cast by the top edge falls on parallel hour lines engraved inside.

❖ At St Mary's **Horham** the scratch dial is incised on a square slab and has Roman numerals cut into the lower part.

❖ **Open Crabbing**
Each summer the **British Open Crabbing Championship** is held at **Walberswick** and is organised by the British Crabbing Federation. Competitors come from near and far and in 2003 a record 728 entrants took part. Up to 3,000 spectators are on hand to witness the event, lining both sides of the Blyth estuary.

For 90 minutes each competitor, armed only with a single line and own-choice bait, catches and lands the non-edible river crabs. The entrants then select the most suitable crab in their catch to be weighed, returning all others to the water. All the crabs have to be kept in a bucket of water at all times and the winner is the single heaviest crab. A fine of £10 is levied against anyone falling in the water and frightening the crabs!

Competition is intense and the best-kept secret of the day is the recipe for the perfect bait. The £1 entry fee is donated to different charities each year and in 2006 the championship celebrated its 25th birthday. The BBC *Country File* team were on hand to record events and Ben Fogle presented the awards.

There are gold, silver and bronze winners for the three heaviest crabs, which vary year to year. In 1981 the record was set at 7.35oz but in 2001 the winning crab was a disappointing 4oz.

❖ **The Suffolk Chair**
The **Suffolk Chair** has a thin wooden curved seat set on a stool frame (which can be elm, oak or mahogany) and is characterised by the design of the back, which has small wooden bobbins set between the horizontal rails. It has a square look and is described as a 'vernacular type' having evolved over the years in the workshops of Suffolk craftsmen. The back design of horizontal lathes with three bobbins is more commonly associated with the Suffolk Chair while the Norfolk version has upright lathes and no bobbins.

The seat is usually only ¼in (6–7mm) thick but nowadays is invariably strengthened by an extra strut underneath. The seat was adequate when oil lamps and candles lighted rooms but when electric light arrived the seats began to fail because people stood on them to change the lightbulbs!

❖ **The Mendlesham Chair**
A more familiar and better established evolution of the Suffolk Chair is the **Mendlesham Chair**, which is a chair with a solid wooden seat, where the back legs stop at the seat and do not continue to form the back. The back is a separate construction built up from the seat, thus making it a Windsor chair.

The creation of the Mendlesham chair is attributed to a local wheelwright, Daniel Day, and his son, Richard, in their Front Street workshop in the village of **Mendlesham** between 1780 and 1820. Daniel was an admirer of Sheraton, in whose workshop he is said to have trained. For many years there were two Mendlesham chairs made by Daniel Day beside the altar in the parish church. These were stolen but have been replaced by two made to commemorate the Millennium.

A feature of the Mendlesham is its very inclined back, which means the user does not tip it backwards, and there is a 'window' at the base of the back frame. The seat is a solid hardwood, usually elm, and fruitwoods, such as cherry, apple or pear, are used for the frame. Complete chairs can be made in a single fruitwood, such as walnut. A feature of all the fruitwoods is that they are light in weight yet dense and strong. Inlaid lining of boxwood also occurs on some back frames.

The **Mendlesham** village sign depicts a Mendlesham chair on its reverse side.

❖ **Finewood Chairs**
There is one firm still making Mendlesham chairs largely by hand, **Finewood of Rendham**. Founded by Albert and Sheila Lain in the mid-1960s the small firm manages to produce around a hundred Mendleshams a year, each one taking about 50 hours to complete. Albert's small team have moved the design on, in that the proportions of each chair are made to the customer's requirements, i.e. height, depth and width of seat. Also, from their experience with restoring originals, where they have noticed carved messages and initials under the seat, they have continued to offer this personalisation and have carved coats of arms, family and military crests, pets, birds, boats and buildings. They are the first workshop to put the Mendlesham style on rockers.

Finewood has a philanthropic approach to business and regularly donates special chairs for charity. In 2002 the Queen and the Duke of Edinburgh included **Bury St Edmunds** in their Golden Jubilee tour and after lunch attended a 'Proms in the Park' concert, during which they sat on two chairs made to the Mendlesham design by Finewood. The Queen's chair had a carving under the seat of two Suffolk Punch horses pulling a plough and the logo of the Royal Agricultural Benevolent Institution, of which the Queen is patron. The chair was afterwards raffled to raise funds for the Institution.

Millennium gifts included a chair to each of the churches in Albert and Sheila's local Upper Alde Benefice (**Badingham, Bruisyard, Cransford, Rendham** and **Sweffling**). In 2006 the team presented a commemorative Mendlesham chair to the Queen on her 80th birthday, which was installed in Windsor Castle until she decides how it might be used to raise money for charity.

❖ **Founding of Modern America**
In 2007 **Finewood** was commissioned to make a high-back

Mendlesham chair for the Queen to take across to Virginia as a gift to mark the 400th anniversary of the landing of **Bartholomew Gosnold** from **Otley** at what became Jamestown (James I granted a charter to the Virginia Company to establish the first colony). The Suffolk emigrants played an important role in the events of 1607 when the English settlement in North America was founded. This is considered to mark the beginning of free enterprise in America because shares of stock were sold by the Virginia Company of London to those investing in the New World. Settlers produced goods such as glassware and also cash crops, the profits going to the shareholders, and Virginian Lotteries were set up in London to raise cash for the settlement. Gosnold is now acknowledged as the 'prime mover of the colonization of Virginia'.

TEN – MISCELLANY

❖ **Bloody Mary at Framlingham**

In July 1553 Princess Mary Tudor heard that her brother Edward VI had died. As the eldest daughter of their father, Henry VIII, she had to act quickly if she was to claim the throne. She knew she had a rival in the 15-year-old Lady Jane Grey, granddaughter of Mary, Duchess of Suffolk (Henry VIII's sister), who lived at **Westhorpe** near **Bury St Edmunds**, and whom Edward had declared his heir. Princess Mary was, by chance, staying with the Catholic Dukes of Norfolk at Kenninghall (just over the border in Norfolk) and she set out for **Framlingham Castle**, which was closer to the coast should her claim fail and a quick exit from England became necessary. Also, the castle could prove useful if she was forced to stand her ground. However, loyal followers met her at Framlingham and she began to assemble her forces for a march on London. Although Mary was Catholic and Lady Jane Grey a Protestant, the country at large thought Mary had the truer claim to the throne and the East Anglian nobility and gentry flocked to Framlingham to join her and show support.

On her arrival in Framlingham a figure of Christ was carried in procession through the market square and into the chapel of Framlingham Castle.

Hearing that Princess Mary was marshalling her followers in Suffolk, the Government sent ships to stamp out the 'rebellion', but they fell foul of storms off the coast and were forced into the Orwell estuary. There the crews heard of the strong support for Mary and mutinied in favour of her and against Lady Jane Grey, whose nine-day reign ended with her execution.

Mary left Framlingham on 24 July and, after spending the night in **Ipswich** at the home of Sir Robert Wingfield, she travelled through Essex to London where she was proclaimed queen.

After a short time many of those who had attended her at Framlingham were regretting it when Mary began her cruel persecution of the Protestant 'heretics', which gained her the nickname of 'Bloody Mary'.

❖ **Melton's Tudor Martyrs**

In November 1558, Alice Driver and Alexander Gouche of **Melton** were both burned at **Ipswich** as heretics in the terrible days of Mary Tudor's reign. They tried to hide from the soldiers in a haystack but were found and poked out with pitchforks. Both were tried and found guilty. When Alice compared Queen Mary to Jezebel, the judge ordered that her ears be cut off there and then.

They were taken from Melton gaol and led to the fire singing Psalms. They are mentioned in John Foxe's *Book of Martyrs*, 'Alexander Gouche and Alice Driuer, 4 November 1558. Brought from Melton gaol at seven in the morning beyng in their prayers, and singying of Psalmes'.

❖ **A Queen in Progress**
In 1561, Elizabeth I made what was called a 'progress' in Suffolk, visiting **Ipswich, Helmingham** and **Small Bridges (Bures)**. In Ipswich she made disparaging remarks about the appalling state of the town's streets and, being preoccupied with the issue of married clerics (of which she disapproved), she expressed great displeasure at what she called the slackness of the local clergy. However, she came again in 1578 and was 'magnificently entertained', everyone presumably hoping to erase the memory of the earlier visit, which had not been a success. On entering the county she was received by '200 young gentlemen clad in white velvet, 300 in black and 1500 attendants on horseback under the High Sheriff'. She visited **Lawshall, Bury St Edmunds, Euston** and **Hengrave**.

So royally was she treated that in August of the following year, 1579, she again visited **Ipswich** and stayed for four days.

❖ It is believed that **Freston Tower**, on the south bank of the **River Orwell**, was built to coincide with Elizabeth I's visit to **Ipswich** in August 1579. It is likely that Thomas Gooding, a wealthy Ipswich merchant, decided to build the tower (construction began in 1578 and was completed the following year in time for the royal progress) so that it was visible from the river. If all the queen could see was the very impressive tower, there was no need for her to know that it was free standing and not attached to a similarly grand mansion or hall. As a cost-cutting measure, or perhaps to save on construction time, the first three storeys on the south side (not visible from the river) are windowless. There are 26 windows in all and a further seven blind ones.

The red-brick tower was not designed to be lived in, as there are no fireplaces and only one small room on each of the six floors that leads off the spiral staircase. There is a viewing platform at the top that affords spectacular views over the river and Thomas Gooding might well have hung banners of welcome to Her Majesty from the arcaded parapet.

The tower fell into decay in the 17th century but was rescued by another Ipswich merchant, John Wright, who saved it from ruin and probably lived in the adjacent Tower House.

❖ In 1765, Robert Sutton advertised in the *Ipswich Journal* that he was conducting smallpox inoculation trials and had hired **Freston Tower House** 'for the reception of persons who are disposed to be inoculated'. He was inspired by the work of Dr William Beeston (1671–1731) of **Ipswich** who had whipped up a storm of protest in the town when he first championed inoculation. When, in 1724, he inoculated three people, he was subjected to vociferous protest from those who believed that far from preventing the onset of disease (especially the dreaded plague) it actually caused it. In reply, Dr Beeston suggested that his accusers, whom he called 'the bigoted high Churchmen' and 'Dissenters', should use their reason. His accusers, however, sentenced to 'damnation' all those who were concerned with the 'heathenish' practice of inoculation.

It would seem that the Freston trials were looked on more benignly. Those attending were required to provide their own tea and sugar and were charged between three and six guineas a week. By 1771 the house had become an inoculation centre 'with opportunities for fishing, fowling, etc...boats and nets provided'.

❖ Romantic legends inevitably grew up around **Freston Tower** and one of the favourites is that the beautiful Ellen de Freston used it for her studies, a different subject on each floor – tapestry, music, painting and literature culminating in astronomy on the viewing platform.

Ellen de Freston is also said to have entertained her suitors on different floors, depending on their eligibility and, presumably, their athleticism.

❖ **The Sport of Kings**
From early in the 17th century onwards **Newmarket** was known as the centre of horse racing, and home to the Jockey Club

headquarters. Charles I took a particular interest in horse racing and by 1627 regular spring and autumn meetings were being held. Unsurprisingly, Cromwell put an interdict on race meetings during the Commonwealth Government, which were gleefully revived at the Restoration in 1660.

❖ Charles II was as enthusiastic a follower of horse racing as was his father, and the **Rowley Mile** racecourse at **Newmarket** is named in his honour. It derived from the King's nickname, which he earned from his hack, Old Rowley.

❖ In 1683 over half of **Newmarket** town was engulfed by a terrible inferno but it was credited with saving the life of Charles II. On the evening of 22 March the King and his brother James, Duke of York, who had been at the races during the day, were planning to spend the night in Newmarket. However, at about nine o'clock a great fire broke out in a stable yard 'near the little stone bridge near the market-place'. High winds fanned the flames and before long the town was ablaze, with almost half the buildings destroyed and the rest badly affected by smoke. The evening's entertainment was cancelled and the royal party decided to return early to London, thereby foiling the Rye House Plot, a plot to assassinate the King and his brother, both of whose whereabouts on certain days in the racing calendar were normally assured.

Around 100 men were supposed to have been concealed at Rye House, a manor house in Hertfordshire, and were to have ambushed the King on his way back from Newmarket on 23 March. Instead, it was they who were ambushed as, once news of the plot leaked out, several arrests were made and the King declared himself 'preserved' from his enemies because of the Newmarket fire.

Historians have suggested that the plot (and even the fire) might have been manufactured by Charles himself as a means of removing a number of strong political enemies from the arena. Others, though, doubted that the King would have done anything that would have resulted in the loss of a day's racing.

❖ **Whoops!**
The large expanse of common land at **Mellis** was used for an enormous muster in April 1644. During the troubled years of the Civil War, Parliament ordered that men should be trained in archery

and battle skills at local level. Practice was clearly required as five men were accidentally shot during the muster. One of them was 'Edward Gibes of **Thrandeston**' who was 'slayne at a muster, being shot through the bowels'. Another, of **Wortham**, was shot in the thighs and three others were 'shot through theyre clothes'.

❖ The two-mile long common at **Mellis** is the largest grazing common in Suffolk. It covers 174 acres (64.4 hectares) and since 1989 has been managed by the Suffolk Wildlife Trust. During World War Two it was cultivated to produce grain and potatoes but returned to grassland at the end of the war.

❖ **The Making of a President**
Hengrave Hall, a few miles outside **Bury St Edmunds**, was built between 1525 and 1538 by one of the wealthiest merchants in Henry VIII's time, Sir Thomas Kytson. Sir Thomas's sister, Margaret (born 1479) married John Washington of Virginia, and was the direct ancestor of the first President of the United States, George Erskine Washington, who took the oath of office on 30 April 1789. When it was built, Hengrave Hall was the largest house in Suffolk with 51 hearths.

❖ Lawrence Washington, half brother of America's first President, served in **Admiral Edward Vernon**'s Expedition against the Spaniards in the 1740s. His admiration for Vernon (known as 'Old Grogram', see Chapter Six, Why is it called that?) was so great that when he inherited an estate at Hunting Creek near the Potomac River, he renamed it Mount Vernon in honour of the Suffolk Admiral under whom he served. Mount Vernon became the Washington family home.

❖ In 1996 a single sheet of paper, with handwriting on both sides, was identified as the work of the American President, George Washington. It was found in an album during a routine probate valuation of books at a house in **Aldeburgh** after the death of a descendant of Sir Thomas Lyell, a geologist who had visited America in the 1840s and was given the page as a souvenir. It was found by accident as the valuer was being shown round the house by the gardener, who noticed it protruding from under a sofa. It is thought to be a missing fragment of the speech Washington intended to give at his inauguration but, in the event, did not. In the draft speech, which originally contained 62 pages, he had distilled his vision of the newly independent country and hoped that it might become a great power. 'The New World is now becoming a stage for wonderful exhibitions' he wrote. Only 13 other leaves of the original speech have come to light over the 200 years since it was first written.

❖ Ancestors of another American President, James A. Garfield (1831–1881) came from Suffolk. The Warrens (from **Nayland**) and the Bigelows (from **Framlingham** and **Wrentham**) were among the original settlers of Massachusetts Bay. New Street Farm on the outskirts of Framlingham is celebrated as the home of one of the Bigelows. President Garfield was the second president to be assassinated, being shot after only six months in office.

❖ **Mulberry Trees**

The mulberry tree growing in the garden of Gainsborough's House, **Sudbury**, was planted early in the 17th century and would have been quite a small tree when the artist, Thomas Gainsborough, lived there (see also Chapter Seven, Writers and Artists). In 1607, James I became very envious of the emerging silk industry of Continental Europe and ordered that mulberry trees be planted to encourage a similar industry in Britain without the need to import the raw material. Landowners were sent mulberry tree seeds and silkworm larvae in the hope that home silk production could begin. The plan failed, chiefly because the mulberry trees took some time to establish and were not those that the silkworms liked. Consequently, they produced little or no silk and imports were still required. However, some trees still survive in Suffolk from that date and there are several public houses that are named after the trees, including the Mulberry Tree in **Ipswich** (now the Milestone Beer House), which opened in 1930 replacing a much older Mulberry Tree Inn. Mulberry House at **Pakenham**, Mulberry Hall at **Burstall** and Mulberry Tree Farm at **Stowmarket** (now a bed and breakfast establishment) all take their name from the trees. A black mulberry is to be found behind a brick wall at **Melford Hall**.

❖ **Historic Silk Mills**

Towards the end of the 18th century, London silk manufacturers chose East Anglia as a place to set up production because of its relative proximity to the capital and skills left over from the by then declining woollen industry. Also, the **Sudbury** area in particular was traditionally renowned for silk production and there is some evidence to suggest that thread and needlewomen from **Glemsford** were involved in the execution of the Bayeux Tapestry in 1067.

Sudbury, Haverhill and **Glemsford** were the main centres of migration for the London silk manufacturers. Initially only the hand loom weavers arrived but after the duty on raw silk was removed in 1824, these were followed by companies setting up throwsting mills at **Hadleigh, Nayland** and **Glemsford**. These mills processed the raw silk by steeping, winding, doubling and twisting to prepare the silk in hanks for the dyers. The workers who wound and thickened the thread were known as throwsters.

By 1840 over 465 workers were employed in the silk mills in the Sudbury area, 217 of them under the age of 13 and the rest nearly all under 19. A few remained in the factory after that age but, as their wages were not increased beyond 19, there were almost no workers over 20. The greatest numbers employed in the silk industry in Suffolk were reached in the mid-19th century when weavers and throwsters totalled some 2,000.

The silk industry originated in China and raw silk is still imported from China and Japan in bales. The mills at Hadleigh and Nayland ceased work towards the end of 1860 but the one at Glemsford has survived into the 21st century.

❖ **Silk Weavers for Nine Generations**
Thread from the **Glemsford Silk Mills** has found its way round the world and into many famous places, including the Royal Palaces of England, the White House in Washington DC, No. 10 Downing Street and Brighton's Royal Pavilion. Glemsford silk was woven into Queen Elizabeth II's coronation dress, investiture robes for the Prince of Wales, and the wedding dresses of the Princesses Anne and Diana.

The machinery in the Glemsford Mill was first driven by a water wheel, the original wooden one being replaced by an iron one in the 19th century. Water from nearby springs was piped under Brook Street into a large pond (now filled in) on the north side of Chequers Lane. Between 1895 and 1905 power looms were gradually introduced and in 1936 electricity took over from the water wheel.

Stephen Walters & Sons, owners of the Glemsford Mill, was founded in Spitalfields, London in the 1720s by Joseph Walters, a

Huguenot artisan. The company moved to Sudbury in 1894. Nine generations of what is still a family business have been silk weavers.

❖ **On the Tread Mill!**
In 1817 the engineer **Sir William Cubitt** (1785–1861) was employed by Ransomes, the principal iron-founding firm in **Ipswich**, when he was asked by the local magistrates to devise a suitable deterrent in an effort to reduce the huge number of criminals coming before them. There had been widespread riots in Suffolk the previous year, caused largely by hunger. Sir William came up with a huge revolving cylinder made from iron and wood, with steps like the slats of a paddle wheel. He called it the 'tread wheel' and it was common practice for people visiting prisons to observe inmates taking up to 50 laborious steps a minute to turn the wheel. Sometimes it was used to grind corn (hence its popular name 'tread mill'), or raise water (to tread water), but mostly the wheel was described by its critics as a 'the most tiresome, distressing, exemplary punishment that has ever been contrived by human ingenuity'. Prisoners were sometimes mangled in the machinery and, in some prisons, pregnant women and old men with hernias were forced onto the tread mill.

In 1819, a tread mill was installed at **Bury St Edmunds** gaol and another in the newly constructed **Ipswich** gaol, which was built according to the recommendations of the philanthropist and penal reformer, John Howard (1726–1790).

Not all of Sir William's brainwaves were so dire, however. He also invented, and patented in 1807, what became the standard design for self-regulating windmill sails, which were used for many years in windmills across East Anglia.

He also engineered the Norwich & **Lowestoft** Navigation system and designed the town's dock schemes.

❖ **The Bulcamp Riots**
In the 1760s there were some in the **Blything Hundred** who were not entirely pleased to see a Poor House, or House of Industry, erected for the benefit of the poor and destitute at **Bulcamp** near **Blythburgh**. In 1764 an Act was passed requiring the Blything Hundred to provide for the maintenance of the poor in all its 49 parishes. In common with other such authorities, the newly appointed board decided to erect a purpose-built establishment.

However, the squalid and degrading conditions of the existing poor houses, and the low status of the inmates (from 1697 the poor had been required by law to wear badges) made the building of a new one so unpopular that even before it was completed it was partly destroyed by a riotous mob, which had to be dispersed by the military.

In August 1765 the *London Magazine* reported that 'some thousand persons' were assembled at **Saxmundham** and **Yoxford** and had attempted to destroy the building known as the Industry House. 'The reason they gave for such riotous proceedings', continued the report, 'is, that the number of hands now employed in harvest work is not sufficient to do the business, and that the poor should be allowed to work in the fields'.

The tumult ended disastrously for the rioters. A party of soldiers was sent from **Ipswich** and used force to quell the disturbance, killing one man and arresting six. This was not the only place where such riots were occurring, as on the same day as the Bulcamp Riot, a similar affray took place at **Nacton**, where a mob threatened to pull down the House of Industry there, but were prevented by a party of soldiers. Damage was estimated at £509.

Despite this the Bulcamp House opened on 13 October 1766 when 56 paupers were admitted. By April 1767 there were 352 inmates and, for the time being, no more serious riots. The Rules and Regulations were numerous, but a notice was published which, it was hoped, would encourage people to see the House in a positive light. Feather beds would be provided for the inmates, married couples could remain in the same room and 'instead of the filthy and nastiness of all kinds to be met with in all or most of the town Houses, the poor in the said house will be kept clean and neat'.

As a precaution against further trouble a guard was appointed who was stationed at the house in a specially constructed guardroom. A fire and candle were to be provided plus one shilling a night. However, shortly afterwards a complaint was made that an inspection by the contractor revealed the guardroom shut up and no soldier on duty. The Commanding Officer at **Halesworth** was notified and a new guard appointed.

In 1834 Parliament made sweeping changes to the Poor Law. The old Bulcamp administration was dissolved and a new body called the Directors and Acting Guardians appointed. Drastic changes were made to the regime, among them a new classification of the inmates. The newly appointed Guardians also decided that alterations should take place to the building, by then called the Union Workhouse, which led to more riots. In December 1835 it was reported to the Guardians that 'a considerable body of men, armed with pickaxes, crowbars and other implements of destruction, were advancing in different directions to attack the Workhouse'.

The High Constable was requested to provide 100 staves for the use of constables who were assembled at the Workhouse. A message was received from the Commandant of the Coast Guard who placed the Preventive men at their disposal and that, if required, he would personally attend. The Preventive forces were used to dealing with armed and mutinous smugglers and the Commandant himself was said to be 'a rough and ready sailor', and 'one who would take a Bear by the Beard with little ceremony'.

All churchwardens in the Hundred were advised by the Union that they were required to notify them immediately 'by a messenger on horseback' if there were any 'suspicious Assemblages' in their area so that the constables were forewarned of numbers.

Although there were minor affrays, such as windows being broken and disorderly behaviour, there were no more serious riots at Bulcamp. However, the 100 staves did not go to waste as the High Constable later appropriated them for the special constables for two days of the parliamentary election in 1837.

❖ **Victorian Feats**

In the Victorian era great feats or unusual physical achievements fascinated people, as did records being set or broken, and any such proposed undertakings were attended with relish and in considerable numbers. The crowds followed the enactment of publicly announced wagers assiduously. The outcome was taken very seriously, especially if it turned out that fraud was involved. The *Ipswich Journal* even ran a column called *Extraordinary Frauds*. People who had been cheated of their money would make their feelings quite clear on the matter.

❖ **The Suffolk Wonder**

On 30 December 1843, the *Ipswich Journal* reported that on the previous Tuesday a great number of people assembled at **Whitton** to witness an extraordinary feat by **Swift the Suffolk Wonder**, who 'for a wager of 20 sovereigns engaged to pick up one hundred stones placed one yard apart, and bring each stone back to the starting post, and walk two miles, all within an hour'.

Swift won with two and a half minutes to spare. Shortly afterwards he was off again and walked seven miles in 56 minutes to the wonderment of his supporters.

❖ **Don the Diver**
On 10 July 1848 the **Ipswich** newspapers declared that 'a most extraordinary feat of diving on record was accomplished here on Monday by William Portuge, better known as **Don the Diver'**. Handbills were distributed saying that this 'intrepid fellow would walk under water from Harwich [in Essex] across the harbour to Shotley Gate'.

Since this was clearly a feat too far, many treated the announcement as a hoax. It was considered an impossible undertaking for anyone to engage in, notwithstanding 'the celebrated feats he had previously performed'.

However, at 12 o'clock on the appointed day, Don the Diver was at his post, suitably equipped for the trip, wearing 'improved air apparatus' provided by Messrs Lewis in the town. It was blowing quite a breeze as he was lowered into the water from a boat and to the astonishment of hundreds of spectators proceeded on his perilous journey. Numerous boatloads of the curious who wanted to witness his emergence on the Suffolk side sailed over his path and, noted the *Ipswich Journal*, the hundreds of spectators would have been thousands but for the doubts that such a thing was possible.

Don the Diver arrived at his destination at 20 minutes past one and was loudly cheered by a large assemblage. Heartened by such support, Don announced his intention to walk under water again, this time from **Languard Point** to Harwich.

❖ **James 'Jim' Smith, Veteran Pedestrian**
In February 1866 an 'extraordinary feat of strength and endurance' took place when **Jim Smith**, the veteran pedestrian, started on 'one of the most remarkable instances of human endurance on record'. He undertook, for a wager of £10, to walk from St Matthew's Fleece Inn, **Ipswich**, to the Bull Inn, Aldgate, a distance of 138 miles, in 36 hours.

He started at six in the morning 'in his old rattling style' and reached Colchester just before nine o'clock. He reached London around 12 hours later, thus performing one half of his task in 15 hours. He stopped for one hour and then set off back to Ipswich. Without stopping for food, Jim reached Ipswich on Tuesday afternoon with two hours and twenty minutes to spare. His arrival excited great interest and a crowd numbering some thousands thronged St Matthew's.

Although he won his £10, Jim was utterly exhausted by the ordeal and, noted the newspaper, it was all the more commendable when it was considered that he would be 50 years old in August. However, having spent the Wednesday in bed he was out and about on the Thursday, going for a walk 'as usual'.

❖ **The Suffolk Stag**
Not to be outdone by Jim Smith, on 26 September 1866, W. Ranson – known as the **Suffolk Stag** – walked from **Ipswich** to London and back in 35 hours and 43 minutes.

❖ **Starvation Attempt**
Mary Elizabeth Squirrel was born at **Shottisham** in 1838, the daughter of an Ipswich tea dealer, Asaph Squirrel. Her grandfather had been Baptist minister for 38 years at **Sutton** and Mary attended **Hollesley** village school. For reasons best known to herself, Mary announced that she would abstain from food and drink for a period of 153 days. Pamphlets were written about this potentially extraordinary feat and, on the strength of her fame, some of Mary's poems were published. Predictably the starvation attempt was exposed as a fraud and in 1852 the family were forced to leave Shottisham and move to Ipswich.

❖ **Walking on Water**
On 20 October 1859, handbills were distributed in **Ipswich** announcing that 'at two o'clock on Tuesday afternoon Mr E.J. Maitland of Worcester would walk over the River Orwell from Stoke Bridge to the Griffin Inn and back. Naturally thousands of spectators made their way to Stoke Bridge hoping to see the 'marvellous performance'. They lined the banks of the river, stood on the tops of houses, the ends of cranes, rigging of ships in the dock and in small river boats, all hoping for a good view of Mr Maitland.

A patient public waited until late in the afternoon when it was apparent that the whole thing was a hoax. As it turned out, it was not so much a hoax as a wager as Mr Maitland had taken a bet that he could draw a certain number to the riverside. His 'walking on the water' story won him his bet.

❖ **Dr Ormonde's Feat Exposed**

In 1896 the hypnotist, magician and author Dr Ormonde (1841–1902) visited **Ipswich** and invited a sceptical public to witness his extraordinary mind-reading abilities. Dr Ormonde (real name Andrew Ormond) operated a successful road show and had at one time been an assistant to the famous magician, Signor Blitz. Among the audience was the Revd Thomas I. Jarrott of Berners Street, who attended with the express intention of exposing Dr Ormonde as a fraud. Unfortunately, his attendance at the Hypnotic Trance Vision meeting backfired on him when, after a heated and entertaining exchange with Dr Ormonde, Jarrott was later accused of being part of the act. He wrote to the *East Anglian Daily Times* saying that he had indeed attended the Ormonde meeting, since when he had been inundated with requests to say 'how the thing was done'. This he would do at a special meeting held at the Ipswich Lecture Hall.

The Hall was packed to hear the Revd Jarrott 'offer criticism on Dr Ormonde' and the feat of mind-reading by the use of a medium. The *Ipswich Journal* declared that it was 'crowded, as it has rarely been, and a throng of people turned away'. Jarrott opened by saying that he had been accused of being part of the act but assured his audience that he had not made a penny out of the proceedings. Another young man had also been accused of participating in Dr Ormonde's fraud by writing down his answers, though Jarrott had no information on this. He said he had tested Dr Ormonde by asking him questions about himself, such as 'What event of importance happened to me in the month of July 1890?' Jarrott revealed that he had been very ill and 'nigh unto death' but Dr Ormonde said he thought the Reverend might be in league with 'the evil one'.

Jarrott then asked 'What number of marks did I obtain at my last examination?' Amid much arm waving, Dr Ormonde again declared that Jarrott had in him 'the spirit of the devil' and was, indeed, 'a devil'.

Jarrott said that in his book Dr Ormonde stated that the four prerequisites for a hypnotist were gentleness, will, patience and persistence, but to the amusement of his audience, he said that Dr Ormonde had apparently left his gentleness behind.

As to the question of mind-reading, Jarrott said he thought that the explanation was that there was 'someone behind the curtain and speaking into a tube put into the hypnotist's ear'. This was greeted with hearty laughter and an enthusiastic vote of thanks was given to the Revd Jarrott.

❖ **Suffolk's Oldest House**
Little Wenham Hall is the oldest house in Suffolk and has the earliest post-Roman brickwork in the county. It was built around 1270 by the de Holebroke family and was an example of a non-fortified manor house with a castellated appearance, although much of the original manor house was dismantled and rebuilt in the 16th century. The lower courses are of flint and septaria but the remainder is constructed with new bricks, not recycled Roman ones. The great hall is 40ft long, with a Tudor recess and deep-seated window, and was formerly approached by a circular staircase in the wall. Here also is found a rare reference to St Petronilla, whose namesake Petronilla de Nerford (née Holebroke) inherited the manor in 1287 (see also Chapter Three, Churches and Chapels).

❖ **William Worby Moves House**
In 1837 the **Ipswich** engineering firm of Ransome and May was doing so well that the works manager, **William Worby**, was summoned into the Old Foundry Road office. He was told that the firm needed to expand as they were finding the old premises cramped and inadequate for the increased production. Worby was charged with finding a suitable site for a new foundry, which he did down by the River Orwell. The construction of the Orwell Iron Works duly got under way, with William Worby directing operations.

There was, however, a two-storey brick house on the new site that William Worby decided should be kept, but it was in the wrong place. It needed to be about 70ft to the right, so as to fit in with the overall site plan. Not a man to be daunted (and presumably not wishing to waste a perfectly good house) he decided that he would simply move it. Being an engineer he worked out how it could be done by the means of well-greased timbers, three bottle-jack screws and a very careful work force. A series of holes, six inches square, were made through the brickwork at ground level through which cantilevers were inserted (wooden timbers about four feet long). The earth, inside and out, was cleared away and, as a precautionary measure, the sides of the house were bound by means of stout planks run up at an angle and fastened together with iron rods. The house was raised up almost three feet and longitudinal timbers slid underneath. It took some time for this to be accomplished as the men were only allowed to work on it when they 'had nothing else to engage them'.

The foundations were cleared, and new ones prepared, and with the house resting on its timbers they were ready to go. Inch by inch the house was eased over the greased timbers, one foot every five minutes. After each move the screws had to be re-fixed and not more than 25ft could be accomplished in a day. Extraordinarily, the endeavour was completed over three days and declared a total success. The house was lowered onto its new foundations 'without sustaining the slightest crack in the walls or ceilings, or even in the papering of the rooms'. The house, declared Mr Worby, was 'none the worse for the experiment to which it has been subjected.'

Completion of the firm's move to the Orwell Works took place later that year and the partners gave a huge party for over 1,500 guests.

❖   Encouraged by the success of the house moving operations, one of the partners at Ransomes, **Charles May** (1801–1860) caused something of a stir in **Ipswich** when he purchased a fully grown tree from the garden of the late Dykes Alexander in London Road and decided to move it to his own house in Bolton Lane (a distance of about a mile). In 1850 the *Ipswich Express* stated that the people of Ipswich 'have wheeled away houses and within the last few days they have applied their moving propensities to a large standard apricot tree'. The tree which Mr Alexander had planted in his garden 56 years earlier, had 'for half a century produced a large crop of roseate and juicy fruit'.

A trench was dug round the trunk, forming a circumference of about 27ft and a ring of stakes was made, all then firmly hooped and screwed together. Planks were then placed under the roots and a 'good strong bottom' was formed. The earth alone weighed around five tons. The girth of the tree was 37in and the circumference of the branches was at least 100ft.

Somehow the tree was levered over the wall of Mr Alexander's garden and on to a wagon. Five powerful horses drew this unusual load through the streets of Ipswich, passing down St Matthew's where the branches frequently swept the fronts of the houses. When the procession arrived at 'the weighting machine' opposite St Margaret's Church an overhead steelyard had to be removed, but eventually the tree arrived at Mr May's house, where it was lowered into the huge hole dug in his garden. 'It is now,' stated the *Ipswich Express* 'together with its old soil, one of the chief and most valuable ornaments of that gent's beautiful grounds.'

Charles May's father, writing to his granddaughter, declared that the operation was 'accomplished without any accident except breaking a window or two…it is planted in sight of the dining room window and will look very nice if it grows'.

Unfortunately the May family left Ipswich the following year, so if the tree survived someone else had the benefit of it.

❖ In 1972 the 200-year-old **Ballingdon Hall** was moved 200 yards up the hill to accommodate improvements to the A131 and the expansion of the Lime Grove Estate. It was also claimed that the owners wanted a better view from their upstairs windows, but if that was the case it failed, since the new site faces north and overlooks nothing more exciting than rooftops. However, for whatever reason, in an impressive display of civil engineering the entire house was raised on a giant wheeled frame, an operation that attracted some 50,000 spectators over the 52 days it took to complete the removal.

Sir Thomas Eden built the Hall around 1593 in what was then the village of **Ballingdon-cum-Brundon** and what is now a suburb of **Sudbury**. It is said that in the 16th century, three evergreen trees once grew on the front lawn of Ballingdon Hall, planted in the shape of a triangle so that any monks who were being pursued by enemies, or were in any kind of danger, might know that they would find sanctuary there.

Among the many film crews in attendance was one from *Blue Peter*, and on hand to witness proceedings was John Noakes (though minus his dog, Shep), which brought an added thrill for the many children who came to watch.

❖ Mustard Pot Cottage, a tiny thatched building, was moved from **Mendlesham** to **Bosmere Mill** (on the outskirts of **Needham**

Market) in the 1970s. The **Stonham Parva** sign bearing a magpie (which stretched the width of the A140) had to be temporarily moved to accommodate its passage. The cottage is now a veterinary surgery and Bosmere Mill has been converted into flats.

❖ The Anchor Inn at **Walberswick** is relatively new and the former inn, which stood in front of the present building, was taken down brick by brick and moved to a position further up The Street in 1927.

❖ In the 19th century it was not unknown for whole windmills to be moved from one site to another. In 1840 the post mill at **Wingfield** was moved to **Syleham** and in 1845 the mill standing on the castle mound at **Eye** was removed to **Cranley**. A smock mill that stood at **Cransford** was re-erected at **Peasenhall**.

❖ **Earthquake!**
On 22 April 1844 the Great English Earthquake occurred, which damaged countless properties in settlements south of **Ipswich** and in the town itself. It was estimated to have been 5.2 on the Richter Scale and lasted for about 20 seconds. The earthquake fault line started in France, crossed the Channel and struck Suffolk and Essex, dying out near **Framlingham**. In **Sudbury**, the earth's movement shook mourners leaving a memorial service at St Peter's Church and afterwards the reservoir was found to be leaking.

❖ **A Family Firm**
Abbott's shop at **Debenham** belongs to one of the oldest surviving family firms in Suffolk. It began life in the 1650s by supplying linen to Cromwell's Commonwealth army and Thomas Abbott later purchased the Green Dragon Inn, where he set up a secondary business as a cordwainer (shoemakers who used Cordovan Spanish leather). By 1707 the family were able to expand into tailoring and drapery, then into supplying fuel for lighting, cooking and heating, finally opening as a general stores offering grocery and household provisions. Henry Abbott of Chancery Lane, Debenham, sells everything from coal to cucumbers and is still run by members of the Abbott family.

❖ **The Mildenhall Air Race**
The 1934 MacRobertson England to Australia Air Race started

from Beck Row aerodrome, **Mildenhall**, and was held in celebration of the foundation of the Australian state of Victoria. The aerodrome had only been opened four days previously, on 16 October 1934, and the runways and hangars were loaned to the Royal Aero Club for the occasion. There were 21 contestants (of the original 64 entrants) in the 12,000-mile race and the prize fund was a magnificent £15,000. Competitors came from England, Holland, America, Australia, New Zealand, New Guinea and Denmark.

The day before take off there were two impromptu royal visits. The Prince of Wales arrived at the aerodrome early in the afternoon and King George and Queen Mary arrived later at about 4pm. They watched final preparations, which had started a week earlier. A post office was set up in one of the hangars and special covers issued, some signed by the pilots. The postmaster was also called upon to witness a number of hurriedly drawn up wills. 70,000 sightseers started arriving at the aerodrome in the early hours of 20 October to see the race start at 6.30am. The *London Letter* columnist in the *East Anglian Daily Times* brought readers a mile-by-mile account of the race and declared that 'few would have much time for thought of anything but the air race tonight. It would be strange if it were otherwise'.

At **Newmarket** the betting got off to a strong start, the race favourites being Charles W.A. Scott and Tom Campbell Black, both retired RAF officers, in their red De Havilland DH88 Comet named *Grosvenor House*. Weather conditions were better than expected and Scott said later: 'Low mists drifted beneath us as Mildenhall passed from sight, and once over the English coast-line we were swallowed in the haze of the North Sea'.

The *London Letter* was the first to bring the news of the death of two British fliers, killed in Italy. 'Perhaps it was too much to expect that a race like that in progress should end without fatality'.

The Comet crossed the Melbourne finish line at 3.34pm local time on 23 October and earned the pilots their prize of £15,000, though both were utterly exhausted. They had covered 11,333 miles in 71 hours, 54 minutes and 18 seconds at an average flying speed of 176.8 mph. The *Grosvenor House* was returned to England by boat, the return journey taking a month to complete.

❖ Miss Ella Lay (1906–2005) was born in **Peasenhall** and was one of only three women to fly in the MacRobertson Air Race, the other two being Amy Johnson and Jacqueline Cochran. She was co-pilot, joint financier and passenger with H.L. Brook, whose aircraft was a two-seater Miles Falcon Gipsy Major, with a cruising speed of 128mph and a range of 200 miles. They left Mildenhall on time but their first problem occurred in Marseilles, where they experienced engine trouble. A lorry backed into their plane at Rome and in Athens they had a 13-day wait for a replacement propeller. Forced landings in Syria and India followed, but they arrived at Essendon aerodrome, in Melbourne, on 20 November. Although they had missed the closing date they were nevertheless presented with the Royal Aero Club gold medal as one of just 12 aircraft of 21 starters to finish.

❖ The parishioners of **Mildenhall** were later accused of being unhelpful and inhospitable to the many visitors who had attended the week-long air race jamboree. The vicar of Mildenhall defended his parish from the jibe that Mildenhall was a 'dust heap' and said that regrettably the authorities could not protect 'our little town from the vulgar journalism, such as the so-called lyric entitled *Less than the Dust*'.

❖ **Elizabeth Hervey's Bolt Hole**
The Manor House in **Bury St Edmunds** was built in the 1730s with no kitchen and only one bedroom. This was because Elizabeth Hervey, second wife of John Hervey, 1st Earl of Bristol, used it as her escape from the Hervey ancestral home at **Ickworth**. The house was built solely for entertainment, mostly gambling, so Elizabeth had no need of a kitchen and only needed a bedroom for herself if she tired of the amusements. Unfortunately she did not enjoy her bolt hole on Honey Hill for long as she died in 1741, less than three years after its completion.

During construction Lord Bristol complained more than once about the cost of the house and wrote to his wife that 'the carriage of bricks, which is at the rate of 1,500 every day, and their weight so great that one of my best wagons is entirely broken down already by them'.

For many years the Manor House was a museum housing, among other treasures, the horology collection bequeathed to the borough in 1953 by Frederic Gershom Parkington. However, it closed to the public in April 2006.

❖ **The Gun Cotton Explosion of 1871**
On 11 August 1871 a series of explosions occurred at the Gun Cotton Works in **Stowmarket** that killed 24 people, injured 72 others and left the factory a complete ruin. The explosion shook the town, blowing out windows not only in the town but three miles away at **Haughley** station. Ten tons of explosive detonated and the sound was heard as far away as Diss in Norfolk. Only the tall, white-brick chimney shaft was left standing amid heaps of 'shattered walls, rafters, tiles, slates, masses of half-burned cotton, iron rods and beams, twisted into the most fantastic shapes, corrugated iron fencing and all the remnants of what had been an hour before an extensive pile of buildings'. Streets were strewn with glass and the leads in the church windows were forced inwards or blown out entirely.

A huge, circular chasm opened up on the site and large trees that had stood thereabouts were torn out by the roots, the fragments scattered around as far as a ruined farmhouse, which stood on the **Ipswich** road some 400 yards from the factory.

At the inquest the painful facts began to emerge and the extent of the heavy loss of life became apparent. Two of the factory owners, Edward Prentice and his nephew, William, had been helping to haul boxes of cartridges away from a fire caused by the first explosion, when a second explosion occurred, killing them both. The inquest concluded that the accident had been caused by sabotage, but no one was ever caught or charged with any offence.

An anonymous 47-stanza poem was published in the *Ipswich and Colchester Times* telling the story of the loss of life and how some had screamed 'The End of Time is come'. Many feared for close relatives:

> For some had husbands, some had wives,
> Some children there employed!
> The first sad thought was, all their lives
> Must surely be destroyed.
> The doleful moans and frantic shrieks,
> Still ringing in our ears,
> In language which too plainly speaks
> What bitter pangs were theirs.

Early in the 19th century the armaments industry was keen to improve the efficiency of gun power. Gun cotton had been invented in 1845 by a German chemist and consisted of cotton dipped in a mixture of nitric and sulphuric acids. Although it initially proved unsuitable as a propellant for weaponry, by virtue of the fact that the reaction was too fast and violent, a British chemist subsequently developed a means to prevent it exploding spontaneously. Obviously, a gun cotton factory was, by its nature, a storehouse for numerous dangerous materials, but was, nevertheless, a source of employment for local people. A directory of 1864 refers to it as 'recently erected by Thomas Prentice & Company, for the manufacture of gun cotton'.

Immediately after the tragedy, the factory was hurriedly rebuilt and carried on firstly as the Patent Safety Gun Cotton Company and from 1873 as the Stowmarket Guncotton Company. The Prentice family sold out in 1880 to the Explosives Company and they, conscious of the risks involved, brought in a rule that no one should carry matches while at work.

❖ **The Vikings**
Formerly the 12th Regiment of Foot, the Suffolk Regiment amalgamated with the Norfolks in 1959, forming the 1st Battalion of the East Anglian Regiment (nicknamed 'The Vikings'), which in 1964 became the Royal Anglian Regiment.

The Suffolk Chapel at St Mary's Church, **Bury St Edmunds** is now the regimental chapel. On the north wall is the Birkenhead Memorial, which commemorates soldiers of the Suffolk Regiment who drowned when HMS *Birkenhead* sank in February 1852. It is said that during this incident the tradition of 'women and children first' originated.

❖ **Birth of the Hovercraft**
The first working model of a Hovercraft, designed by the engineer and inventor **Sir Christopher Cockerell** (1910–1999), was tested on **Oulton Broad** in 1955. Sir Christopher had bought a boat-building business on Oulton Broad in 1950, living at nearby **Somerleyton** in a caravan. He had begun to experiment with a theory that a heavy vessel could be supported on the water with a cushion of air. With the help of an empty cat food tin inside a coffee tin, an industrial blower and a pair of kitchen scales he made the first mock-up model of what was to become the hovercraft.

The first prototype, *Saunders-Roe – Nautical One* was launched in 1959 and crossed the English Channel in two hours.

Sir Christopher also coined the word hovercraft, a word that was chosen to represent 1959 in the 100 words selected to encapsulate the 20th century in the millennium edition of the *Collins English Dictionary*.

❖ **Rare Letter Box**

There is a very rare 'Ludlow' letter box at **Bawdsey** that bears the insignia 'E VIII R', a reminder of the very brief reign of Edward VIII who abdicated after only 325 days as uncrowned king. Suffolk played a vital role in his relationship with Wallis Simpson, the twice-divorced American for whom he gave up the throne in 1936. She resided at **Felixstowe** prior to a 17-minute court hearing at **Ipswich** in which she obtained her *decree nisi*, allowing her to marry the king the following year.

The Letter Box Study Group have declared that the 'Ludlow' type wall box is the only surviving one of its kind in the United Kingdom and letter box aficionados travel hundreds of miles to view it. The box is now on the property of a private home that used to be a sub post office, but collections are still made daily.

❖ **The New Face of M&S**

In 2005, a chance sighting of the sixties fashion icon Twiggy at the Crown Hotel in **Southwold** led to a revival of the fortunes of the high street chain, Marks & Spencer. M&S marketing boss Steven Sharp, who lives in the town, was having lunch with his wife when she told him, 'Don't look round, but Twiggy has just walked in.'

Twiggy, who also has property in Suffolk, was approached and agreed to front a new marketing campaign to win back women customers in the key 35 to 55 age range. Twiggy later joked that she had been 'off duty' at the time Mrs Sharp had spotted her, 'wearing no make-up, a winter coat and a cap' but Mr Sharp, apparently, was captivated and the gamble paid off.

❖ **America Wants Her Daffodils Back**

In April 1964 two men from the Ministry of Agriculture went into the garden of Miss Mea Allen's garden at **Walberswick** and took some soil samples, the first step in obtaining an export licence for an old-fashion daffodil now known to botanists as the 'John Tradescant' daffodil. It is a golden, many petalled American daffodil (also known as the Great Rose daffodil) and when in full bloom looks like a rose with tiers of petals but no trumpet. They were brought to Suffolk from Virginia in 1621 but had subsequently become extinct in America. The only surviving bulbs were those in Walberswick.

In 1964, as the occupier of Tradescant house, Mea Allen wanted to send some of the daffodils to a friend in America in appreciation of the help she had given her when writing her book *The Tradescants, Their Plants, Gardens and Museum 1570–1662* (1964). Miss Allen told the *East Anglian Daily Times* 'Just as you get antique furniture, so you can get antique plants'. However, she had not realised that there were so many regulations to be observed, but was happy for the various soil samples to be taken so that the daffodils could be sent off to her friend, Mrs James Bland Martin, President of the Garden Club in Virginia.

The Tradescants lived in Walberswick and were travellers, naturalists and royal gardeners. John Tradescant (1570–1638) travelled widely in Europe and is believed to have introduced the Cos lettuce to England. He was gardener to Charles I and was succeeded in the post by his son, John Tradescant the Younger (1608–1662). Between them they introduced into England many new plants including the Algerian apricot, the lilac, acacia and the Occidental plane. It was John the Younger who undertook three plant collecting trips to Virginia and brought back the multi-petalled daffodil.

Thomas and Robert Tradescant also resided in Walberswick Street in London, named after the Suffolk village where their family cultivated and nurtured the numerous plants brought back from foreign parts.

* According to the writer Norman Smedley, the **Suffolk darts board** differed from the regular pattern in the arrangement of the numbers.
* **Blunderston** still has a very rare circular, brick animal pound, where stray animals were kept until their owners collected them.
* Columbine Hall in **Stowupland** is one of the few houses in Suffolk where every owner from 1290 onwards is known and documented. These include a murderous family, a rumoured illegitimate grandson of Henry VIII and a farmer called Harry Potter. Dating from around 1390, Columbine Hall was named after a Norman, Thorney de Columbers.

Viking raiders are reputed to have attacked an 11th-century version of Columbine Hall during the battle of Stone Bridge at today's **Old Newton** (which once consisted of the ancient settlements of Dagworth and Stow). During World War Two it housed members of the Womens' Land Army.

❖ The growing stone of **Blaxhall** has been a legend in the village for several generations. It is a circular sandstone boulder, 5ft wide, 2ft high and weighing 5 tons, which stands in the yard of Stone Farm. The story goes that it was ploughed up in the 19th century and put in the yard when it was 'only the size of two fists', since when it has grown to its present size.

❖ In St Mary's churchyard, **Bungay** is a stone called variously the Druid's Stone, Devil's Stone or Giant's Grave. It was taken out of Bungay Castle many years ago and, having danced around it and knocked on it 12 times, young girls would place their ears against it to hear the answer to questions.

❖ Toppesfield Bridge, **Hadleigh,** is the oldest bridge in the county still in use. It was built originally in the 14th century but was enlarged to twice its original width in 1812. The River Brett would appear to have been widened and straightened at that point but once through the town it reverts to a meandering stream that joins the River Stour at **Higham.**

❖ **Walberswick** was the first village in what was then the county of East Suffolk to form a Women's Institute. A committee was formed at a meeting in September 1918.

❖ Nailed on to a beam in the Crown public house in **Hartest** are 24 florins and a farthing. The men who went to fight in the trenches during World War One saw them nailed there the night before they left home. Every man going to war took his wife, girlfriend, sister or mother for a farewell drink in the Crown. Every woman who had a man going to war nailed a coin to the pub beam, a florin for those who could afford it and a farthing for one woman who could not. When the men returned from the war the coins were retrieved. While there are more holes than coins, there are still 25 left on the beam. It serves as the village war memorial though there are no names to go with the coins.

❖ In 1942 sawdust became a valuable fuel in **Ipswich.** It was a plentiful waste product from the various sawmills in and around the town and it was reckoned to have replaced about 800 tons of coal during World War Two. Its success meant that it continued as a fuel until 1948.

❖ A moor is a very rare thing in Suffolk but there is one at **Middleton**. In 1908 Middleton Moor (an open, public space known elsewhere as a green) was the scene of a remarkable event, namely an open-air baptism in the local pond. During February **Yoxford** was visited by 'No Sect' preachers – two women who proceeded to hire a cottage in Brook Street. They knocked on doors and visited houses, not only in Yoxford, but also in the surrounding neighbourhood. They organised open-air meetings and, since there was not very much else going on, a large number of people turned up. Several converts were made and on Tuesday 25 February the baptism of six new adherents took place, these being immersed in the pond on the Moor.

Since the afternoon was bitterly cold, and rain was falling heavily all the time, it was a sterling test for the new converts. The spectators were cold but intrigued and photographs were taken that were later sold as postcards. A long service was held prior to the immersions, the *East Anglian Daily Times* reporting that 'the conductor [gave] an exhaustive explanation of the object of the gathering. The candidates – four males and two females – bore their part in the ceremony remarkably well'.

It is not recorded if any of them later developed pneumonia but there was a similar service held afterwards, also in the cold and rain. The newspaper declared that the immersion ceremony 'has caused quite a commotion in the neighbourhood'.

Middleton Moor was also a popular camping place for gypsies and the venue for prizefights.

❖ The word moor describes an early form of an open green and although there were one or two others, Middleton is the only one to survive. Hodskinson's 1783 map of Suffolk shows one at **Friston**.

❖ **Middleton** was also the home of the Weeping Prophet, John Barham, who lived at Rackford Farm. He was a Master Thatcher but as a lay preacher in the local Baptist chapel was famous for his flailing arms and loud, booming voice as he imparted the Word of the Lord.

❖ The Benedictine monks of **Eye** were once in possession of a book of great antiquity, the *Book of the Gospels*, given to the Episcopal See at **Dunwich** by St Felix, who established the See of East Anglia there in 632. Eye Priory was founded in 1071 by Robert Malet, who also held the Manor of Dunwich and, when that town was lost to the sea early in the 14th century, the book was brought to Eye where it became known as *The Red Book of Eye*. It was seen in the 16th century by the topographer John Leland, who recorded that it was 'written in great Lombard letters' and upon which 'the common people were accustomed to swear'.

At the Dissolution of the Monasteries in 1539 the book was sold and described as 'an old masse Boke, called the redde boke of Eye, garnysshed with a lytell sylver on one side'. Shortly afterwards *The Red Book of Eye* disappeared and its fate is unknown. There is still hope that it might one day be discovered and returned to the ancient borough of Eye.

SELECT BIBLIOGRAPHY

Cautley, H. Munro *Suffolk Churches and Their Treasures* (1954)

Dymond, David & Peter Northeast *A History of Suffolk* (1995)

Fincham, Paul *The Suffolk We Live In* (1976)

Hadfield, John (ed.) *A Suffolk Garland for the Queen* (1961)

Jobson, Allan *North-East Suffolk* (1940)

Jobson, Allan *Suffolk Villages* (1971)

Mee, Arthur *The King's England: Suffolk* (1949)

Mortlock, D.P. *The Popular Guide to Suffolk Churches* (3 volumes) (1990)

Pevsner, Nikolaus *The Buildings of England: Suffolk* (1961)

Pursehouse, Eric *Waveney Valley Studies, Gleanings from Local History* (*c.*1965)

Scarfe, Norman *The Suffolk Guide* (1988)

Smedley, Norman *Life and Tradition in Suffolk and North-East Essex* (1976)

Suffolk Federation of Women's Institutes *The Suffolk Village Book* (1991)

Wilson, Derek *A Short History of Suffolk* (1977)